Naturism in the United States

Naturism in the United States

Frances and Mason Merrill's
Nudism Comes to America

Edited and introduced by
Paul Rich

WESTPHALIA PRESS
An imprint of Policy Studies Organization

Naturism in the United States:
Frances and Mason Merrill's
Nudism Come to America

Also from Westphalia Press

westphaliapress.org

PREFACE TO THE NEW EDITION

THE BIGGEST PUBLIC RELATIONS PROBLEM that nudism has faced over the years is public voyeurism over what is really a minor part of the movement's program. It is certainly not about taking off clothes, as can be seen in the ensuing pages. Naturism is undoubtedly a better term than nudism to describe the movement recounted in this admittedly unusual book. It is not a matter of skinny-dipping gone wild. The shedding of garments is only a small part of the story, as nudists generally are in pursuit of a simple life shorn of what they regard as unhealthy influences such as drugs, smoking, liquor, and synthetic foods.

They are much more likely to be found discussing schools of yoga than ogling pornography. In fact, most of us practice nudism, at least in the shower. But modesty, or what passes as modesty, comes early in life and so do bathrobes and beach towels. This is unsurprising since prudery is closely connected with modesty and has been since Adam and Eve grabbed fig

E

leaves in the Garden. Those who wish to go about undraped are compelled to seek out communities of the like minded. Hence the American Association for Nude Recreation American Sunbathing, the Naturist Society and the proliferation of nudist beaches.

Knopf published several titles related to nudism and having such a distinguished publisher undoubtedly gave Frances and Mason Merrill a degree of protection from comstockers. The reader will have to decide on the strength of their case, but nudism persists as an organized movement that challenges our conventionalism.

Paul Rich

F

OTHER NUDIST BOOKS AVAILABLE IN THE STAR SERIES

AMONG THE NUDISTS
by Frances and Mason Merrill

The experiences of a young American couple who tested the theory of nudism by actual practice in European camps. *Illustrated.*

ON GOING NAKED
by Jan Gay

The author, a practising nudist long before the movement began, investigates organized nudism here and abroad and approves. *Illustrated.*

NUDISM IN MODERN LIFE
by Maurice Parmelee

A discussion of the urges that lead people into nudism and of the effect it has upon men and women and their relations to each other. *Illustrated.*

STAR BOOKS PUBLISHED BY
GARDEN CITY PUBLISHING CO., INC.

NUDISM
COMES TO AMERICA

NUDISM COMES TO AMERICA

FRANCES AND MASON
MERRILL

*"I will go to the bank by the wood
and become undisguised and naked,
I am mad for it to be in contact with me."*
WHITMAN

ILLUSTRATED

Garden City, New York
GARDEN CITY PUBLISHING
Company, Inc.

PREFACE

B̲UT FOR THE CONTRIBUTIONS FROM NUMEROUS AMERICAN nudists, who might suffer from being identified, this book could never have been written. To them we express our gratitude, both for the information which they have given us, and for the photographs (from nine widely scattered states) which adorn these pages.

Two of the illustrations we owe to the kindness of Constance Towne and her dance students. For permission to reprint the poem "Down with Clothes" we are indebted to Ralph Cheney and his publishers, William Faro, Inc. Our obligations to Dr. Howard C. Warren, of Princeton University, whose assistance and advice made the psychologists' chapter possible, and to David C. Heaton, who surveyed the law, are especially great. We regret the impossibility of mentioning the other contributors and thanking the distinguished scholars and scientists who went to the trouble of answering our questionnaires. But our collaborators—named and unnamed—must be exonerated from any responsibility for the all too evident shortcomings of this book, for which we alone are to blame.

FRANCES AND MASON MERRILL

New York City
February 1932

CONTENTS

┉┉┉┉┉┉┉┉┉┉┉┉┉┉┉┉┉┉┉┉┉┉┉┉┉┉┉┉┉┉

NUDISM
COMES TO AMERICA

INTRODUCTION

ALTHOUGH FEW PEOPLE IN THIS COUNTRY HAD EVEN heard of nudists up until about a year ago, probably most Americans have heard at least rumours of them by now. In fact some have become nudists themselves, else there would be little excuse for this book. Yet it is evident, from the way "nudist" is commonly used in the press, and from discussions of the subject, that the word is bandied about by many who have no idea of what it really means. In the newspapers, a nudist is anyone who takes off his or her clothes for any purpose whatever—for instance, to appear on the burlesque stage. To be sure, journalistic usage is no criterion of the meaning which even the journalist actually intended to convey. Reporters and head-writers undoubtedly realize that Earl Carroll is not a leader of the nudist movement. "Nudist" has simply become newspaper argot and joined those numerous vocables which, because they fit neatly into headlines, serve as symbols for a heterogeneous and often incompatible lot of ideas. The unfortunate thing is that these exploited words may come in time to take on the debased characters their users have made them play.

To the public, nudism is still shrouded in misconceptions in spite of the fact that it is rapidly becoming a *fait accompli* in

Introduction

various parts of the United States. The most common and real confusion regarding its nature—and one at times arising even among those who are aware of serious and truly laudable motives for undressing—is the belief that the nudists wish to do away with clothes altogether, at once, and for all purposes and climatic conditions. Naturally enough, those with such a conception have reason to mistrust the nudist movement and put down its adherents as fanatics, impractical if not actually crazy, and ridiculous in any case. It is for that reason that we are here briefly defining nudism and its aims, and summarizing the movement as it exists in Europe. Those who are familiar with the movement and its principles are expected to skip this introduction. Others too will probably do likewise; but if the uninformed persist in their ignorance, the blame henceforth will be theirs.

Apparently it cannot be repeated too often that the ideal of the nudist is not a "return to nature," in the sense of a wholesale scrapping of modern civilization; indeed it is not even an immediate sloughing off of all its garments. It is merely the correcting or counteracting of some of civilization's evils through the laying aside of clothes, *not* when the latter are useful, but when they are detrimental. The nudist does not aspire to ride naked in the subway, nor to walk down Fifth Avenue in the costume of Lady Godiva. He realizes that clothes serve a valuable purpose in the subway—that, in fact, the most practical costume would be a complete suit of armour augmented by a gas mask. And he knows that while protective armour is less necessary on Fifth Avenue, little benefit can be derived from exposing his epidermis to an atmosphere so largely compounded of dust, soot, and monoxide gas that no ultraviolet rays can penetrate it from November to April, and not enough to be effective even during the periods of the sun's greatest intensity. Neither is it his ambition to face the icy winds of our winter plains or the raw fogs of our northern coasts clad only in gooseflesh.

Introduction

What the nudist does believe is that the artificial conditions of our machine age have robbed man of light and air that are not only valuable but essential to his physical well-being. In the rush of our mechanical progress, we are coming more and more to incarcerate indoors an organism still adapted to an outdoor environment. We even, as one writer aptly puts it, "travel in sun-proof boxes"—which, incidentally, are often air-proof as well. Although much of the action of the sun and air on the human physique remains a mystery to science, the experiments of modern medicine, chemistry, and physics have demonstrated conclusively that various pathological conditions, such as rickets, result when the body is deprived of the sun, and that certain of the solar rays, as well as the free play of air on the naked skin, have definite beneficial effects on the blood, bone structure, musculature, glandular system, and general metabolism. The nudist, by restoring to the body as far as possible its natural environment of sun and air, would safeguard his health and strengthen his resistance to disease. Because there is scientific ground for believing that the action of light and air is much more effective if the whole surface of the skin is exposed, and because the body for the greater part of the time must be shut away from sunshine and air, he proposes to make the most of those elements, whenever he can, through complete nakedness.

Thus far in the emancipation from clothing go many people, scientists as well as laymen, who are by no means nudists. The nudist goes further and thereby encounters opposition and in many countries comes into conflict with the laws and conventions. For he stubbornly insists on more than the privilege—available only to a favoured few—of sneaking off for solitary sunbaths; he demands the right to absorb his sun and air in the company of his family and friends, regardless of their age or sex. His time for outdoor recreation is limited at best, as is the time he can possibly devote to social life; if he is condemned to solitude, or even to the companionship of his

[5]

own sex exclusively, sunbaths and exercise become mere hygienic duties rather than recreation, both diminishing their benefits and tending to reduce the time given to them. What is more, such segregation of the sexes, the nudist feels, does positive harm in that it prevents humanity from enjoying the psychological advantages of nakedness, which to him are at least as important as the physical advantages.

Slavery to clothes, which make a mystery of the unclothed body while stressing the very sex differences they purport to conceal, has warped man's mental health. Our bodies, and particularly the sex organs, have come to be deemed so disgraceful that their very sight is not to be borne, but curiosity is stimulated and imagination inflamed by the draperies that veil them. The forbidden fruit of mere physical sex differences has come to assume an undue importance, and nakedness is regarded as an aphrodisiac subject to pornographic exploitation. As a matter of fact, anthropologists long ago discovered that the real aphrodisiac is dress. It is generally conceded now that clothing originated not from modesty nor even for protection against the elements but from a belief in magic or a desire for ornamentation. The trinkets with which the savage decked himself were originally talismans and charms rather than coverings of his shame. Modesty came afterward and, according to that dangerously radical work, the *Encyclopedia Britannica*, is "a feeling merely of acute self-consciousness due to appearing unusual." There is ample proof, both in primitive cultures and in high civilizations such as those of Ancient Greece, Japan, and contemporary Scandinavia, that a lack of modesty is by no means incompatible with sexual morality. Indeed the evidence seems to corroborate the statement often quoted in regard to African tribes that "chastity varies inversely with the amount of clothing."

Modern educational psychologists are alive to the dangers of training children in our taboos on sex and nakedness. They are aware that sexual impulses are often exaggerated or even perverted in the battle between suppression and human instincts, that pruriency is latent in the eternal conflict between dress for concealment and dress for decoration. Without ever having heard of nudism, progressive parents are accustoming their children to nakedness in the family in the belief that thus the new generation may be given a saner, cleaner, and a happier attitude toward sex and be spared much of the torture of adolescence and the maladjustment of maturity. The originality of the nudists lies in the discovery that nakedness can be psychologically helpful to adults as well as to children, even when those adults have been trained in conventional modesty and exposed to conventional pornography for years. The nudist believes that through the practice of nudity the normal adult—not the abnormal, of course, or those relatively few who have been corrupted beyond hope of redemption—will, in a surprisingly short time, be purged of his accumulated obscenity and develop a healthy sexual attitude. The body will no longer be vile and shameful, and the idea of nakedness will cease to be an erotic stimulant. Sex attraction and the desire for its physical expression continue to exist in man naked or clothed, but the undiscriminated and purely artificial seductiveness that results from concealment of the body will disappear. Sex will become neither a fear-shrouded sin nor an all-devouring obsession but a joyous and normal part of life.

In fact, to the practising nudist, so natural and simple a thing is the naked body, and so obvious is its rightness, that he is inclined to be impatient of theorizing on the effects of nakedness not only by its opponents but by those who devote themselves too ardently and solemnly to the many philosophical and psychological arguments in its defence. He resents having his sane and sensible practice made ridiculous by over-fervent and fanatical advocates, and its real advantages blurred by extravagant claims or confusion with mystic and utopian vagaries. The nudist does not pretend that nudism is a panacea for all the ills of civilization—that it will banish all disease, solve our economic problems, end unemployment, and outlaw war. Enough that it makes a tangible, though more modest, contribution to a good life. Unless he is introspective and given to the analysis of himself and others, he is satisfied to observe that he feels better for the practice of nakedness and enjoys life more; he has lots of fun going without his clothes and suffers no sense of sin or remorse. The main thing, the thing that keeps him a nudist as no conscious and dutiful pursuit of physical or mental improvement possibly could, is the sheer joy of nakedness and freedom from clothes. That he can appreciate this despite the inhibiting years of modesty and an environment in which nudity is infamous—and, too, without being a rebel against conventions in general—is in itself significant. The nudist believes that nakedness will increase the health, beauty, and morality of mankind; he knows by experience that it makes for happiness.

In view of the fears often expressed, it is not amiss to dwell on the fact that the nudist is no mere exhibitionist. He does not wish to compel those whose modesty would be offended to gaze on him in his naked state, for nothing makes him more resentful than to provide a spectacle for non-nudists. He dislikes the presence of inquisitive people who are unwilling to join him, and he rigidly excludes from his parks the Peeping Tom. For himself, the psychological benefits would obviously be destroyed if his nakedness were made to serve as a parade, a mere bravado in the face of superciliousness, shocked horror, or base prying. If he proselytizes, it is only in order to share the advantages he has experienced and above all to secure freedom and toleration for himself and his kind. Any prohibition of clothing that would bestow on it the charm of the forbidden is far from his mind. While hoping that humanity will, for its own good, come to embrace his doctrines, he aspires to set up no nudist dictatorship. Only a zealot would expect psychological benefits from compulsory and universal nakedness while our present conventions and prejudices are dominant.

Introduction

There is not space here to take up the chief moral and æsthetic arguments that have been advanced against nudism. Most of them, as well as the nudist refutations, will be found in the body of this work. For few if any possible objections have been overlooked by the American opponents of nakedness, and it would be unthinkable to omit them in any study of nudism in this country. What must be slighted in such a cursory survey as this, however, is the nudist movement abroad. Although the claims of the nudist are being tested in practice on American soil, the European movement, owing to its greater extent and longer experience, is a more effective demonstration and the only one proper for those who demand concrete proof on a large scale and over any considerable length of time.

In spite of much that has been printed in this country, the ideas of the American public regarding the scope of nudism abroad are on the whole still vague. It is generally known that the movement is widespread in Germany; but the fact that it is most frequently referred to as the "nude cult" reveals a misconception not only of its nature but of its extent. The word "cult," except when used in its literal and rarer sense of "worship" or (to quote Webster) the "rites and ceremonies of a religion," connotes something limited to a select and freakish few. Obviously nudism is not a religion and has no rites or ceremonies—unless undressing in the most informal and expeditious manner possible is a "rite." It could be a cult only in the sense (to quote Webster again) of a "great devotion to a person, idea or thing, especially such devotion viewed as a sort of intellectual fad." But nudism in Germany has long since passed the stage of an intellectual fad. Its adherents number hundreds of thousands and include all classes and types of people—aristocrats, intellectuals, burghers, and workers, young and old, reactionaries and radicals. The identity of the nudist is significant, for if he were necessarily an eccentric or a misfit in society, the validity of his beliefs would be vitiated.

[9]

Introduction

The typical German devotee of Naked Culture, or Free Physical Culture as he often prefers to call it, is an average citizen, in no way exceptional in background, education, or individual make-up. As his practices have legal protection and a certain amount of support from various municipal and governmental authorities, it is unnecessary for him to be a social rebel. As long as he restricts his naked activities to reserved territory or unfrequented spots in the country, he is free from interference, while the worst that befalls him if caught off these preserves is a modest fine. There is still opposition from some quarters of course, particularly in the conservative and Catholic South, but nudist parks thrive even there, and in most parts of the Reich they are a matter of indifference to their non-participating neighbours. Every German city of any size has its nudist club or clubs; Berlin alone is said to have over thirty of them. Many of these clubs are branches of large federations that have parks throughout the Republic, some even with affiliated clubs across the national borders. It has been reported recently that the three largest federations—the *Reichsverband für Freikörperkultur*, the *Liga für freie Lebensgestaltung* (both "bourgeois" societies), and the *Verband Volksgesundheit* (a Socialist and Labour organization)—have formed a sort of cartel. Each association has its own publications, and there are quantities of independent periodicals devoted to the cause.

The club parks and the club gymnasiums maintained in some cities are naturally restricted to members, but there are a few public parks run on the principle of summer resorts or *pensions* and open to nudists unaffiliated with any organization. The outstanding example is the park at Klingberg, which attracts many foreign visitors. In Berlin, two large swimming pools—one of them belonging to the city—are reserved at certain hours and days for people who wish to bathe without suits or sex segregation. Two other enterprises are worthy of special mention. One is Dr. Fränzel's co-educational school at

Introduction

Glüsingen, in the Luneberger Heide, where pupils and teachers
practise nudity; it is licensed by the State. The other is Adolf
Koch's system of gymnastic schools for workers, affiliated with
the *Verband Volksgesundheit*. Koch has gymnasiums in Berlin, Hamburg, Barmen-Eberfeld, Breslau, Ludwigshafen, and
Mannheim, where young workers of both sexes, naked as
Greek athletes, exercise and sun themselves under ultraviolet
ray lamps.

The fact that many of the German nudists do not belong to
any association but practise their doctrines either in public
parks, such as at Klingberg, or privately at home, or on tramps
through the forest as *Wandervögel*, accounts for the impossibility of obtaining accurate statistics as to their number. Un-
official estimates have run into the millions. In any case, the
nudists are numerous enough to be representative of the population in general. Nor is this large movement a mushroom. It
is true that it has been protected legally only since the war, but
it began with the present century. In Germany one meets
nudists who have "practised" for twenty years. By 1914 the
movement had assumed healthy proportions and was spreading
rapidly. It was blighted by the war; but in the difficult years
that followed, it revived and flourished under a government
which, if it did not foster, at least did not try to extirpate the
growth.

Switzerland, Austria (or more properly Vienna, since outside the Socialist city opinion is hostile), Holland, and Belgium all have their own nudist organizations as well as branches
of the German leagues. The groups in these countries lack legal
status and are comparatively small, but they are vigorously
expanding. Switzerland deserves special mention as the home
of the pioneers in heliotherapy, Bernhard and Rollier. Auguste
Rollier is the "bright, particular star" in the field of heliotherapy, and it is hard to exaggerate either his achievements at
Leysin or the influence of his medical use of natural sunlight.
To the mountain republic also belonged Auguste Forel, the

eminent psychiatrist who advocated nakedness for its psychological and educational benefits. The movement in France, though more recent, is noteworthy as the most striking refutation of a charge frequently made in order to discount the undeniable success of German nudism—namely, that Naked Culture is fundamentally Teutonic and unadaptable to other peoples and races.

France does offer greater obstacles to nudity, particularly on account of her paradoxical prudery regarding nakedness—the result of religious training and of the prevalence of pornographic nudity—and on account of the *esprit gaulois* that sharpens the weapon of ridicule. Nevertheless, the *Amis de Vivre*, the sole large bona fide French nudist society, has in less than five years established active branches in Paris and a number of provincial cities. Marseilles has two, and Bordeaux, Nice, Lyons, Strasbourg, and Toulon have their own parks. The Paris group, after renting estates for two summers in the neighbourhoods of Evreux and of Rouen, has just bought a permanent centre more accessible to the metropolis and plans to keep it open the year round. There are also branches in the North African colonies—at Algiers, Casablanca, and Oran—as well as several in Belgium, one in Spain (Barcelona), one in north Portugal, and one in Greece (Piræus). The *Amis de Vivre* publishes a fortnightly illustrated periodical, *Vivre Intégralement,* and a number of books on nudism and related subjects. It has the patronage of many outstanding physicians, psychologists, and literary celebrities, and its doctrines are constantly discussed in the general press. Legal sanction is still lacking—except for one of the Marseilles groups, which is given the use of an island belonging to the municipality—but the French government has taken one step, not far in the direction of total nudity, to be sure, though daring for a country notoriously backward in matters of hygiene and physical education. In the person of the Minister of Public Health, it has extended its blessing to the semi-nudists, the *Naturistes,* who

Introduction

have an island in the Seine and one in the Mediterranean, where the uniform amounts to a fig-leaf and, for women, a brassière. Incidentally, this costume, reminiscent of the music-hall, has impressed some French observers as more ridiculous, less æsthetic, and even more indecent than none at all.

Yet, though the rise and spread of the *Amis de Vivre* in France has effectively demonstrated that it is as possible for a Latin as for a German to be a good nudist, nudism can scarcely be said to have had a real trial among the Anglo-Saxons of Britain. Theoretical discussion has been considerable, and a number of books have been published dealing with the subject. A few years ago a "gymnosophical" society was started for propaganda and actual practice, but it was forced to disband. Since then several nudist associations with practising clubs have sprung up. Their activities are necessarily clandestine, and it is difficult to penetrate their wall of secrecy. Public nakedness is still severely penalized, as two brilliant Cambridge graduates, one of them last year's Senior Wrangler, were reminded when they played tennis *à la nature* on the fairly secluded courts of Pembroke College in Grantchester—Rupert Brooke's Grantchester where "they bathe by day, they bathe by night" and "shadowed waters fresh lean up to embrace the naked flesh." Women in the neighbourhood complained of naked flesh on the tennis court, and the guilty Cambrians were each fined the anything but modest sum of £3, 15s, 3d, and costs.

England, however, has made a contribution to a greater hygienic interest in sun and air bathing. Not only have the therapeutic achievements in the use of these forces by Sir Leonard Hill and Sir Henry Gauvain won international renown, but Sir William Arbuthnot Lane, as head of the New Health Society, and Dr. C. W. Saleeby have done much to popularize the knowledge of the hygienic value of light and air. Dr. Saleeby has campaigned doughtily for cleaner air in British cities—air more pervious to light—and for a better utilization of the little sun vouchsafed the inhabitants of the foggy isles. It is scarcely necessary to remark that nakedness from the æsthetic and psychological standpoints has long had an ardent British champion in Havelock Ellis.

In the Scandinavian countries and Russia, nudist practices have existed from time immemorial. The bathing suit is an importation that has gained small ground in Scandinavia except on the public beaches near those cities subjected to foreign influence, and in Russia it can scarcely be said to have gained any. Under the Soviets the practice continues that flourished under the Czars, when even the aristocrats on the fashionable Crimean beaches bathed nonchalantly in the nude. There is no Scandinavian or Russian nudist "movement" for the simple reason that there is no need for it, nudity there being just a custom, commonplace and accepted. The Swedish who doff their clothes on the front porches of their seashore homes and stroll stark naked to the beach—guests and hosts, men and women together—no doubt wonder why all the pother over nudism. The growth of the European movement affects Scandinavia chiefly in that it may protect native customs from an invasion of alien modesty, while the U.S.S.R., whatever the modesty or immodesty of the rest of Europe, is undoubtedly safe from any such conquest under the present order.

International co-operation among the nudist societies has had considerable agitation in Europe, and there have even been a couple of international congresses attended by delegates from many countries. Although the League of Nations may not establish a Committee for International Nudist Co-operation in the immediate future, nudism itself is a reality that long since has transcended national boundaries.

PART ONE

NUDISM COMES

ENTER THE NUDISTS

I N ITS CUP OF SURROUNDING HILLS, THE WATER WAS BLUE AS the July sky overhead except in streaks where, brushed by the gentle summer breeze, it shimmered with a million dancing points of light. The smooth curve of the opposite shore, three-quarters of a mile away, was as distinct as the part in a head of dark hair, marking the line between the green wall of trees and their reflection in the lake. In the whole scene the only living soul was a lone fisherman in an anchored boat, fifty feet from the nearby bank.

Even he was motionless. Behind him, unheeded, his rods lay idly across the bow, lines drifting listlessly along the boat. Obviously his mind was not upon his sport. Hands to face, elbows resting on his knees, only his back was visible. Like a modern Thinker, or a lump of clay, he sat hunched out there in the brilliant sun. But finally he moved, drew from his pocket a handkerchief, and mopped his brow. As he did so, he disclosed a pair of binoculars in his hand. Then pocketing his handkerchief, he resumed his pose and trained his glasses on the opposite shore.

Over there, across the dazzling lake of light, nothing but forest was to be seen. Minutes passed while the naked eye failed to find an object for the fellow's gaze. Then, as he suddenly straightened, something moved far in the darkness of the woods, something light that now and then caught a ray of sun deep in the shadow of the trees. In a moment several dim objects could be discerned, moving slowly, coming down the hill in the direction of the lake. As they advanced, these objects gradually became more distinct until, on nearing the border of the woods, they took on form—human form, naked forms.

Now the fisherman's back was taut, leaning forward, his feet widespread and braced against the thwart, glasses tightly clutched before his eyes.

Soon twelve or fifteen of these shapes could be perceived, coming down to the lake by a zigzag path. Now their figures could be clearly seen—men and women, boys and girls—their light bodies flashing between the trunks of trees in sharpest contrast with the black surrounding woods. Reaching the water's edge, they paused, some crouching, other sitting on the bank, apparently bent on removing shoes. Then, hanging towels on nearby trees, they took to the water, one by one— some wading cautiously, hesitant as if afraid, others charging in headlong with much splashing and hilarity. The sound of their voices came clearly across the intervening space.

Very shortly all were in. A few began tossing and swimming after a brightly coloured waterball. Three or four youngsters climbed atop a rock near the water's edge and dived, only to emerge, climb, and dive again. Two girls swam out from the shore laboriously pushing a couple of huge, white, peeled logs, which they straddled with many duckings and shrieks for a game of water-polo. Still others were content merely to swim serenely or to float about.

From this distance, they seemed to remain close together, to keep a rather compact group. But in a little while one was seen to have drawn away from the rest, to be already well beyond the group and a considerable distance from the shore. He was swimming strongly, as if bent on crossing the lake. Yet, if that were what he had in mind, he had veered considerably from his course, for he was not coming in a direct line from the group.

In a few more minutes his progress was noticeable, and he was getting close enough to be clearly seen. He was advancing with a powerful crawl. But this he shortly modified to an equally effective though quieter side stroke so that, coming up behind the bow and outside the field of the binoculars, he nearly reached the boat unnoticed by the fisherman.

At length the latter heard him, lowered his glasses, and turned about. Seeing the advancing head and arms, he half arose, but settled back, laid down his glasses, and reached for his oars. Then, as if in afterthought, he leaned over and stowed the binoculars in a duffle-bag, straightened, and waited with every sign of uneasiness.

Reaching the boat, the swimmer grasped the gunwale and raised a brown face and bare shoulder above the bow. "Doing any good for yourself today?" he panted, smiling amiably.

The fisherman, grinning ever so faintly in his turn, paused as if studying the tanned face before he replied: "Oh, not much. They don't bite through the day."

"Do you fish this lake often?" came back the same good-natured voice.

And the fisherman with less hesitance answered: "Yes, 'bout every other week."

"You live around here then, I guess."

"No, Hanover," and the fisherman's calmer drawl, like his figure, seemed more relaxed, registering relief and more self confidence. "I'm a fireman there and get every other Sunday off. I generally spend 'em fishing here."

Then, as if suddenly inspired, he added hurriedly: "Don't you want a bottle of beer? I got a couple cooling in this gunnysack."

"No, thanks," jovially answered the swimmer with a broadening grin. "I just came over to see if the glasses were bringing you any luck." And, unhooking his arm from across the bow, he turned and set out for the opposite shore.

* * * * * * * *

This is not a scene, real or imaginary, from any *"Freilicht-park"* in Northern Germany; nor is it some suitless bathing beach in Scandinavia. Rather, it is an actual scene in our own New England, in these United States of last year. And the people are authentic Americans—at least some of them with long lines of American progenitors.

The naked bathers are American nudists, not *Lichtfreunde* or "gymnosophists" or anything else equally exotic or mystical, and the fisherman is probably a more or less normal American too, with a typical curiosity regarding nakedness. His interest in these nudists is in no sense practical; he probably has no desire whatsoever to join with and be one of them. Perhaps he has scarcely heard of nudism except with accompanying sniggers and winks, and as for taking off his own clothes anywhere except to prepare for bed or a bath—no matter how much he may have felt the urge at times—that, in all likelihood, is to him quite unthinkable, for such things in his world are just not done. His primary interest, as evidenced by his binoculars, is simply one of seeing a forbidden sight or receiving certain visual stimuli and enjoying their emotional effect.

Courtesy of Constance Towne

II

NUDIST NEWS IN AMERICA

A YEAR AGO THIS SCENE WOULD HAVE BEEN FAR MORE BE-
wildering to the curious fisherman. Although his ideas of the
motives for such conduct are doubtless still vague, and he probably considers the immodest beings themselves mildly insane
if not outrageously immoral, he knows at least that they are
"nudists" and connects them with the foreign "cult" that has
lately been in the limelight. For a year ago, scarcely a word had
been printed in this country concerning the German nudist
movement except in a few fantastic tales from foreign correspondents of the daily press. These yarns were too preposterous; the public could only refuse to believe them or dismiss
such practices as the antics of a completely crazy and negligible sect of fanatics. Whether the correspondents who sent
back stories of the arrest of thousands of Germans for practising *Nacktkultur* on the public promenades of Berlin, or of
French nudists petitioning the Prefect of Police for permission
to appear *à la* Godiva in the Paris streets, were giving rein to
their fancy, or whether they had trusted to unfounded rumour
on a subject which they deemed unworthy of research, American readers were not to be blamed for snorting at the nudists
and forgetting them at once.

In the course of the past year, however, these startling tales

[21]

have practically vanished from our papers. They have been replaced by soberer and more accurate accounts from reporters who have taken the trouble to investigate, at least superficially, the activities of which they write. Americans now know enough about the movement abroad to detect absurdities and to be eager for authentic information. An instance of nudist news in the manner of the newer realistic school appeared in the series of articles on the German nudists by Julia Blanshard, syndicated last September by the N.E.A. Service of the Scripps-Howard papers. The fifth article of Ruth Seinfel's series on "Young Germany," which ran in the New York *Evening Post*, the Boston *Post*, and elsewhere around October 16th, also dealt with the nudists and the closely related *Wandervögel*. Although anything but complete treatments of the subject, both of these were free from inaccuracies and misemphasis, and revealed that the writers had taken pains to talk to nudist leaders in Berlin and learn something of the purpose and procedure of these organizations. Julia Blanshard had visited at least one nudist camp. Recent stories from France, such as William P. Carney's report in the New York *Times*, July 5, 1931, of the endorsement of the Naturists at Villennes by the French Minister of Public Health, distinguished between the Naturists and the total nudists—two separate groups always hopelessly confused by the Romantic school of nudist news.

Nowadays, when our journalists direct a really ambitious flight of the imagination to naked gatherings, they select the American scene. Their range here is somewhat limited by the ease with which the public detects a palpable hoax too close to home, but the journalists who would exploit the clandestine existence of the American nudist are assured of considerable freedom by the latter's need for dodging publicity. Reporters realize that there is slight danger of nudists publicly denying false statements, much less correcting erroneous reports or countering with authentic information about their group. If the reader fails to find the naked clubs that are luridly depicted in his tabloid, the paper has a defence in the fact that such clubs are secret—so secret that only its reporters could ferret them out, and they of course cannot tell all they know. Incidentally, this is an opportunity for conveying the impression of a journalistic honour of which the paper is actually devoid. True, the tabloids would prefer a good, spicy nudist story based on actual fact. They would like nothing better than a real nudist club to expose, and no sense of honour would stand in the way of the exposure. Their zeal in hunting down rumours of modern Adams and Eves is truly commendable, and there are no limits to the time and money they will devote to running them down. In one instance, reporters and photographers who failed to gain admittance to the grounds of a nudist club in northern New Jersey, or to see anything but people in ordinary sport clothes, returned shortly in an airplane. Although they came near to knocking the chimney off the club-house, naked forms were still invisible. But the finesse of these detectives was inferior to their persistence, for the plane was conspicuously labelled with the name of a notorious New York City tabloid.

Thus thwarted in its pursuit of facts, sensational journalism has had to fall back on fiction. Though no attempt has been made to verify the story in the New York *Daily News*, June 1, 1931, that "60 Shy Nudists Cavort in Briny" on Long Beach, it is reasonable to suspect that upon investigation this naked group would dissolve into thin air. "New York's 3 Nude Cults" described in the *New Broadway Brevities*, August 24, 1931, were traced and proved to be the creations of the writer. The tales widely printed last November, of the nudist group vainly petitioning the authorities of Carmel, California, for permission to establish a park there, may not have been all hoax, but Californians who looked into the matter could find no signs of the reported organization. The unreliable nature of American nudist news confines it largely to the lower order of journal, except in cases authenticated by the appearance of the sun-worshippers in court. An exception was the authentic, though discreet, story in the New York *World-Telegram*, November 3, 1931, of the activities of the American League for Physical Culture. But even such genuine nudist news was eschewed by the New York *Times* as not "fit to print" until the arrest of members of that group last December. With nudist tales serving the press up to the present chiefly for pornographic appeal, there was some justification for the purity of the *Times*.

Incidentally, this mentor of morals in news had less prudish standards in advertising. In April 1931 it not only carried a large announcement of a nudist book, adorned with a cut of a naked man and woman, but virtually—though doubtless inadvertently—endorsed it with the following statement printed in large type immediately underneath: "AN ADVERTISER IN THE NEW YORK TIMES is in good company, for exceptional care is exercised by the *Times* in the acceptance of all advertising. The *Times* standards are high and are generally recognized and accepted as the most strict and thorough of those of any newspaper."

Last December 8, the word "Nudist" leaped into the New York headlines and ran out over the Associated and United Press wires to papers throughout the country. The arrest of twenty-four members of the American League for Physical Culture in their gymnasium almost in the shadow of the Times Building shook the *Times* out of its silence and provided a Roman holiday for the Hearst papers. The *Times* carried a detailed though naturally sober account of the raid on an inner page, but to the New York *Evening Journal* it was the news of the day, the flaring banner head, "NAB 24 IN TIMES SQ. NUDE CULT RAID," dwarfing even Mrs. Culbertson's story of the first round of the bridge battle. The *Journal's* nudist story began on the front page and wandered into several inside columns adorned with a photograph of the defendants snapped in night court. The other papers carried less spectacular accounts, but none of them overlooked it save the *Herald-Tribune*, which was probably caught napping. Any suspicion that the latter had grown purer than the *Times* was dispelled when it printed the story of the nudists' aquittal.

Most of the papers lapsed into silence again until the trial, but the *Journal* continued its saturnalia throughout the intervening week. Every day had its "nudist story," the findings of what the *Journal* called a "survey." All the papers and letters found by the police in the "raid" were published, and various unwarranted conclusions drawn therefrom. The newspaper employed every subterfuge of the detective to learn more about the members of the arrested group, or of any other nudist group, and reportorial imagination supplied details when clues failed. Extracts from nudist books were printed as if they were information vouchsafed by nudists in personal interviews. Three times the City Editor sent a "lady reporter" to the wilds of New Jersey to interview a man because a letter addressed to him had been found by the raiders, although he knew nothing whatever about the case. The reporter-sleuth was also commissioned to find the site of the American League's summer farm. She promptly discovered "unmistakable landmarks of the Adams and Eves" (discarded leaves of the fig-tree?), although none of the nudists could recognize their camp in her description. And of course when the case was dismissed in court, December 14, the nudists again "made" the *Journal* with front page headlines and their picture in court—but the backs of their heads only, since the magistrate had restrained the photographers.

The Boston *Post* on December 10 published a column story under a New York date line that purported to give the history of the American League for Physical Culture as well as of other thriving, but nameless, groups through the five boroughs—a tale that appeared to be a distortion of the distorted *Journal* "survey." These categorical assertions in the final paragraph give an idea of the authenticity of the information: "The nudists, for the most part, are middle-aged men and rather fat, matronly women, according to available reports. . . . Some of the nudists are exhibitionists, others really are seeking physical improvement, and a lot of them are just thrill-seekers." Actually, the average age of the twenty-four people arrested, as shown on the police record and published in all the New York papers—including Mr. Hearst's—was thirty-two, and exactly half of them were under thirty. So much for the fat, middle-aged! And, as it is psychologically impossible for either exhibitionists or "thrill-seekers" to be anything but bored with nudist clubs if they find no other attractions in nakedness—so much for the motives!

The New York *World-Telegram* as usual took a middle course between the sobriety of the *Times* and the extravagance of the *Journal,* carrying two fairly impartial stories in the interval between the arrest and the trial—an ostensible interview with an anonymous defendant, and one with Maurice Parmelee. Although the exoneration of nudists in court was not nearly such a delectable news bit as their arrest *in flagrante delicto,* all the New York papers noted the magistrate's decision, under headlines varying from "Free New York Nudists" to the *World-Telegram* masterpiece, "Nudist Caper Left Cops Cold." But none of them commented on it editorially or bestowed either opprobrium or merited laurels on Magistrate Goldstein. The *Herald-Tribune* after the arrest did publish a letter from Poultney Bigelow protesting at the police raid—a communication that may have accounted for that paper's taking note of the trial. Shortly thereafter the Bridgeport (Connecticut) *Herald,* on the Sundays of December 20 and 27, ran two long nudist stories (one an interview with Constance Towne at whose school in Stamford girls occasionally dance in the nude), which demonstrated effectively that a story on nudity is not necessarily sensational even in a sensational paper. The first article appeared on the front page under an alarming banner head, "PINK PANTIES BUST ELDERS' MARRIAGE," but the "pink panties" fortunately had nothing to do with the nudist tale, which oddly enough was straightforward and fair.

Both stories were likely dull reading for inveterate Fishermen.

The rotogravure section of the *Times* and other reputable journals is reflecting the evolution toward nakedness. On Sundays the reader of our most conservative paper is exposed to the scandalous sight of Lindbergh's bare torso, of Bernard Shaw in nothing but a pair of "bathing drawers," or of Noel Coward in a fig-leaf. To be sure, American Sunday newspapers have not yet published the photograph that has appeared in European nudist periodicals of Havelock Ellis taking a sunbath clad only in his noble beard. Fig-leaves may be deemed imperative for some time to come, but progress is indicated when the reputations of our heroes can survive the display of naked chests, which are still unlawful on many of our beaches.

No less a transformation is apparent in the attitude of our magazine editors—and of their readers, if editorial policy is, as they say, but a reflection of public interest. Before 1930, no record of an article on European nudism is to be found, at least in the better known and established monthlies or weeklies. It is true that there were articles on the benefits of sunbaths and ultraviolet rays, generally written from the medical point of view and appearing chiefly in scientific periodicals or in the health departments of the women's magazines. Those that were published in general magazines also emphasized therapeutic and hygienic effects, but if they mentioned the European nudist movements it was in such oblique fashion as this reference by E. E. Free, the chemist, in an article on "These Ultraviolet Rays" in *Harper's Magazine* for February 1929: "Is the habit of unclothed sun-bathing, which persistently makes headway in Europe despite convulsions of the mores, to be deemed scientifically respectable or the reverse?" Although the allusion would be decidedly obscure to anyone unacquainted with nudist activities, Mr. Free's reply to his own question is significant: "On the whole the answer of science must be that anything which relieves the human skin from its role of a shameful secret is worth helping. . . . It would be better still, everything in modern physiology indicates, if most of the world's work could be done out of doors and much of it at least in summer out of clothes."

The pioneer article on the practice of nudity from what might be called the lay point of view, where the pleasures and psychic factors of outdoor nakedness outweigh its purely hygienic considerations, was Stuart Chase's now famous "Confessions of a Sun-Worshipper." These "Confessions," which doubtless will occupy the place in American nudist literature that Rousseau's *Confessions* have in Romantic literature, appeared in the *Nation* as early as June 26, 1929. But Mr. Chase's declaration of sartorial independence is an individual and isolated expression, in no way connected with European nudism. He arrived at nudism by himself, out of his own experience with bootlegged sunshine. Not that he was blind to the decided trend that was evident in America even in 1929 toward acquiring tan and liberating the body from its prudish prison of clothes; he remarked in fact: "I have been associated with many reform movements in my life and it is with considerable astonishment that I find one actually gaining ground." And he concluded with an appreciation of the possible benefits that a naked mode might bring our civilization, as well as a firm determination to be a sun-worshipper himself regardless of what the rest of his countrymen may do: "If the republic wants to go native, and can hold to it with any fidelity, it will probably do more than any conceivable action to balance the inhibitions and pathological cripplings induced by the machine age and the monstrous cities in which we live. If it but wants a new fad to play with and presently to toss aside, I know how to outwit the law; to find the sheltered spot where comes the sun and wind, and men come not."

As far as we can discover, the first article dealing specifically with the foreign nudist movement appeared in the August 1930 issue of Dr. William J. Robinson's *Critic and Guide*, a one-man journal concerned chiefly with medical questions and sex hygiene. Dr. Robinson related his favourable impressions of the German nudists. The second article on the subject seems to have been in the November 1930 issue of an obscure travel magazine, *Nomad*, inaugurating a series dealing with the various countries that nudism had already invaded. Of this series, the first two, by C. Hooper Trask, a foreign correspondent of the New York *Times*, were devoted to "The Nude Cult in Germany." The February article, by H. Lucius Cook, described "Physiopolis," the semi-nudist or Naturist centre near Paris, and the March article dealt with "The French Nudists." In April "Sun Worship in England" was discussed by C. M. Kohan. All of these articles were free from misemphasis and were reasonably accurate in their statement of facts. In regard to the magazine's editorial policy, however, they represented not sympathy for nudism but an attempt to prop up a tottering financial structure with new and rather sensational material. They served the purpose to the extent of attracting considerable attention and exhausting the supply of the magazines on the news-stands immediately on publication, but not to the point of saving the *Nomad*, which shortly went into bankruptcy leaving some of the nudist contributors unpaid.

Before the second *Nomad* article had appeared, the anything but obscure *Cosmopolitan* was in the field. In the December number, Karl K. Kitchen, newspaper columnist, told how "I Went Back to Nature for a Day." But Mr. Kitchen displayed neither the knowledge of the subject nor the open mindedness of his less widely known *Nomad* colleagues. Although he admitted that in the course of his day at a *Freilichtpark* near Berlin he "did not see a single untoward gesture, let alone anything anyone could object to," he persisted in calling such parks "dubious Gardens of Eden." He was extremely careful, moreover, to preserve his own columnar modesty. "They feel," he said of the nudists, "that they derive great benefits from such sojourns in the open and I am convinced that they are right, with the reservation that a pair of bathing trunks for both men

and women would be beneficial from a practical as well as from
an æsthetic standpoint." This attitude he reinforced later in
his New York *Sun* column with an assertion that "After all,
there should be standards of taste and decency as well as de-
portment—even among back to nature lovers." No one could
disagree with this were it not that, by "taste and decency," Mr.
Kitchen means bathing trunks. There are people who do not
consider bathing trunks, or any sort of a fig-leaf, essential to
taste and decency—people quite as well qualified to pass on
æsthetic and ethical questions as is a newspaper columnist.

In January 1931, *Living Age* published an article "On Going Naked," by Edmond Jaloux, who viewed the nudist movement from the superior eminence of ridicule. Typical of the
feeling of the distinguished French critic is the remark that
"It is in Germany that Nudism has made most progress. This
is due first of all to the fact that the Germans have no perceptible sense of the ridiculous." For M. Jaloux, the subject of
nudism served merely as a springboard for a plunge into the
perilous sea of modern devotion to sport and outdoor life in
general. He saw shoals in even less extreme forms of physical
culture and sun-worship. "The struggle for youth, health, and
beauty," he opined, "has in it those elements of courage and
energy which only become a danger if they confuse the end
and the means. Greek and Roman paganism had the city as
their ideal. Where is our paganism going? Alas, I am afraid it
is nothing but a fashion and that another fashion will replace
it."

In March the *Outlook* offered the report of William B.
Powell's encounter with "Adam and Eve in Germany"—a
meeting as brief and even more uncongenial than Mr. Kitchen's.
Mr. Powell gave more information than did the latter, though
he made the error of dating the origin of the movement in 1920,
whereas it would have been nearer correct to have said 1902.
While he did not demand bathing trunks for decency, he cried
out for them to preserve the world from dullness. The nudists

were so decent as to bore him. Apparently he expected something exciting and naughty and was disappointed to discover only ordinary folk conducting themselves in a perfectly respectable and humdrum fashion. "It was anything but glamorous or intriguing," he sighed, regretting no doubt the seductive near-nakedness of the "Scandals." "I am glad I went to the *Nackt* Club, but I never want to visit one again," was his conclusion. "The sight was mainly unpleasant, not shocking. If everyone there had been selected from the youth and beauty of the land (which you seem to find at the German beaches of the natural variety), that would be one thing. But with half of the people fat and forty (or over), I must admit that as I left the grounds I was grateful that *Nackt* Clubs have not reached America yet, and I said, 'Thank God for Clothes.'" Incidentally, we should like to ask Mr. Powell why beaches of the "natural variety"? What is "natural" about putting on clothes in order to bathe?

The "Paradise Regained" by the nudists was viewed with less alarm by Paul Morand in the September 1931 *Vanity Fair*. M. Morand at least appreciates the pleasures of life out of doors and out of clothes. He depicted enticingly the delights—the "sheer glory," he called it—of naked bathing in the sea and sun, the tang of salt on the bare skin, and the joy of sleeping unclad under a tropical sky. But he could not hurdle the old æsthetic obstacle. "To how many sorry sights would we be condemned, were we to go naked in the interests of beauty?" he lamented. "Imagine Chaplin without his shoes, the Pope without his robes, Marlene Dietrich without her silk stockings, Mussolini without a uniform! We are unsightly during the major portion of our lives. We should think of more than our own health and comfort. We should consider the æsthetic sense of others."

One might reply that whatever the undoubted merits of Charlie Chaplin's shoes, beauty is not one of them, and that Marlene Dietrich stripped not only of her stockings but of all her scanty draperies would be scarcely a sorry sight. As for the Pope and Mussolini, nobody insists on their joining the nudists.

M. Morand's historical accuracy was as inadequate as his grasp of the æsthetic question. According to him: "Near Paris about five years ago, the New Adams chartered the island of Villènes [*sic*] at Poissy in the Seine; but they could be seen from the banks (and what is sinning if not being seen?). The police made them put on at least those little triangles of black cloth which are the fig-leaves of the twentieth century. The result was a Schism: the confirmed advocates of pure Nudism retired to a park surrounded by walls; and last year they founded the Sparta Club, an austere name calculated to silence the Gallic witticisms of Frenchmen." The Naturists of the Doctors Durville would be indignant at the implication that they ever tried appearing at Villennes without their fig-leaves, and the *Amis de Vivre* of the Sparta Club would with equal reason resent no less hotly the idea that they are an offshoot of the Naturists. Some of the blame may be shared with the il-lustrator, Dignimont, who drew "Adamites at Villènes in the Seine, Poissy, France" completely minus fig-leaves, and with a detail that might be even more criminal in the eyes of the Dur-villes—two pipes and a pouch of tobacco beside an Adam reading *Le Journal!* The coffee pot in the picture might be given the benefit of the doubt; it could contain Kaffee Hag or some other caffeinless vegetarian brew. Fortunately the illus-trator omitted a wine bottle, taboo at Villennes though not in the Sparta Club. But of course, it is too much to expect strict attention to detail from one who dashes around the globe with the breathless speed of what Professor E. P. Dargan has called Paul Morand's "international steeple chase"—and, no one does who is acquainted with morandese.

The nudists have not yet broken into the so-called Quality Magazines, but it is safe to say that the editors of the latter would no longer display abject terror if a writer approached them with an article on the subject, even if they are not solicit-

ing such stories after the fashion of the lesser and more specialized periodicals. The *Dance Magazine,* for instance, in December 1931, had an article on the "nudist cult that may become a
movement." Under the title "Among the Sun Faddists," Richard Sylvester related his experience at the Egestorf nudist
park near Hamburg and described the European movement in
general. At the end of this were several paragraphs under the
caption "The American Movement," in which Gilbert Parks
discussed the beginnings here and pointed out the relationship
between nudist activities and dancing. Both writers presented
authentic information and were sympathetic in their viewpoint. The *Magazine,* however, took pains to explain why it
was offering such inflammable material and in a box statement
declared: "The *Dance Magazine* presents these two articles . . .
so that its readers may understand what is back of this great
demand for unhampered life. The dance plays an important
part in the pastimes of nudists, and dance teachers may be
called on in the future to direct nudist activities. The *Dance
Magazine* publishes these articles for the information of its
readers, and does not necessarily subscribe to the opinions expressed therein."

Modern Living, a health magazine of naturopathic doctrines,
has carried a number of articles related to the subject. The first
one, "Nudity," describing the European nudists, appeared in
June 1931. In August, Harry Salpeter discussed nudity in Russia through an interview with Mrs. Eve Garrette Grady, who
pointed out that nudity is neither new in Russia nor proletarian
in origin, but that it is a perfectly natural and commonplace
custom encouraged by the Communists on the ground that
shame and false modesty are essentially middle-class. In the
November issue, P. V. Keyes, in "Nudity Wasn't New 500
Year Ago," gloriously jumbled mediæval religious cults of nudity, nature cults, and the modern movement. In tracing the
origins of the latter, he went back to a Hebrew cult that existed before the birth of Christ; but he omitted all reference

to the Greek cultivation of nakedness, which in spirit is much closer to the modern movement than were any of the countless nude religious sects of history. In December *Modern Living* also carried an understanding account of the German movement by C. Hooper Trask, who concluded on a note of prophecy regarding the prospects for nudism in America. He believes that in some respects we do not need a nudist movement here so greatly as did Germany, for the reason that we already have more sunshine and more hygienic habits of living. But he finds one important contribution that nudism could make in this country—that is in "relaxation in matters of sex." For, "there is no question," he said, "that it helps to relieve the terrific erotic tension which is one of the banes of modern life. America, with its Puritanic shackles to throw off, might find in nudism the Mecca of its seeking."

It is somewhat surprising, though a matter for congratulation, that Bernarr Macfadden has not yet taken up the championship of nudism. The American nudists may well tremble at the thought of what he might do to their cause since, as Dr. Morris Fishbein has justly remarked, Macfadden, in his advocacy of physical culture, has already "taken what should be a beautiful search for health, for vigour, and for strength and made it an ugly and discouraging thing to every rightminded individual." *Physical Culture* published a series of brief articles last summer on the French and German movements, but fortunately Mr. Macfadden has shown no signs of sponsoring the nudists in America. Perhaps he realizes the lack of pornographic appeal to total nudity, for—to quote Dr. Fishbein again—"It needs no reading of the Macfadden publications to convince any sound observer that the appeal of all of them is sexual and erotic." Then, too, perhaps this spiritual saviour of man's physical being would hesitate to embrace nudism after his audience with the Pope in Rome last year, for it is not to be hoped that the Holy Father who urges his daughters to cover even their necks and arms and ankles will issue an Encyclical approving the practice of nakedness.

This sketchy survey by no means exhausts the serious discussions of nudism that have raged in American newspapers and periodicals for the past year. The great bulk of these arguments, however, appeared not in special articles on the subject but in book reviews. The reviewers of the recent works dealing with nudism have in almost every case used the books merely as a point of departure for a consideration of the subject in general and an expression of their own views in particular. On the whole, the professional literary critics have received the idea with more favour than did Messrs. Powell and Kitchen. But a treatment of the opinions set forth in reviews, not being "nudist news" strictly speaking, belongs elsewhere and will be taken up as a phase of the reception of nudism by the American public in general.

The first book on nudism to be published in the United States, *Among the Nudists,* was brought out in April 1931. But the first book actually written was Maurice Parmelee's *Nudity in Modern Life, or the New Gymnosophy,* although it did not appear on the American market until September 1931. The history of this work is significant of the changing attitude of this country. Early in 1927 an American publisher was ready to bring out Mr. Parmelee's book; in fact it had been set up and printed, and a circular announcing it had been sent out. One of these announcements, however, fell into the hands of the gentleman who was then United States District Attorney of New York, and who was sincerely shocked by the naked photograph illustrating the circular. He served notice on both the author and publisher that if this book, "inciting to crime," were brought out, he would prosecute; that in fact, unless they promised not to bring it out, he would prosecute them for publishing the circular, which he held had already violated the obscenity laws.

In all probability the book would have been cleared in court, for there is nothing "spicy" about it, "gymnosophy" being to

Nudism Comes to America

Dr. Parmelee, as Harry Hansen says, a "most serious subject." Moreover, the fact that since 1915 the Society for the Suppression of Vice has not had a single conviction of a book published by a reputable publisher and sold openly indicates that nowadays literary "criminals" have a good chance of escaping legal punishment. Incidentally the U. S. Custom officials found no grounds for excluding an identical English edition of *Nudity in Modern Life*, published in London in the fall of 1929. Yet the mere threat of the District Attorney was enough to frighten the publisher, and the author was unable to find another to assume the risk. But four years later, after *Among the Nudists*, with even franker illustrations, had escaped any attempt at suppression or censorship, Alfred A. Knopf issued Parmelee's book, printed unchanged from the original plates of the suppressed edition, the sole alterations being in the title—which was changed to *Nudism in Modern Life*—the preface—to which less than a score of words were added—and the illustrations, which were increased in number. Some of the pictures were even more "daring" than the originals, as they included front views of the human figure, but the censors and moralists made no protests. The Secretary of the New York Society for the Suppression of Vice did request one bookdealer to close copies of the book that were open in a window, but he made no attempt to stop the sale or even display so long as the covers were modestly shut on the illustrations. And nothing has been heard from the former District Attorney.

The remaining nudist book published in 1931 belongs to a different category, although the bookstores do not agree on just which category this is; at one shop it is on the "Humour" counter, and at another it nestles beside Eugene O'Neill in the case labelled "Drama." Tom Cushing, the author of *Barely Proper*, calls it "An Unplayable Play," but that is a misnomer. True, it is unplayable by the Theatre Guild or the company of a Broadway producer, but there are amateur groups in existence who can stage it privately in authentic nudist costume without

Courtesy of Constance Towne

the slightest shock to the audience or embarrassment to the actors. One club, in Mr. Cushing's native New England, is planning in fact to put it on this coming summer for the entertainment of its members, who can appreciate the genuine humour of the encounter between a conventional young Englishman and the nudist family of his German fiancée. Indeed, there is nothing to offend even ardent nudists, for as a Chicago reviewer has pointed out, the "play makes fun of the nudists but more fun of the anti-nudists."

Since the non-nudist hero is characterized as "humorous and a good sport only until he reaches the borders of 'the things that aren't done' . . . when he turns into what might be called 'Mrs. Grundy's model son,' " one does not expect him to be immune from his creator's ridicule. And much of the laughter at the expense of the nudists is actually at the expense of their Germanness rather than their nakedness. They talk a surprising amount of sense for a nonsensical play, and "going starko" triumphs in the end. Although the heroine, for the sake of her love, is ready to wear heavy tweeds in England and think "horrid thoughts," it is the hero who makes the final sacrifice and casts off his trousers. The prospective producers of this play see only one obstacle—the difficulty of keeping their leading man out of the sun so he will fit the lines that describe his skin as "white—like grass under a plank."

Nudism figures in another satire that reached the American public in January 1932, the *New Crusade,* by Anthony Gibbs. This was, of course, an English book, and significant in this country only in that it appears in an American edition. The *New Crusade* is a nudist movement, but the satire is directed at the press and the methods used to put over the Crusade, as well as at the English public on whom it is put over, rather than at nudism. Nudity is made ridiculous solely because of the Crusaders' tactics, and at that it is not so funny as it might be. The book is an excellent object lesson in how nudism should not be promoted; we hope the American movement heeds the warning and keeps the hands of Mr. Hearst and his brethren off. Nakedness, incidentally, does not triumph in the *New Crusade*, as it does in *Barely Proper*, for in the end Mr. Gibbs's hero, the New Adam, returns with relief to his old unhygienic ways and his pyjamas.

As a result of all the recent publicity, "nudist," unknown in America a year ago, has become a "tabloid word" and supplied American humorists with a new subject for their quips and jibes. Nudists have attained the status of mothers-in-law and hen-pecked husbands. The columnists, from Walter Winchell to F. P. A., have all made nudist jokes, and jest columns have carried extended "News from the Nudists," with items about absent-minded professors seen wandering around with their trousers on. Humorists such as Corey Ford and Robert Benchley have devoted whole articles to parodies of nudist literature. The cartoonists have seized on the new joke with no less avidity, and as early as last May a cartoon, "The Probable Origin of the New Nudist Movement," was syndicated the length and breadth of the country. One of the first issues of *Ballyhoo* showed a glimpse of the "Windermere Nudist Club" with a skinny gentleman explaining to a fat one, "Yeah, I've signed up for the depression." Comic artists now have a chance to display their skill at drawing nudes, particularly gnarled or bulbous ones. A shapely nude is not very funny, but naked Germans, shaped like seals, are comic. Naked lissome damsels and athletic young men still belong to the commercial artists who illustrate the soap advertisements, but "Noodism" has even reached the funny papers. "The Smythes" carried it into homes all over America on the Sunday of August 16, 1931. A year ago, a nudist joke would not have occurred to our humorists— or, if it had, they would have been forced to explain it to their readers. The fact that Icarus, in his "By-Products" in the Sunday *Times*, should think of dividing German public sentiment as "38¾ per cent for Hitler, 54½ per cent for the Bruening coalition, 22 per cent for Schmeling, 6½ per cent for the Nudists"; or that there should appear in "The Lion's Mouth" of *Harper's Magazine* the simile "as uncomfortable as a nudist at a convention of Methodist bishops," indicates that the nudists are not only deemed funny but well known.

The nudists are cropping up, too, in another and very different specialized field—that of the business publications and trade journals. The clothing merchants and manufacturers are beginning to speculate on how a healthy nudist movement will affect their industries. To be sure, the alarm they feel is faint and scarcely serious as yet; they have launched no organized attack on the naked heresy, as no doubt they would had it reached formidable proportions. To them it is still only a comic threat. Yet they are beginning at least to wonder. Last August *Advertising and Selling* was curious enough to solicit an article on the question, "If Nudism Comes to America, What Will it Mean to Business?" But the attitude of the commercial interests, as well as that of the humorists, will have further consideration later, along with other typical American attitudes toward this new immigrant, nudism.

III

INFORMAL NUDIST PRACTICE

Apparently there are a good many Americans who are nudists without knowing it. Some, without ever having heard of nudism, have nevertheless been practising it as a mere matter of course, about in the manner of the inhabitants of Russia and most sections of the Scandinavian countries. Others, perhaps thoroughly aware of the nudist movement in Europe today, are regularly enjoying, very consciously, the benefits of nakedness and yet have never thought of joining any sort of nudist organization—many in fact would not consider such a thing, holding with John Langdon-Davies that they "do not need a secretary and a treasurer" to help them take off their clothes.

Such an attitude is all very well for those comparatively few so fortunate as not to require assistance. Even so conscious and conscientious a sun-worshipper as Stuart Chase has said: "I shrink from the Teutonic organization of the modern nudists. I like to sun-bathe when the mood seizes me, and I enjoy the adventure of finding a proper spot, with due regard for (a) sun elevation, (b) wind, (c) bugs, (d) spectators." Realistically enough, he hastened to add, however: "But I realize my good fortune in having more time and space than the average workingman. If he and his family are to sun-bathe at all, they

Informal Nudist Practice

must have the facilities organized." Alas, the same thing is true for many hundreds of us who cannot claim even the honour of being so-called workingmen.

Up in the West Seventies—and likely in many other sections of New York City—there is a gigantic apartment building crowned by four penthouses. Recently the landlord there obtained four thoroughly desirable tenants in the form of four families of friends on the condition that he give them the exclusive use of the entire roof. As a result, if one were permitted to go up there now—almost any time, day or night, in comfortable weather—he would find the children of those four families playing, or the adults sun-bathing or lounging about or working, all wholly free of clothes. Here in fact is a group which, though lacking any formal organization, constitution or by-laws, is a nudist "colony" in a truer sense than any ordinary nudist camp or park could possibly be; here the people are thorough-going Adams and Eves even to the point of living their day-to-day lives, instead of just their holidays and vacations, in a state of complete nakedness. Yet for how many people is such a thing possible? Penthouses are notoriously expensive places to live, and only the well-to-do can possibly afford such facilities for nudity.

A much more rudimentary but commoner form of nudism in America today is a growing practice on the part of families privately. Of late years a rapidly increasing number of parents have made complete nakedness a habit with their children, in the privacy of their homes, not so much on account of the physical benefits or comforts to be derived as on account of the educational effect upon their offspring. Modern, progressive educational theory demands a greater frankness than formerly in all matters relating to sex, and many psychologists have pointed out the value of unembarrassed nudity on the part of parents as a means of saving their children from prurient-minded curiosity and shame regarding the human body. Such practice can be, and often is, a joyously free and unself-

[41]

conscious—even though deliberate—thing; or it can be an extremely self-conscious and altogether joyless procedure, depending upon the attitude of the adults who institute it. We have heard of cases where it was positively painful to both parents and children because of the awfulness with which the body was viewed, sometimes subconsciously, by those who sought to set the example. Nakedness here became a sort of horrid medicine, to be taken dutifully. But it can be the simple, natural, entirely proper state, under suitable conditions, and conducive to better mental as well as physical health. An example is presented by the California physician who recently stated: "My interest in nudity dates back to the raising of my family—three boys and a girl—when the policy was adopted that no one in the family should ever pretend a modesty in front of any of the others. At home we walked about in our dressing rooms or the bathroom without any restraint." He added that he is "convinced such a policy has had its beneficial effect."

We have been much amazed at the number of people who have written in this manner. The practice is apparently quite common in America. A good many people fail to indicate in their letters—if in truth they themselves know—the precise motive that lies in back of their nakedness. But as a general rule, those who are discovering with the greatest surprise the fact that they have been for a long time nudists of a sort have been inspired in their nakedness principally by a desire to give their children a saner sex education. Even of those who in their letters do not attribute their practice specifically to educational purposes, few have indicated any clear appreciation for the health benefits or the physical comforts, and fewer still the sheer joyousness of being free of clothes. It is as if their inherited or acquired puritanism forbade them any such appreciation—as if they were too ascetic to think of enjoying the health, much less the mere happiness and ease, of nudity.

Naturally there are exceptions. One man described how

Informal Nudist Practice

"For several years on my own property [in Southern California] I have been accustomed to do my gardening and all outdoor activities completely nude, keeping a garment or two conveniently at hand in case of an unexpected caller. . . . [Likewise] the family has been accustomed to drive to a fairly secluded beach and spend the day on the shore and in the water sans bathing suits. I have no doubt that hundreds of other families in California follow the same practice." And, as if to prove his own thorough appreciation for both the physical and psychological benefits of nudity, he cited numerous health and vacation resorts in the mountains of California and Arizona offering "sun treatments" and made the prediction that they "will soon realize the greater benefits to be derived from nudism than at present derived from passive sun-bathing; and those who 'take the cure' at such places will by dissemination spread the movement throughout the country at large. Once addicted to the drug of air and sunlight, the urge of free recourse to its nepenthean qualities becomes a craving that is determined to find relief."

Other Californians have borne out his testimony regarding family practices out there. "When we moved to Pasadena," wrote one of them, "we rigged up a small sun parlour on the roof where we used to spend some time nude regularly. . . . We expect to go back there and we hope to arrange our back porch and garden so that we can practise nudism at all times (the climate allows this) without causing our neighbours too much real suffering." And this man explained: "For me the sense of freedom which comes from air and light striking the naked body means much more than just something physical. It means freeing oneself from a lot of superstitions, fear, and hypocrisy." In other words, he finds the practice of nudity educational for adults no less than for children. Yet at the same time he appreciates the purely physical advantages, stating: "At our ages [middle age] elimination is not so good as when younger, so that the need of a healthy skin is, I think,

[43]

quite vital, and nudism contributes toward this."

Nor do all these veteran family nudists bask in California sun. It was a New Jersey woman who, writing for herself and her husband, reported: "We have been taking sunbaths and practising nudism for the last ten years, at first without any knowledge of such a movement anywhere, and later on reading *Lachendes Leben* [a German nudist magazine] we found out that it was far advanced in Germany. Being sincere sun-worshippers, we have put all our energy, ambition, hard labour, and means into building up a beautiful private place in the country, where we have so much freedom that we can attend to all work inside and outside completely nude."

These are typical instances of family nudism prompted by an appreciation for one or more of the benefits or advantages of nakedness. It happens, too, that they are all examples of quite long standing. But there is plenty of evidence of a new and rapidly spreading interest in nudity, on the part of not only families but groups. We have received letters from all over the country bearing reports similar to the following: "Last Sunday in New Hampshire I began to plan for a little *'Spielplatz'* at my summer home and shall soon have the trees cut down to let in the sun and allow of a deck-tennis court, where we can play naked." Again, "each Saturday and Sunday now finds a canvas stretched around two sides of the orchard," reported a professional man from Ohio, "and four or five healthy young folks [his children with their wives and husbands and friends] sun-bathing and romping about." And last summer a technical man from upper New York State, on learning of the nudist movement abroad, wrote: "To-day I planned and began a small legal solarium in our yard. Our three daughters, the youngest sixteen, are delighted. My wife approves, and does so cheerfully." He went on to say that he himself had "been a secret nudist for many years, but I cannot help despising those who make secrecy necessary. The secrecy takes such a lot from the beauty of it all. Why cannot the members of my family go out and lie on the grass without fearing the police, the church, or the Klan?"

This same man later made the plea: "Why cannot someone start an organization right now? Make it possible for those of us who so need the sun to get its full benefit this vacation? It is such a simple proposition for the rich, but for those of us on an ordinary salary it has so far been impossible. If only the ministers knew how much so-called sin and disease this movement would abolish, they might wake up." And here he adds a second point to the logic of nudist organizations. First of all, there is a need of facilities—in the form of established places and times for the practice of nudity for those who otherwise find the joys and benefits of nakedness unattainable. And secondly, there is need for the organized strength of all nudists to fight for the personal liberty of taking off their clothes—to gain the right, ironically enough, for one's family to go out and lie on the grass of their own lawn, if they are lucky enough to have one. Such an organization need not and should not make itself obnoxious by proselytizing or trying to convert the world to nudity. Let the prudes keep the sanctity of their pallid skins if they prefer them. But it behooves us, as a minority, to form some sort of a union in order to gain the power of collective bargaining. Then, having won a status for ourselves and our practice, we can sit back with the attitude of *not* "Why nudity?" but "Why not nudity?"

However, there are people who, lacking the private means and organized facilities for nudism in America, already find opportunities for enjoying the freedom from clothes. They are what might be called casual nudists in that they have no regular place or time for their naked activities but make the most of every chance for sun-bathing and swimming and playing games in the nude. We have heard from or of scores of them, who find such occasions on the lonely sand dunes along the southern shore of Lake Michigan, or the still deserted sand spits of outer Long Island. They even defy the angry

[45]

shades of the Puritans and strip themselves in secluded coves on the Cape of the Sacred Cod. Many of these casual nudists are young people who are members of hiking clubs that have no express purpose of nudity. Some of these clubs are nominally even church organizations and are sponsored by persons who would be shocked into prayers and denunciations by the very thought of their protégés engaging in anything as sinful as nakedness, especially in mixed company. Other clubs, though free of even the vaguest religious affiliations, are sufficiently reputable to rate weekly announcements in the columns of our better metropolitan newspapers.

It may be that only a few of the members of such a group— perhaps only a dozen or so out of a total of say thirty or forty —prefer to sun-bathe and swim in the nude, the rest of them being still too conventional. In such cases, when the time comes for the club to rest or stop for a swim, these dozen or so boys and girls wander off a short ways together for their hour or two of freedom. Sometimes this is done stealthily, with every precaution lest the others learn the purpose of this exclusiveness. But in at least some clubs, if our reports are to be taken for anything, there is no secrecy whatever, these young people apparently considering the matter merely one of personal choice. In at least one instance, the leader of the club, a young student of law, frankly declares the intention of the nudist contingent and joins them. Once the club has arrived at the place where they are to swim, he announces: "Those of you who want to wear suits may stay here; the rest of us will go up around the bend." In another instance the leader is a young woman engaged in social work. She too joins the nudist faction each week in its temporary withdrawal from the rest of the group, and their purpose, although unannounced, is perfectly understood and taken for granted.

That such goings-on are not only unknown but wellnigh unthought of by most of the parents and elders of these young people is highly probable. Thus it was with the utmost amazement—though fortunately in this case not horror—that a New Englander of the older generation recently discovered such a practice within the circle of his own family. But, once he had digested the admission of his niece, just graduated from Smith, that she "and her brothers and their girl friends for a number of years had taken off their clothes and played games together in secluded spots, as opportunity offered," he readily concluded there was a possibility of nudism coming to America.

Nor should it be thought that all casual nudists are of the younger, and presumably rasher, generation. Though their guerrilla mode of attack on the old taboos may seem too perilous to the most timid souls, it is not utterly disdained by some thoroughly reputable people of maturer years. An illustrious American artist, who is no longer a callow youth, disclosed this fact in his account of how he and his wife "went to the beach with a group of hearty German craftsmen whom we had recently met, solid citizens of whom for the welfare of this country one wishes there were more. One, a blacksmith, was in reality a worker in ornamental iron. Another was a shipbuilder, another a noted decorator. With them were their families, types such as one might expect: an older Frau of comfortable proportions, and those of greater youth and slighter weight; a pair of young lovers much occupied with each other, and a flock of children. After food came time to swim, and we all went in without conceding a fig-leaf to our national grundyism. Afterward, instead of scurrying off in shame to some dark corner, as even I had expected we might, all gathered about the fire to dress." And he added, "this is but one example of what is happening everywhere, unimportant save in that it is symptomatic of a change in our national attitude toward the body."

Apparently among the class more given to social entertainment and the English style of week-end parties, the custom of dispensing with bathing suits for swims at private beaches or pools or in secluded spots after dusk is likewise increasingly prevalent. The staider bourgeoisie frequently take it for granted that such naked bathing parties are inevitably wild orgies—as some doubtless are, especially when the water is accompanied by a flow of stronger beverages. But there is evidence to prove that this is not necessarily the case. An American poet of distinction, who has had no experience with organized nudism but who has participated in such impromptu parties, wrote: "I myself enormously enjoy being on a picnic, or at a country house with a few friends, and having everybody use swimming as an excuse for taking their clothes off." That such experiences were new to him, he attested: "Five years ago I had never been to a nude party." Likewise a young woman told us of her stage fright recently on discovering that the other members of a beach party she attended took it as a matter of course that the bathing suit was obsolete. There is no doubt that aquatic garments were threatened even before the idea of systematic nudism reached the shores of America; not only have they been steadily shrinking, but the moral necessity of even their remaining scraps was being questioned.

It is quite true that the majority of these instances of informal nudism we have cited are largely mere chance practice, generally of an impromptu character, and might almost be dismissed as meaningless as far as an American nudist movement is concerned. But it happens that, along with them, there are a number of known instances in which, though still without any organization in a formal sense, nudism is being tried out in a very deliberate and systematic fashion in this country. The purposive character of some of these essays is well illustrated by the report from a professor in one of the Canadian universities, who wrote: "The difficulties of practising nudism here are probably very much the same as in the United States, but nevertheless I can report progress. During five weeks of last summer I sponsored a little practising group which finally included four women, five men, and five children. We merely went to a fairly secluded beach on a nearby lake and undressed, sometimes spending nearly the whole day in and out of the water. We had to keep bathing suits handy for quick donning in case of disturbance, but enjoyed the freedom of the sun and air immensely in spite of that."

It takes only a few such letters, from widely separated and independent sources, to disclose that there is a genuine sentiment for nudism in America. People are definitely interested, not in the mere theory or the "philosophy" of the thing but in actually trying it out. What is even more significant is that at least some of them have long since passed the experimental stage with it. One day we received a letter from a youth who said he was interested in nudism "because about three years ago I became associated with a group of boys and girls who practise [it] in a remote part of the Bear Mountain Region." This we immediately dismissed as being either a case of misconceived nudism or an instance of confusion between fact and fancy. We frankly doubted that boys and girls had been practising nudity for any "proper" purpose for a period of three years in this country. But within a short time we had word from a somewhat older, though still young, business man, who stated that "During 1927, 28, 29, and 30 I attended a mixed nude camp near —, Pennsylvania." And something about the tone of the letter, as well as the specific details it contained, made us less certain the writer was a victim of either misunderstanding or imagination. When, therefore, still other reports followed—of "a little group" here or there, in the East, the Middle West, the South, on the Pacific Coast, that had been spending vacations in the nude "for years"—we began to realize that genuine nudism was a fact in America, and that there were indeed Americans entitled to call themselves bona fide nudists.

There are other Americans, too, who have not yet put their nudism into practice on American soil, but who are experienced none the less. Many last summer went straight to Europe on learning of the existence of the German Edens. Some who had already planned trips abroad altered their itineraries to take in a *Freilichtpark* or two. Not a few decided to go for that express purpose. Klingberg, the German park that has received the most publicity in this country, had a record attendance despite the depression which affected the parks catering solely to members of German nudist organizations. Americans outnumbered all the other foreigners at Klingberg, and an English-speaking table became a regular institution in the dining room. Typical of last summer's tourists were three Stanford University students who, having read *Among the Nudists* on shipboard, headed straight for Klingberg, without further inquiry, as soon as they landed in Germany, arriving at the *Freilichtpark* one night unannounced and without reservations, bearing the book as their introduction. Fortunately for them Klingberg had not been disguised in their source of information as it was in a French book on the same subject, for they might have had some difficulty in buying a railroad ticket to a mythical "Nackendorf.'" Probably ere long Baedekers and other official guide books will be forced to list the nudist parks among the attractions of the localities they describe; already a reputable American travel agency has arranged a tour of the principal nudist centres of Europe for this coming summer. Even now either the United States Line or the Hamburg-American Line might steal a march on its chief competitors by advertising its final port as "The Gateway to Klingberg."

A number of these American tourists to the lands of naked men might have hesitated to go to similar Edens in America even had they known of any existing here. It is easier, of course, to be daring on foreign soil, safe from the tongues of one's disapproving neighbours; many, who in Rome do as the Romans do, would never dream of playing Roman in their own home town. On the other hand, many have regretted that they were not offered the same opportunity in their own land, and would have preferred to take off their clothes in the United States had they known where to do it without being arrested.

Informal Nudist Practice

No doubt numerous Americans who have had the courage to strip themselves in Europe and taste the joys of unhampered light and air will now be emboldened to go naked at home.

IV

ORGANIZED NUDISM

B<small>UT BY NO MEANS ALL NUDIST PRACTICE IN THIS COUNTRY</small>
today is of a private, incidental, or even casual character. There
are a number of flourishing groups or clubs in America founded
expressly and primarily for the purpose of promoting nudism.
We are not referring here to any such pseudo-nudist outfits as
the so-called "Olympian League," which may have sprung
into life and assumed for a day some of the ear-marks of nudist
organizations while, in reality, merely utilizing nudism as an
excuse and means for a quite different end.

Only last fall the Olympian League suddenly blossomed
forth with a big advertisement in the *New Republic*. Beneath
the heading "Nude Culture" and a few lines of text about the
"ancient gymnosophy of the Greeks," the Adolf Koch Schools
in Germany, and the nudist movement abroad, there followed
what was ostensibly a solicitation of mail orders for *Among
the Nudists*, Parmelee's *Nudism in Modern Life*, the English
translation of Hans Surén's *Man and Sunlight*, and Saleeby's
Sunlight and Health. At the end, however, with all the emphasis
of a full stop, came an invitation to "Send only one dollar for
a year's subscription to The Olympian, America's nudist magazine." Perhaps to some readers sincerely interested in nudism,
this sounded promising. If so, they were doomed to disap-

pointment when they sent for and saw "America's nudist magazine." The very advertisements it carried disclosed its purpose and appeal: "Art Photos. Undraped and unretouched poses. . . ." and "French Art, postcards—the kind Paris is world-famous for—in true colours. . . ." generously interspersed with "Would you like a pretty, wealthy sweetheart? Stamp for particulars. . . ." or "If you want a rich husband, send for my big FREE list of descriptions. . . ." et cetera. And the motive behind the cheaply printed leaflet, as behind the alleged organization for which it was the ostensible organ, may be judged from the well-grounded report that its combination founder-owner-manager never had practised nudism himself, and that not until long after he had set himself up in this business had he established contact with, and sought to join, an authentic nudist club in New York—and was refused membership.

Fortunately there is evidence to disprove that the development of nudism in this country must be necessarily along such sublime Olympian lines. For some of the genuine nudist groups, with thoroughly valid ideas regarding nakedness, have been in existence and functioning now for a year or more, their members of both sexes practising nudity in common moreover, without any of the evil consequences, moral or otherwise, predicted by the opponents of nudism in America. No one knows the actual number of such groups today—certainly we lay no claim to knowing; nor do we pretend to present here anything like a survey of them. In fact we shall not attempt even a catalogue of all those groups which we ourselves do know or have had authoritative reports upon. This should not be taken to mean that we deem those unmentioned as any the less significant. In some cases it will be because we lack specific enough information as to their character—their form of organization, mode of practice, or their membership. In other cases it will be simply for lack of space and to avoid repetition. For our purpose here is to present only a few typical specimens of the different kinds of American nudist associations.

There is, first of all, the oldest and largest nudist club of New York City—probably, too, among the oldest and largest in the United States aiming primarily at the promotion of nudist practice by both sexes in common. Originally formed in December, 1929, by a handful of German-Americans, who either had been initiated into *Nacktkultur* in Germany or at least had learned of it there, this association has thrived and grown to a present membership of nearly two hundred men and women, with a waiting list of nearly a hundred more—this, too, in spite of its being encumbered with the ambitious and ambiguous name of "American League for Physical Culture." (No, Bernarr Macfadden neither has, nor ever has had, anything whatsoever to do with it!) While still essentially a German-American group, it contains today many members whose forbears are what is known as old American stock.

And what, then, are these people? Radicals? No indeed! With the exception of possibly half a dozen or so Communists and a somewhat larger number of Socialists, they are very bourgeois. In fact, the American League for Physical Culture counts among its members many who are ultra-conservative in matters of politics, economics, and religion. At least three of them either are Protestant clergymen or have been; several are teachers or professors in the public schools or universities; and there are business and professional men and women, artists, writers, musicians, students, clerks, and labourers. Socially, as well as economically, politically, and in almost every other way, they are a heterogeneous lot of people, but they are distinctly homogeneous in their views regarding nudity. As a group they are consciously democratic to the point of accepting anyone who is, as they say, "psychologically prepared for the practice of nudism," stating specifically in the "Principles and Standards" of their organization: "We invite to our membership persons of character of all ages and both sexes. Our purposes are not exclusively physical or cultural or æsthetic but rather a normal union of all these. We make no tests of politics, religion or opinion, provided that these are so held as not to obscure the purpose of the League. It is intended that the American League for Physical Culture shall be thoroughly representative of the whole social order."

Married couples are given preference in matters of membership and are encouraged to join together. In fact a man or wife alone may become a member only upon filing the signature of his or her marital partner to an affidavit that reads as follows: "I understand the purpose and customs of the American League for Physical Culture and have no objection to my wife (husband) joining." It is the plan of the club, moreover, to keep the membership more or less evenly divided between males and females by the simple method of relegating to the waiting list any preponderance of applicants of either sex. Minors are eligible only when at least one of their parents or a guardian is a member. And non-residents can, at the cost of a nominal yearly fee, obtain membership privileges whenever they come to New York, and receive throughout the year the small mimeographed "Bulletin" that each month carries official announcements of meetings and business affairs of the organization and bits of news regarding individual members.

Requirements for admission to the League are intended to discourage Fishermen. There is a duly appointed committee to receive and act on formal applications for membership. These not only call for full particulars regarding the life, character, and habits of the candidate but demand the signing of a statement that reads: "I hereby apply for membership in the American League for Physical Culture. I am familiar with the League's ideals of health, morality, and clean living, and I accept them for myself. I will faithfully observe its principles and customs, and agree to surrender my membership card if suspended by the Board of Governors. I understand that the Board of Governors is not obliged to give any reason for suspending a member from the League." And that there may be no chance for misunderstanding, the ideals and principles referred to are set forth in an accompanying page as follows:

Our goal is the healthy mind and the healthy body.

Sun, light, and air are vital conditions of human well being. We believe that these elements are insufficiently used in present day life, to the detriment of physical and moral health. For the purpose of health and recreation and for the conditioning of man to his world we offer a new social practice, based on the known wholesome value of exposure to these elements and in the spirit of naturalness, cheerfulness, and cleanness of body and mind that they symbolize. We aim to make the fullest possible use of sun, light, and air by a program of exercise and life in the open in such a way as will result in the maximum physical and mental benefit.

We believe in the essential wholesomeness of the human body and all its functions. We therefore regard the body neither as an object of shame nor as a subject for levity or erotic exploitation. Any attitude or behaviour inconsistent with this view is contrary to the whole spirit of the society and has no place among us.

The practice of our physical culture tends towards simplicity and integrity in all ways. We counsel for our members the sane and hygienic life. We reserve the right to impose abstinence from stimulants and intoxicants at our meetings and on our grounds.

During the winter months, the American League meets regularly several times a week in a gymnasium in the midtown of New York City. There they gather around eight o'clock of an evening, men and women with a sprinkling of adolescents, for two or three hours of exercise, games, and a swim in the adjoining pool. For the first half hour, all remain conventionally garbed in bathing or gym suits. It then being assumed that all are in who are coming that evening, the doors are locked, the compromise clothing is dispensed with, the teacher for the night takes charge of the gym floor, and the real evening's program begins. The exercises are a combination of gymnastics and rhythmics, generally done to the count of the leader or to music on the piano. They may begin with a few minutes run about the room, first slowly, then faster, then slowly again but in wide strides, or short ones but on the toes. Then the steps are co-ordinated with certain body motions—bending first forward, then back, then to the side—and with various arm movements. By a progressive integration of motions, the class is led gradually into what is a virtual dance, a sequence of group movements—raising of arms and legs, bending or swaying of bodies and heads and necks, this way and that—while, as a unit, the members perform an intricate pattern of steps across and back and around the floor.

Forty minutes of this formal exercise, and the teacher withdraws. Rather, he himself now joins the group in various games or individual exercises. A net is hastily stretched, and a game of volley ball draws the interest of many. A few gather in one corner about a rowing machine; two or three may move to another corner and there industriously set to work with a set of pulleys and weights; still others, forgoing further exercise, go at once to the shower room and thence to the swimming pool. Within another hour all will be, or have been, at the pool, where fancy and plain diving, races, water ball—and, in the youngsters' shallow end, furious water fights—hold sway until almost eleven o'clock. At that time all dress and, again looking as staid as any person you may meet upon the street, they depart for their respective homes, neither to return nor perhaps to see one another again until the following Monday or Wednesday or Friday night.

But it is during the summer months that the American League for Physical Culture takes on its greatest life. Then, in addition to the gymnastic sessions in town—which few except the most ardent physical culturists attend regularly—the members have their "park," a farm within commuting distance from the city, where they gather for week-ends, holidays, and even vacations. Located the first year in lower New York State, since then in northern New Jersey, their farm is really the centre of the League's interests. Nude exercises and games and swimming in a city gymnasium are all very well, provided nothing better is possible—such things do help to keep the club together during the winter months—but real nudism calls for open air and sunshine, and that blissful freedom of nakedness out of doors.

On the day set for our first visit to this authentic American nudist park, we drove out with friends and members in order to learn the way. It being a hot afternoon in early summer, we were glad to get away from the city, and the hills and woods of northern New Jersey looked good. The road was thronged with others who had also felt the call of the country, with picnic parties and week-enders, but after two hours of driving, we turned off from the main highway with its heavy Saturday afternoon traffic. As we did so, we passed a little house set back in a wide shady lawn, from the porch of which a heavy man in shirt sleeves amiably shouted a greeting of some sort and waved.

"The constable, our nearest neighbour," one of our friends informed us with a chuckle.

"Constable!" We started at the thought. "But he doesn't know where we're bound of course, or what's going on!"

"Sure," laughed both of our companions in unison, and one of them added: "I think he'd even join us if he could get off duty for week-ends. As it is, he plays a kind of private police-man—helps steer snoopers and outsiders away."

Less than half a mile up the lane and we entered the yard of a farmhouse. It was quiet and peaceful back there away from the auto road. But lacking so much as a sign of chickens or livestock, the place looked ominously still, almost abandoned.

We turned in bewilderment to our companions: "But where is everyone? Saturday, and nobody out here!"

Organized Nudism

"Oh, everyone is out in the park—everyone but young Jim back there; it's his turn to guard today."

Looking back toward the gate, we now discovered beneath a shady elm, a husky young man we had failed to notice. Barefooted and dressed in a pair of shorts, he was stretched on his belly in the grass, a book propped against a stone in front of him, apparently engrossed in reading, while kicking his bare heels in the air like a boy. We then learned from our friends that, out of deference to convention, nudity is allowed only in the "park" proper, an area well back in the centre of the farm and which, being completely surrounded by woods, is screened from every possible view except a bird's-eye or an airplane. Hence the sight of what goes on there can neither shock nor corrupt the morals of any outsider who has not first violated the innumerable no-trespass signs that mark the boundaries of the property.

By this time we had rounded the corner of the farmhouse and halted before an open shed. Apparently built to house farm implements, it was filled now with a dozen or so automobiles.

"You see, at least some of the crowd are out," one of our companions declared. "I expect some came even last night. More will be here yet today, and tomorrow. . . ."

It was then explained how all the members reached the place. Some, as ourselves, arrived by automobile; others by train, then afoot from the nearest station; and on Sundays, at a certain hour a special bus—the property of one of the members of the club—came from the ferry in Jersey City.

After parking the car, we proceeded to a round of inspection of the barn, granaries, and the like, that had been converted into transient quarters, and the house, the entire downstairs of which except for the kitchen was given over to tables and chairs for the dining-room. In the orchard we even discovered a number of pitched tents, the private property of members who preferred to keep camping facilities always ready for their arrival. Then we ourselves went upstairs in the house, got out of our town clothes, donned bathing or gym suits and sandals, and, armed with blankets and towels, were ready for the park.

Back through the farm-yard and across an open field we went, then down hill to the woods that enclosed the nudist area. Already we could hear voices and singing through the trees ahead of us. Soon we came to a gate beyond which were numerous neat little piles of various sorts of clothes—bathing costumes, bathrobes, gym suits, shorts, and what-not—and we in turn doffed, folded up, and added to the collection the brief garments that we wore. Completely unclothed now except for our sandals, we entered the prescribed borders of the park. A few more steps along the shady path and we emerged upon a clearing, to be greeted by at least two score nudists, young and old.

Out in the centre, on open ground worn bare of a single blade of grass, were half a dozen young men and three or four young women playing a game of volley ball. Their light tanned bodies, gleaming in the sun as they leaped and ran for the ball, stood out sharply against the dark bank of trees beyond. And across the far end of the field two more robust males balanced, crouched, and swung their beautifully bronzed bodies, like pictures of Ancient Greek athletes, as they hurled a javelin back and forth to one another. But by far the greater number of people were lounging in the sun or shade along the border of the clearing. Off to the left, on blankets spread in a wide circle around a girl who strummed a guitar, sat a mixed group of men and women, young, old and middle-aged, who were singing a song of the *Wandervögel*. Nearer were smaller groups, pairs, and trios, soberly talking or happily laughing together. Out immediately in front of us, in the bright sun, three naked babies, ranging from one to four years old, rolled and tumbled happily about on two or three blankets spread side by side, while across the two ends of this blanketed playground their mothers lay stretched out as if asleep. And to the right, some-

Organized Nudism

what removed from the others, lay a naked man and woman, their blankets and themselves half in and half out of the sun, she softly reading aloud from a book she held in the shadow, while he lay gazing up into the tops of the trees.

We were welcomed warmly on every hand and at once invited to join each group, in song, play, discussion, or quiet conversation and repose. But, it being our first visit to this American nudist park, we could scarcely settle down—enticing as was a sunbath in this open glade—until we had explored everything; above all we must see the swimming pool. So, proceeding on across the field, we again entered the woods by a path that meandered down the hill. Again there were voices ahead of us, shouts and sounds of hilarity. Soon we came to the brook, and then to the dam that made the pool. Ten or fifteen nudists were already there. Some were having a furious water fight, while the others watched and applauded from the opposite bank.

Less than two hundred feet in length and scarcely deep enough for diving except with the greatest care, the pool nevertheless was inviting with its clear water, icy cold from the dense shade of the wooded brook. Breath-taking, its very iciness was a tonic; to feel it slipping freely, uninterrupted, along our naked skins gave the thrill of an electric bath. We felt an irresistible impulse to strike out and swim with all our might, to throw all our power into our strokes, to kick and thresh the water with a veritable frenzy of force. It was as though our bodies were suddenly supercharged with energy. But such tempestuousness is short-lived, and in a few minutes we clambered out upon the bank, lungs heaving and flesh tingling with the cold, to lie in the sun upon the warm leaves and grass. Under the influence of the hot sun and air on our wet skins, we began to relax involuntarily. It was as though our very muscles had attained a state of flux; our bodies settled, flattened, like that of a cat ensconced upon the hearth, and we lay inert, completely filled with a delicious sense of peace and the luxury of contentment.

Nudism Comes to America

Nevertheless, in a short time the afternoon shadows commenced to grow and the air in the shade began to cool; so rising and donning our sandals again, we climbed back up the path to the clearing and the volley ball field. We found that game had attracted more players in our absence—some of them men and women no longer young—and as we spread our blankets for another rest in the sun, still more arose and began a less strenuous game of quoits.

It was interesting, as the sun gradually sank in the west, to see how the different people reacted to the evening chill. To many who, like ourselves, were less used to outdoor nudity, this chill was immediately perceptible, the slight mist that began rising from the ground as soon as the sun had dropped behind the hill very quickly forcing them to get up and move around. But some, more accustomed to doing without their clothes from having spent vacations in the park—men and women easily identified by the bronze-like colouring of their skins—were far less susceptible to the cold. In fact one couple, who had lived out there for a month or two, seemed wholly indifferent to either the damp or chill. Not until long after the sun had set did they resort to clothes, and even then it was not, they said, because they felt any physical need for them. Nor was it layers of fat that made them impervious to cold, for both of them were unusually thin. Interestingly enough, too, it was these same pigmented ones who later displayed a similar obliviousness to heat, being generally the last to quit games in the midday sun and seek the shelter of the shade.

At length the crowd in the clearing began to thin. People departed in twos or threes, by the path to the gate where the clothes were cached. Soon we too set out and, on our arrival back at the farm, found everyone attired in some sort of clothing. Most of the women were wearing gym or bathing suits; most of the men were only in shorts, for the air up there was still hot as compared to that of the valley below. Many sat or stood about, visiting in small groups around the yard, and a

[62]

number of both men and women were at work in the kitchen or on the back porch, peeling potatoes and making other preparations for supper.

To those wont to object to the organized, regimented character of the nudists' activities, this kitchen of the American League would have been a comfort and a joy. True, it was a communal affair. Coffee, for example was strictly socialized— a sufficient amount, in huge pots, always being brewed to serve all who wanted it—and there were various kinds of cooperation between members. But in general, the kitchen was ruled by the principles of anarchy, pure and simple. With facilities and room strictly finite and the demand relatively infinite, needless to say there resulted a staggering—or straggling—of meals. It was not a case of "first come, first served" so much as it was a question of come early to find any chance of serving yourself at all. No wonder that few indeed went in for roasting or baking of any sort, and that some were content with the proverbial sandwiches or canned pork-and-beans of American picnickers. Probably these conditions explained why so many of the members had set up their own tents and camps in the orchard, where portable stoves and bonfires were now being put into use. Next year, however, the leader assured us, things would be different, for they expect then to install a cook who will prepare and serve all meals, with perhaps a little volunteer help from the members.

Supper over, there was little to do but sit around and rest. A few young people went for a stroll down the country lane; three or four energetic souls began recruiting players for another game of volley ball in the park once the moon should rise, as it shortly would, and out in the darkness of the front lawn, a fresh chorus of singers gathered, to begin a long repertoire of old songs. Their voices, low pitched and unobtrusive in the open air, mingled with the numerous minute noises of the night—the creaking of crickets, the distant croak of a frog, and an occasional faint call of some bird or the hoot of an owl

[63]

deep in the woods of an adjoining hill. Everything seemed conspiring to lull us into silence and repose, and conversations lapsed as we sat there in the darkness watching the flit of fireflies down the hill and waiting for the moon to rise. The latter event, coming at ten o'clock, was the signal for many to retire to their cots, their bedrolls, or their blankets on the grass beneath the trees; but the singing continued at least until we ourselves went to sleep.

From this typical day at the park, it will be seen that the American League for Physical Culture is an extremely harmless and innocent group which should scarcely be objectionable to even the most peace-loving community. Its members engage in no sort of active propaganda; much less do they stage demonstrations to agitate their ideas of life. But neither are they deceptive or even covert regarding their nudism. Though they do not recruit, they welcome new members to their association and gladly explain their views to anyone who has the interest to inquire about them. Thus it was they themselves who furnished the facts last fall for the New York *World-Telegram* story already cited in Chapter II. This was a frank statement of the group's history, aims, and activities, furnished by one of the officers, with the express agreement that it was not to be exploited or "played up," and that the editors in return would refer any resulting inquiries they received to the group itself to answer in whatever manner seemed suitable. That this forthright policy has stood the League in good stead is fairly proved by the public relations it has on the whole enjoyed during the nearly three years of its existence. As already shown, even the local constable tacitly approves of them on their farm. Likewise the farmers of the vicinity have given evidence of their goodwill. It may be true that the latter are interested primarily in selling their produce and supplies to the city visitors, but they can scarcely be ignorant of what these summer guests are doing in their midst.

Only on two occasions have the American Leaguers met

with embarrassment by running afoul of legal difficulties.
The first time was in the summer of 1930, when their park
was raided. This was a result not of a scandalized and incensed
community but of a woman's jealousy. The lady in question
had a summer boarding place in which business was not what
she thought it ought to be. Assuming that the nudists' farm
was a similar establishment, she was both annoyed at its thriving patronage and curious to learn the secret of its success. So
one Sunday morning when a young man appeared at her door
—a new member seeking directions to the farm—she generously offered to drive him there, which she did. And, disdaining
the "Entrance Forbidden" sign upon the gate, she brought up
in the very yard of the farmstead, beside the swimming pool
where some dozen naked mermaids and mermen were disport-
ing themselves. She at once beat a hasty retreat—straight to the
police station. Just what she told the authorities was never
learned, but shortly a car appeared out of the lane that led to
the farm-yard, and before it had fairly stopped, four policemen jumped out, with guns drawn as for the capture of some
desperate band of criminals in a "Western" movie.

On the farm that year there was no particular area exclusively designated as a nudist "park," for the whole property
was fairly secluded and screened by trees. Hence this day, as
usual, found most of the members scattered throughout the
woods. Only half a dozen men were down by the pool, a few
yards from the farmhouse— they and six women. It can
scarcely be said who was the more surprised or taken back,
hunters or hunted; both alike stood dead in their tracks, staring
at each other in utter stupefaction. But suddenly one of the
women dived into the pool. Another slipped quietly into the
water from atop the dam, letting herself down slowly while
she gazed solemnly at the little group of officers.

The latter, once out of their car, had taken in the scene,
stopped, and then rather fumblingly pocketed their guns.
Finally one of the nudists, a portly man, made a dash for the

nearby house, and a policeman at once set out after him, both on the run. The nudist, without stopping, shouted back plaintively: "I'm going to get my pants!" at which some heartless wretch laughed—and the spell was broken. Nudists and police alike advanced, and the officers made it clear that the nudists were under arrest and must come to the nearest town as prisoners.

In town the local magistrate immediately held an informal hearing. Fortunately he was curious as to the motives for this unconventional procedure and open-minded enough to heed the explanation, a New York paper later quoting him as saying: "They are well dressed, well educated, well bred. I think the men are brokers or business men in New York City. . . . When I asked them why they persisted in their nude sunbathing, with the women side by side with the men, they told me: 'Nature doesn't segregate the sexes, so why should we? Women work and play by the side of men. There's nothing shameful about nudity. The sun's rays give us health and purify our minds.' " Moreover, His Honour was properly impressed by the fact that the culprits were all married couples— a lucky chance indeed, since there were a number of unattached youths and maidens about the place who might have fallen into the police dragnet.

But he held that it was not for him to make distinctions between nakedness for commendable purposes and ordinary indecent exposure. His duty compelled him, he said, to fine them five dollars each for disturbing the peace, and ask them to wear legal covering hereafter, at least in those sections of the farm accessible to the public. He took pains to explain that as far as the State law is concerned a mere pair of trunks was sufficient, nothing being required above the waist, even for women. He intimated, too, that if the defendants wished to protest their case by bringing a charge of trespass against the complainant, they might very well have the best of it. But as the defendants were anxious above everything else to avoid publicity, lest it jeopardize their standing in their respective businesses or communities, they decided to let the matter drop. Nevertheless, they very frankly gave their own names and addresses for the magistrate's record. And their trust was rewarded, for when the metropolitan tabloid reporters appeared, hot on the trail of a sensational story, the names were so garbled as to be unrecognizable by inquisitive neighbours or employers—a very natural and explicable accident since many of the names were Germanic in origin and rather complicated as to spelling.

The second time they were troubled by the law was last December, when the New York City police broke into their gymnasium "a stone's throw from Times Square," as the tabloids liked to point out, and arrested seventeen men and seven women on a charge of "indecent exposure." This too was ostensibly the result of a woman's wrath, since the raid was prompted by an anonymous letter purporting to be a wife's complaint of her husband's attendance at such scandalous gatherings. But, quite aside from the fact that neither husbands nor wives are singly eligible for membership in the American League without their spouses' written approval, the leaders of the group have quite conclusive evidence that such a letter, if actually received, was written not by an outraged woman but by a disgruntled man who shortly before had had his membership retracted on account of his character. Not only did he when ousted threaten to "get" the group, but he is said later to have boasted of his revenge. Of course the extra-legal status of nudism in this country today makes it particularly vulnerable to just such tactics on the part of enemies.

But whatever the source of the "tip" that set them on the trail of the League, the police, according to their own subsequent testimony, went to the roof of the building and, peeking through a crack in the skylight, saw in the narrow strip of room visible below two or three naked men or women doing rhythmic exercises. So what they did was to go downstairs and,

[67]

thougn unarmed with a warrant of any kind, crash in the door and arrest everyone—incidentally displaying, their victims later said, not only much vile temper but a great air of moral superiority that led them to handle some of their prisoners very roughly and to berate all of them with language of the most abusive sort. In this connection there may be significance in the nudists' account of how this attitude suddenly changed to one of respect, once they had dressed and appeared in the class symbols of conventional clothes. They said that by the time they had arrived at the station, the police were nearly apologetic, expressing the hope that their prisoners would forget any unpleasantness that might have occurred. Obviously clothes make the man in the eyes of our policemen.

The trial, which followed in a week, must have been a sorry disappointment to the prudes, for the case was dismissed, not for any lack of evidence but for lack of grounds. City Magistrate Jonah Goldstein, before whom it came, held that mere nude gymnastics, such as described by the police, while unquestionably *wilful*, did not constitute an instance of *lewd* exposure as specified in Section 1140 of the Penal Code, under which the case had been brought. Though insisting that he was offering no brief for nudism and did not wish to become involved in any controversy regarding nudity, he declared that "Not by any stretch of the imagination could it be called lewd when all they [the nudists] do is gymnastics and it is not a cover" for something else—this after having forced the police to admit upon the stand that they had seen nothing to "arouse sex desire." Thus blocked, the prosecuting attorney asked the court to recharge the defendants, arguing that for men and women to be together "in a semi-public place stark naked" itself "openly outrages public decency" in violation of Section 43 of the Penal Code. But this, after reading the law, Magistrate Goldstein refused to do. "While not putting the stamp of approval on nudity," he declared the statutes "aimed at lewdness," which had not been proved.

[68]

Organized Nudism

It is worth noting here that even in the earlier case where the American League became embroiled with the law, this question of lewdness possibly saved the nudists from a considerably heavier penalty. For even the country magistrate—perhaps on account of his being so impressed by the "respectable" character of the defendants—quickly recognized the absence of any "lewd intent" in their activities. Hence, although they were then too first charged with indecent exposure under Section 1140 of the Penal Code, His Honour changed the charge almost at once to disorderly conduct. Whether that too could have been overthrown was not found out, for the defendants preferred to pay their fine rather than incur the publicity of fighting for an acquittal.

ⱳⱳ

V

RESTRICTED NUDIST GROUPS

Perhaps in time the American League for Physical Culture will be seen to have had no small influence on the nudist movement in America. Not only is it among the oldest but it is probably the largest single organization in this country aiming directly at the promotion of nudism, and up to the present it is more or less setting the pace. But there are several respects in which it is not serving as a model. As has been shown, it is avowedly democratic in character; while scrutinizing with great care the "moral" character of candidates for membership, it strives to make no discrimination on any other grounds, its creed being to welcome all comers who, as they say, have a proper mental attitude toward nudity. Not all of the several nudist clubs formed or starting in this country are following this broadly catholic policy. With most of them there are certain other things to be taken into account besides the question of whether the candidate is "psychologically prepared" for the practice of nudity. As a general rule, some degree of selectivity is being exercised, and memberships are restricted more or less to one or another type of person.

This does not necessarily mean that there is an inherent element of snobbery in American nudism, although there inevitably is in some instances. An example is that of a reported

[70]

Restricted Nudist Groups

Los Angeles group that holds forth on the roof of a very large apartment hotel in the heart of the city. They are said to boast that their club is a "closed corporation." But, in truth, it is not a club at all, properly speaking. It is merely a "set" that has gone in for sunbaths and tanning, a member of which, happening to have control of this apartment building, has supplied convenient facilities for sun-worship. From a man who has visited them we learn that no dues are charged, but that one or more members contribute from time to time whatever there may be need for. Nor are there any opportunities for games or exercises on their roof, only sunbaths—and, cocktails. Probably there are numerous such groups out there, as well as in New York and elsewhere. But, generally speaking, the membership restrictions in nudist clubs are not of this nature. Distinctions are not as a rule along class lines but are made to conform with certain—though often vaguely defined—personal standards; they have to do with matters of sociability rather than social differences, and take into account such factors as the cultural and intellectual character of the candidate. While a proper attitude toward nudity is still the prime requisite for membership, congeniality with the other members is considered likewise necessary. Social philosophy, rather than social rating, is the chief criterion.

A rather extreme example of this sort of restriction is the case of a small group of New Yorkers who last year joined hands in acquiring a large farm on the New England coast line a few hours out of the city. Just seven families comprise this group, and theirs too is a closed corporation. But in their case there are certain extenuating circumstances for any apparent snobbery. First of all, they are writers or editors of that lucky variety who can earn a living by work outside of the city. Hence their prime need is not a club in the country affording opportunities for social intercourse; rather what they require is a quiet place in which to work, or to relax from work, and a country home where their children can spend at

[71]

least their summers in healthful open air and sun. Their group comes near to being a colony of intimate friends and brother craftsmen. Desirous of escaping New York during the summer, and yet not being people of such affluence as to make private country estates attainable, they very sensibly decided to throw in their lots together. Since all of them happened likewise to appreciate the joys and advantages of nakedness, at least for sunbaths and swimming, they resolved at the same time to get a place that would permit it. So, they took a ten-year lease on an old farm with a mile and a half of sea-shore, and posted the land side with "Private: no trespassing" signs. One room was delegated to each family for its own use, care, and responsibility, the rest of the big house being kept for the use of all in common, maintenance, rent, and living expenses to be pro-rated; and the place is there now for any or all of the members to go to whenever they wish, with a long stretch of sheltered and secluded cove of extraordinarily fine white sand for nude swimming and sun-bathing.

A still different sort of exclusiveness—and one which at a glance constitutes more nearly a case of class distinction—is exemplified by another Los Angeles group. Being a temporary and more or less experimental project, it is now disbanded; but its members, according to last reports, are preparing to reorganize on a permanent basis and acquire a place of their own for the regular practice of nudity. It was fostered originally by a man of means who wished to try out his ideas with the view of interesting some of his acquaintances in the practice. Yet from the beginning it differed both from the other Los Angeles group—the roof-top nudists—and the small New England coast group just mentioned in that this was not a closed corporation but a regular club, open to anyone with the proper qualifications. It was the extraordinary character of membership requirements, however, that gave the club its exclusiveness. While a proper attitude toward nakedness was here too a prime requisite, and sociability or congeniality was a factor, eligibility was a question, finally, of whether one could pay monthly dues of twenty-five or thirty dollars. This fact alone, if no other, would have given the club both a character and goal different from that of the American League, for instance, which with its nominal fees requires a large membership to maintain its farm and gymnasium.

This Los Angeles club was made up of people given to expensive things; their tastes were for luxuries, not the simple life. Also, the mountain property where they gathered for their nudist practices, although temporarily donated for the purpose by the sponsor of the experiment, was, according to all accounts, appropriate to high dues, being a private estate with costly grounds and an outdoor pool. The club, however, was not a commercial project. In fact all the revenue from dues—and perhaps more too—was expended on club services, including that of a special swimming teacher and even a professional masseuse, as well as an athletic and physical director. And the success of the venture may be gauged from the fact that, beginning with only eight or ten members, it grew within the three or four months of its existence to an active membership of about thirty-five, men and women together—all of whom are now sufficiently enthusiastic to be planning, as has been said, to reorganize and acquire their own club property. It is probable that when they do, their new club will follow more or less the elaborate lines laid down in this trial organization and therefore be limited to people with means.

A sort of happy medium between this organization, with its financial requirements, and the broadly democratic American League of New York is the "sun park" that was instituted last year on the North Pacific Coast, about ten miles from the centre of one of the larger cities—a "wooded shoreland" of something over a hundred acres, two of which "are in grass with scattered shade trees that serve as a screen against aviators." Actually this is not yet an organized club. As the proprietor and sponsor of the place himself says, "We are allowing this [matter of club organization] to evolve. At present, on account of property ownership and financing, as well as for individual and family protection, the whole activity is closely under my own supervision and control." But he explains that there are "no restrictions on colour and creed, etc. Any person who would be a pleasant companion under the circumstances will be considered."

Such a rule of course might be made highly restrictive if rigorously applied. To anyone too critical, not many people would qualify under any circumstances as "pleasant companions." The record in this case, however, indicates that probably considerable latitude has been exercised, for the owner's report continues: "Starting in July [1931], we had about thirty regular participants by September, ranging in ages from two years to eighty-one. Our Sun Park is very new but our membership cross-section is very wide. Teachers, nurses, social workers, a police officer, a minister, and various unlabelled persons make up the roster. We expect to more than double it next summer." As they have not yet organized formally, the question of dues has not risen and there has been no initiation charge. But "reasonable fees for a season and single admission charges will be determined before next May."

During this formative period when the place has been something in the manner of a private enterprise, "Visitors properly sanctioned and referred to me," as the owner explains, "are especially welcome, but until I can be sure of their good faith and acceptability they will probably think me very non-committal. . . . We are very careful not to be talked about. When some member desires to suggest a new member, there can be enough talk between them on tanning, sun-bathing and nudist books, etc., to find out that the new member would be receptive. Then the new name is submitted for consideration, and if we are favourable, the old member is authorized to inform and invite the prospect. . . . If a prospect or member desires to withdraw, he is honour bound to refrain from divulging any information whatever about our Park, it members or customs." And writing at the end of the season, he said: "Every participant is enthusiastic. Not a regrettable thing has happened except three bee stings at important places. This with all our happy memories gives hopes for our future"—hopes which call for the possible addition of guest cottages, as well as more playgrounds, to augment the present equipment of "tether ball, quoits, put-golf, swings and hammocks."

Still another group in California, differing from the others there as from the "Sun Park" of the Pacific Northwest in that it neither enjoys nor apparently feels the need for any sort of financial sponsorship, has "more than fifty" adherents who have a regular camping place, though one for which they pay nothing. It is because they exercise a sort of squatter's right on this land—whether with or without the owner's knowledge and consent we cannot say—and hence their park costs them nothing, that they have got along so well economically. This group, incidentally, antedates even the American League in point of actual nudist practice, having been enjoying clothesless freedom for week-ends and vacations regularly for a period of more than three years. However, we have accorded the New Yorkers seniority as a nudist organization, holding that they are probably the first such in America, because this California group is not organized in any formal sense even now. In truth its members do not aspire to have it become an organization, although their history clearly indicates that they have enjoyed—what is far more important—a high degree of direction. Their group is in principle autocratic, not democratic, and evidently has been fortunate in its choice of autocrat. The latter explains: "So far we [himself and his wife] have merely gathered a group of our friends on an invitational basis, trying each time to pick a crowd that would be congenial. Our only control of conduct is our ability to pick our guests and to leave out anyone who might prove a misfit"—a thing that has happened, he says, only twice.

"We have often discussed the advisability of forming a club," he continues, "but hesitate for several reasons. Any elaboration of our plan would increase the cost and thus keep out some of our most valued members. Also the question of 'discipline' might arise, which is hardly possible as long as the inmates [*sic*] feel that they are guests. . . . So far most of our complexes in new members seem to be nothing more serious than unreasoning ingrained modesty, which we usually cure in forty-eight hours by treating everything as such a matter of course that participation seems more comfortable than resistance." And, as to the personnel, he says: "Our interests differ widely. Painting seems to cause the most discussion, as we have several artists. Several of the girls are dancers, some write with moderate success, and we have one playwright, an opera impresario, two architects, two flyers, several newspaper and advertising people, plenty of musicians, and too few good cooks." He adds that after several "parties" they now practically bar drinking, and "most of us don't miss it [while some] of the gang are really interested in diet and physical training, using the camp as a rest and relaxation from plenty of the other kind of stuff in the city."

His own description gives a graphic picture of their activities: "Our great sport is swimming and surf-board riding. We have one of the finest beaches on the Pacific Coast all to ourselves. We usually collect on the sand as soon as breakfast is cleaned up and stay there until late afternoon. The camp is run on a strictly communal basis, each person paying his share and doing whatever work he is asked to perform. This means just the essentials of living, wood gathering, water carrying, cooking and cleaning up. Tents and sleeping quarters are so scattered as to give privacy. A 'civic centre' with movable canvas wind-breaks is the hub of activity."

It will probably be noted that none of these restricted nudist clubs is really self-sustaining; either their facilities for nudist practice are contributed by someone who sponsors the project, or the group has been fortunate enough to "find" a park (where it was never lost) and therefore pay nothing for the use of it. None that has been cited is up to the present free and independent in the manner of the American League for Physical Culture. However, it should not be assumed that a restricted club cannot be made self-supporting once it becomes sufficiently established. Perhaps what is potentially the soundest as well as largest organization of this character—one making no distinction of class, creed, or colour but restricted to members who will be congenial—is in the East. Its park, which for present purposes will have to be known simply as "the Hill," is a tract of over twelve hundred acres of lakeside and woodland in New England, a short journey by train or automobile from the nearest large city. That membership in it is not extremely expensive is witnessed by the fact that it is made up largely of artists, writers, scientists, several university professors, and younger professional men and women, although it includes too a number of older and less impecunious people, such as architects, doctors, economists, and lawyers.

The Hill was formerly the country home of a wealthy portrait painter. It was acquired only some three or four years ago as a club property, though not at that time with any view to the practice of nudism. The idea then was simply to make a large tract of natural woodland available for camping and vacationing; the residence was converted into a club-house, and cabin sites sold to members who wished to build summer bungalows. The depression coming on about that time, the original club never fully materialized, many of the pledged and prospective members withdrawing, but last year it so happened that a great majority of the sixty or seventy members who had joined discovered a common interest in nudism; so they promptly decided to make their place a nudist park.

The property, for many reasons, lends itself admirably to such a purpose. In the first place, it is one large hill overtopped and overlooked by nothing in the vicinity. In the second place it is secluded, being off the principal highways. Moreover, it is private, being protected on two sides by large private estates tolerating no trespassers, and shut off on a third side by an impenetrable marsh and dense thicket of bull-briars, so that the sole means of approach is through the main entrance. But most happily of all, it is bordered by two lakes, one private and one public, in such a way that an imaginary line across the property agreeably divides it into nudist and non-nudist domains, each with its appropriate bathing facilities. For it must be borne in mind that not all of the members are themselves nudists. Those who are not, however, are open-minded and willing that those who care to should be; likewise the nudists try to be liberal and tolerant of those who are faddishly addicted to clothes for their games, sunbaths, or swimming. Hence a section of the park is set aside for each kind of psychology, as is an appropriate bathing place. The nudists, naturally, have the private lake on their end of the property, while the non-nudists—being given to dressing up—are much happier on their public beach, where they can be assured of a larger audience before whom to display the beauties of their swimming suits.

The place has the typical New England atmosphere—a quiet scenic beauty and the tone of permanency. Rocks, grey and moss covered, and stone fences are everywhere. Giant hemlocks and oaks, pines and cedars, and a few ailanthus and tulip trees, interspersed with growths of beech and maple and elm, cover the surrounding slopes that fall away on every side to the lakes and marsh, while up out of the centre of this circle of woods rises the bare crest of the hill, standing high and alone with only here and there a tree. This grassy plateau, crossed and criss-crossed with stone fences and sprinkled with clumps of fragrant bay, looks out upon the whole countryside of rolling wooded hills and the distant ocean. The club-house, vine-covered, built of stone, sprawls across the highest point of the plateau, its upper windows giving a view above the intervening trees of the wide expanse of an historic valley below.

Because the Hill is a considerable distance from the metropolitan areas in which most of the members live, it is for the majority of them a vacation place, rather than somewhere to go for merely a week-end. And yet, even last summer—the first season of nudist activities there—frequently saw as many as thirty or forty nudists gathered for a Sunday. There were always a number of vacationists—people out for anywhere from a week to a month or more—and every week-end, when the weather was good, at least a few would come for even a day or two. Thus far it has been the practice of most of the guests to depend on the club for their accommodations. Meals are served at the club-house, and large comfortable rooms are available there or in the smaller farmhouse just below, at reasonable rates by day or week. Both houses are equipped with running water and baths. But even last summer some of the members provided their own accommodations, either for the sake of economy or through preference. A few pitched tents in the woods, convenient to some of the several springs of fine drinking water. Others erected temporary quarters in the form of huts, or bought some of the numerous small farm buildings and converted them into rustic cabins. A number purchased lots and plan to build summer, or even all-year-round, houses this year or as soon as they can afford them.

Perhaps it should be explained here that, as a natural heritage of the club's original plan, there are two means of acquiring membership. One is through the purchase of non-profit-sharing stock; the other is through the ownership of land. A share of stock in the club corporation costs $125 and may be converted at any time, along with a small additional payment, into a building site, which one then owns outright. Both plans carry full membership privileges, at a subsequent cost of very nominal yearly dues.

As in the case of the farm of the American League, though for a different reason, nudity is not practised promiscuously

all over the Hill. Here it is not a matter of protection or for
any danger of being seen, but it will be recalled that not all of
the members are nudists, and it is deemed proper that those
few who are not—perhaps a dozen in all—should not be em-
barrased by their own clothes and by being forced to see
people with none. In any case, with something over two-thirds
of the twelve hundred acres reserved for them, the nudists
have no great need for more space. Therefore in and around
the club-house, the nearby farm buildings, and on the area
which lies between them and the front of the property, nudity
is discouraged for all but the smallest children. One passes
around the club-house, through a narrow screen of woods at
the rear, and out a rustic gate in an old stone wall before
shedding the minimum attire for the club-house and its vicinity. Nearly always, if the weather is fine, the ground and rocks
just beyond this gate are dotted with small piles of clothing,
though rarely are any nudists otherwise in evidence. To find
the latter themselves, it is necessary to strip and go out some
distance upon the hogback—out along that open stretch of
hill-top where, if no place else, there will be a breeze to cool
the naked skin and inspire that ecstatic sense of freedom which
is one of the joys of nudity.

There is intentionally a minimum of regimentation to life
on the Hill. Meals at the club are, of necessity, served only at
more or less set hours; but when it is a question of activities,
absolute informality is the only rule. For it should be borne
in mind, the membership here is made up largely of people
who view this as their place of rest; most of them are fleeing,
not wanting, compulsion of any kind. Hence formal exercise,
while taken conscientiously by a few, is looked upon as wholly
a matter of personal choice, just as are games, swimming, or
sleep. Swimming is about the only universal activity engaged
in with any degree of regularity—and it is done to anything
but a count. Some members are in and out of the water half
a dozen times a day. Still unsatisfied, a certain economist who

comes from New York every Saturday for the week-end invariably sets out for the lake again about ten at night—carrying a lantern if the night is too dark for him to find his way through the woods. His insatiable aquatic appetite forces him to go alone for his final night-cap dip if no one will join him, and he is always up again for a swim before breakfast. But the great majority—perhaps on account of the steep and arduous climb back up from the lake—manage somehow with two swims a day, one in the morning and another in the late afternoon.

Often by nine-thirty or ten there is a cry raised for swimmers, and a few abandon their games, sunbaths, books, talk, or slumbers for the path that leads toward the lake. From then on for the next hour or so, others from time to time may follow, departing in pairs, trios, or singly. But as a rule it is eleven or eleven-thirty before there is any concerted interest. Then suddenly someone cries out, "Let's go!" and there is a general stirring. Sleepers arouse themselves, stretch, and get up from their blankets; games are brought to an end as quickly as possible; and a straggling line sets out over the ridge and plunges into the woods in the direction of the lake. Down through the deep shade of damp woods, the path zigzags over and around rocks, across fallen trees, under wide-swinging loops of ancient grape-vines, and past a moss-bordered spring where it is the rule to lie down and to drink without benefit of a dipper. In the woods the air is chill to the bodies just come from out the heat of the sun, and the nostrils and throat tingle with the cool-stinging smells of balsam and pine, moist earth, rotting wood and old leaves. Off down the forested hill ahead, in the soft green filtered light, the naked bodies of the procession faintly gleam—white, tan, or brown—except when caught by an occasional chance ray of sun, when they flash amid the black trunks of the surrounding trees. Soon down through the leaves ahead come glimpses of water in the lake below.

Nudism Comes to America

The path ends at the foot of a giant hemlock that leans far out above the lake. Its branches, drooping from high up the trunk, hang to the water twenty feet from the bank, forming a shady room that is a most natural bathhouse. Through this the nudists enter the lake unseen by the owners of the opposite shore. Not that the latter are unaware or perturbed— they themselves sometimes have guests who forgo the use of bathing suits—but since bare skins are not the invariable custom over there, the nudists too prefer to be circumspect, for they appreciate amicable neighbourly terms and do not believe in flaunting their own nudity. Several take up the unending pastime of diving for rocks with which to build a future pier. One or two go in for a long-distance swim across the lake, or for lessons in new strokes. A few are content with a brief plunge, after which they set out to climb the hill again. These will later be found in one of the numerous clearings along the way, where they will have stopped to rest and acquire another shade of tan. Soon, however, the distant boom of an East-Indian gong will be heard, thumped from the roof of the club-house half a mile away, and then all will come out and start up the hill, ravenously eager for the coming meal.

So the days are passed at the Hill, varied perhaps by strolls of exploration through the woods below the brow, along faint trails where ferns softly brush the naked legs, or where less welcome blackberry briars catch and claw. The grounds are so extensive that even after many visits one can still make expeditions of discovery. The evenings, though not "nudist" except for the few who insist on a midnight swim, have their charms, and the congeniality of the group is here no small factor. On chilly nights they gather in the large living-room of the club-house to chat before the fire, or in the "studio" to listen to some of their excellent musicians. At times, hilarious "shows" are staged by those with a flair for dramatics or a talent for light verse and satirical skits, that do not spare the foibles of the other members. On warmer evenings they linger on the porch or lawn, these city dwellers, drinking in the silence of a country night where there is no reminder of civilization save, far below and miles away, the lights on the sea and the winking of a lighthouse. But when there is a full moon, the visitors at the Hill find it almost impossible to go to bed, eager as they are to make the most of the morning sun. Some wander down the path to see the moon on one of the lakes; others are content to sit before the club-house gazing at the distant arm of the sea that has become a sheet of silver. The most memorable concert perhaps was on such a night when a violinist, unaccompanied, played Hungarian airs—sobbing laments and wild rhapsodies—on the moonlit lawn. But whatever the program at the Hill, strict informality prevails. There is no dressing-up, no "parties"; one is "dressed" for the most elaborate of the festivities if he but have on shorts and a shirt and a pair of sandals.

ꖥꖥꖥꖥꖥꖥꖥꖥꖥꖥꖥꖥꖥꖥꖥꖥꖥꖥꖥꖥꖥꖥꖥꖥꖥꖥꖥꖥꖥꖥꖥꖥꖥꖥꖥꖥ

VI

WHO ARE THE AMERICAN
NUDISTS?

─────────────────────────

W HAT KIND OF PEOPLE ARE THESE AMERICANS WHO WEL-
come nudism? The question is pertinent because if nudism
appeals only to the freakish or eccentric in this country, the
American movement can be considered as nothing but a passing phenomenon, unlikely to take root in our soil. It is becoming fairly well recognized that the German nudists are on
the whole normal, respectable, even conventional people. But
Nacktkultur has social and legal sanction in Germany. Might
not the case be quite different in the United States, where the
movement has no official standing? Moreover, are not Germans
and other foreigners—even the respectable ones—tempera-
mentally different from us, or peculiar at best? Taking off
one's clothes in company is so contrary to all our established
customs and habits of thought that it appears to be an extremely radical, if not absolutely abnormal, procedure. The
simplicity and naturalness of such behaviour is scarcely apparent to anyone who has not tried it, and the theoretically
converted nudist who has not yet been initiated to the practice
is apt to dread the first step and suspect that he is after all the
victim of a fantastic nightmare. Consequently the average
person, no matter how much thought he may have given to the

arguments for nakedness, is justified in feeling that nudists in this day and age must be peculiar persons indeed.

Those who have never met American nudists are not illogical in conceiving them as (1) just plain "nuts," (2) health fanatics and "back-to-nature" extremists, (3) social misfits who are ready victims of any promised panacea, (4) faddists who adopt every craze for its novelty, (5) born radicals, the rebels and protesters who espouse a cause merely because it is contrary to the established order, (6) the ignorant and uneducated who lack high standards and a sense of propriety, or (7) sexual psychopaths, especially exhibitionists. There may be other categories of putative nudists still more unsavoury, but the company here enumerated is clearly one that a discriminating person might hesitate to join. While we hope that in describing the American nudist clubs we have not given the impression that they are made up of people belonging to any of the above classifications, it may not be out of place to scrutinize them more closely—not only these particular nudists but others throughout the country who have expressed their approval of the nudist practice. We shall endeavour to present true portraits, neither embellishing the pleasant features nor suppressing the unpleasant. While we cannot cite names and addresses, we can give assurance that our nudists are all actual people and not creatures of our imagination.

In all frankness, we must admit that any movement deviating from long established custom has its "lunatic fringe," and that nudism is no exception either here or in Europe. It has attracted cranks, extremists and faddists, even the pathological. But—and this is the thing that has astonished all unbiased observers—it has drawn relatively few of them. The fringe is so thin as to be negligible. Because the majority of nudists are sane, and because they are moderate in what they expect from their practice, the fanatic is apt to find he is not so much at home among them as he had supposed, and he is apt to drift away—in all likelihood berating his erstwhile companions for their lack of zeal, their inconsistency in refusing to go all the way back to nature in everything, or their near-sighted *terre à terre* view of a great spiritual or social doctrine, as the case may be. The faddist of course is soon bored, and so are most of the psychopaths who have not previously been requested to leave on account of their obnoxious conduct. And yet, even with all these elements weeded out, the body of nudists might remain, while mentally competent, too radical and Bohemian for staid and respectable people, or too ignorant and crude for the meticulous.

The models who sat for our composite portrait are two hundred men and women, less than half of whom are members of the particular clubs we have described. Those that do belong to the clubs in question are all people who either became interested in nudism before learning of the existence of the clubs, or who were instrumental in starting clubs of their own. In other words, we have omitted the "converts" made by the organizations, as well as those who were drawn into the movement largely through the influence of friends. Other than that, we have exercised no selection—have neither taken the most impressive people nor rejected the least attractive. Our group takes in nowhere near the total number of American nudists of whose existence we know—including, for instance, less than fifty of the two hundred members of the American League for Physical Culture. Rather, our two hundred merely represent approximately the number of nudists about whom we happen to have fairly complete information, those who have told us in letters something about themselves or whose acquaintance we have made personally. The determining factor in making up this group, aside from the reservation made above in regard to the club memberships, has been nothing more than the amount of available information.

This amount of information of course is not uniform in every case but varies somewhat with the individual. Some correspondents have been very specific on the subject of their family life but have omitted all reference to their business or education. Others have dwelt on their academic careers but failed to mention whether they were married. And many have given no indication of their ages. But while our data might be inadequate for a strictly scientific set of statistics, the gaps in it are not large enough to render the portrait unrepresentative or hazy.

Geographically, our two hundred nudists are fairly well scattered throughout the country. Seven of them are Canadians, from five different towns in the provinces of Alberta and Ontario. The other 193 reside in 21 states: Alabama, Arkansas, California, Connecticut, Delaware, the District of Columbia, Illinois, Indiana, Louisiana, Maine, Massachusetts, Michigan, Missouri, New Jersey, New York, Ohio, Pennsylvania, Texas, Virginia, Washington and Wisconsin. They seek the sun on the stern and rockbound New England coast, the languorous Gulf of Mexico, and the radiant shores of the Pacific. They live in the sophisticated metropolis, the Babbitt-ridden Middle West, and the darkest Fundamentalist South. Our list would seem to exempt from the taint of their presence only the heights of the Rocky Mountains. We can offer no explanation for the purity of the Rockies. With the New England strongholds of puritanism and the Southern fastnesses of reaction yielding their quotas of nudists, it is difficult to erect any theories on the basis of regional liberalism or conservatism.

New York, to be sure, has a preponderance of the known nudist population, the majority living either in New York City itself or in the suburban towns of Westchester or Long Island. But the State outside of the Metropolitan district has a goodly number of nudists residing in such cities as Albany, Buffalo, Ithaca, and Rochester. Viewed strictly according to state rather than metropolitan lines, the largest nudist populations we have found are in the following states, arranged in order of numbers: New York, New Jersey, California,

Connecticut, Massachusetts, and Illinois. If, however, New York City with its environs is considered as a distinct entity—a separate state as some people think it should be, if not a separate nation—and if the dwellers in the suburban towns of New Jersey as well as New York are subtracted from the nudist population of those states and added to that of New York City, the ranking would be as follows: New York City, California, New York State, Connecticut, Massachusetts, and Illinois. New Jersey has dropped far down the list, doubtless because there is comparatively little of that state not within commuting distance. Yet Connecticut, with a somewhat similar geographical relation, strangely enough holds its rank even when all commuters are bestowed on New York City, nearly all of its nudists living beyond commuting range. Perhaps Connecticut belongs with Massachusetts and, if suburban, is a suburb of Boston, for eighty per cent of the Massachusetts nudists live either in Boston itself or the neighbouring towns.

But that does not solve the problem of why certain regions are more strongly "nudist" than others. The huge nudist population of New York City might be attributed in part to the sophistication, the individual freedom of action, and lack of censorship of the city—its wickedness, if you will. But how does that apply to Boston, where nude statues are draped and unblushing literature suppressed—the Modern Athens where the shades of Puritans still stalk in the Hibernian guise of Pericles the policeman? There is no accounting for the fact that more of our nudists are in Boston than in Los Angeles or San Francisco, or indeed than are in Chicago. In short, the only possible conclusion, logical or not, is that the American nudist may live practically anywhere in the United States. He may speak with a nasal twang, a consonantless drawl, or a harsh burr.

Of course the nudist may be an American and speak with a foreign accent—and many of our countrymen, looking on nudism as a "foreign cult," take it for granted he does. But what is the percentage of unadulterated Americanism among our nudists? Their names, in the first place, are almost overwhelmingly Anglo-Saxon in derivation. In fact, not more than fifty out of the two hundred are Germanic, Scandinavian, Italian, French, Slavic, or other un-British origin. Names, to be sure, do not tell the whole story; a good number of the nudists without Anglo-Saxon surnames come from families that have been American for generations, and that left their foreign speech behind in the early days of our colonization. Likewise, Anglo-Saxon names sometimes belong to recent British immigrants or have newly replaced more exotic and unpronounceable cognomens. Measuring Americanism, then, not by name but by recentness of arrival in our midst, we find barely 31 of our 193 in the United States who are not quite Simon Pure Americans—who are either naturalized or, if not foreign born themselves, of foreign born parentage. One of the seven Canadians owns to an un-Canadian, though equally British, ancestry, having been born in Australia.

The national origins of our 31 hyphenated Americans are typically varied. As one would expect, the largest number— twelve in all—are Germanic, and, as one would not expect, the next largest—nine—are British. There are two Scandinavians and two Russians, and the rest are lone delegates of Austria, Hungary, Holland, France, Italy, and Armenia. It should be remembered that 81 of our nudists live in New York City or its suburbs, and the New Yorkers include all but a scant half-dozen of the less than 100 per cent Americans. Not knowing the exact percentage of foreign born in the total population of the United States, we cannot say whether our 31 out of 193 is an unusually high proportion for the country as a whole, but we know that it is not so for New York. Hence it can be asserted without exaggeration that the average American nudist, outside of New York City at least, is native born and of native ancestry. An extraordinarily large number of them have spoken of Puritan forbears, of "New Englandish" or "Old American" ancestors—ancestors who doubtless lie uneasy in their graves.

Nor is the age of the average nudist to be taken for granted, though unjustified assumptions are often made on that score. Some people are sure that the nudists are limited to the wild and reckless younger generation. Innumerable people, in discussing nudism, have been surprised to find, as did a well-known psychologist who sounded out his friends and acquaintances, that "it is not always the conservative and elderly people who disapprove of this movement, nor the young and liberal who approve." Others, having discovered this, go to the opposite extreme and imagine the majority of nudists to be middle-aged, if not elderly. Thus Harry Hansen, literary critic of the *World-Telegram* and *Harper's Magazine*, blandly asserted that "Many of the cultists are middle-aged; hence their testimony [on sexual questions] is not important." Of course "middle-aged" is an elastic term; to extreme youth it may mean thirty, or even twenty-five. The older we grow, the farther we stretch the boundaries of youth. Where Harry Hansen places these frontiers may be divined on the basis of his own age, especially since he makes it clear that he is still one of the young people. He goes on to say: "At the present stage of the cult they [presumably the middle-aged] are more aware of their bodies and of the temptations that lie in dress than we are. It will take a generation before young people can take nudism naturally." Mr. Hansen's "middle-age"— since he himself is well over forty—probably does not begin until about fifty. It will be interesting to see whether our composite nudist is that old or older, especially since Mr. Hansen sees so much significance in this question of years.

Our entire group, unfortunately, cannot be used for these vital statistics; the youth or senility of many can be only a matter of conjecture. The ages of 132, however, are known to us, many of them exactly and others within a few years, enabling us to place them as, say, between twenty and thirty, or between thirty and forty. It should be noted that none of our two hundred is under eighteen. Many of them have children who are also nudists, but children have been omitted as dependent for their nudism on their parents. We find the 132 determinable ages distributed among the age groups as follows: 6 between eighteen and twenty; 37 between twenty and thirty; 41 between thirty and forty; 24 between forty and fifty; 22 between fifty and sixty; and 2 over sixty. Thus 84 out of 132—or nearly two-thirds—are under forty; half of these, or one-third of the total group, are under thirty. By cheating a little and including children, the average age could easily be lowered; but even without counting minors, our typical nudist is under forty—still in possession of his mental faculties, granting he ever had any—or old enough to have a little common sense but safely outside of Mr. Hansen's category of self-conscious middle-age.

Sex is no less significant. Our two hundred is anything but evenly divided between the sexes, for we have 142 men and 58 women. On the face of it, this would seem to indicate that American women take to nudism less readily than do their men folk—that female modesty, or female vanity, still persists. But this is where the statistical method reveals its dangers. Other evidence does not fully corroborate these statistics, as it does in the case of ages. The membership of the nudist clubs, for instance, is found to include a larger proportion of people under than over forty, but it also proves to be quite evenly balanced between the sexes. Some of the clubs make it a deliberate policy to keep the numbers of the two sexes about equal, and they manage to do it without too great a struggle. Furthermore, those who have discussed nudism widely have not found the opponents and the advocates divided along sex lines, with the majority of men for and the women against the practice. One ardent nudist we know, who frequently argues his theories with a large circle of acquaintances, insists that the contrary is true—that the women are generally favourable and the men opposed or indifferent.

There is one factor, however, to be taken into consideration here. The friends with whom this nudist has talked over the matter are nearly all married couples, and it seems fairly well established that married women take much more readily to nudism than do single women. This is not to imply that the clubs are without single women; a large number are to be found there. But usually the unattached female has had to overcome considerable initial resistance, and in most cases it was the influence of married friends that brought her there in the first place. We shall not endeavour now to examine possible reasons for this greater hesitancy on the part of unmarried women, but merely to offer it as a probable fact—a fact that explains some of the discrepancy in the proportion of the sexes in our two hundred. For single men are more susceptible to nudism—or perhaps are more daring—than are unmarried girls. Only eight of our group of 58 women are single (that is to say, have never been married, for in addition to these there is one widow and one divorcee), while there are 26 bachelor men.

There is still another explanation for the male predominance in our group. Many of the married men who have given detailed information about themselves have entirely neglected to say whether or not their wives accept nudist doctrines. Quite possibly most of these wives too belong on our nudist lists, but we have not ventured to put them there without proof of the fact. Another large class of our male correspondents have failed to give even any inkling of whether or not they have wives at all. For some reason, nearly all of our correspondents have been men; even when the letters speak for the wives as well and are really joint letters, they are most frequently written by the husbands. But this may indicate not that the men have greater interest in nudism, but merely that they are the letter-writing sex.

In any event, we have 48 married women, 8 spinsters, and

2 who are widowed or divorced. The marital status of the men, however, is as follows: 72 married, 26 bachelors, 5 widowed or divorced, and 39 unknown. This gives a total of 103 men whose marital status can be considered, while we can take into account the entire 58 women. An extremely interesting and revealing fact is that all but one of the 48 married women are the wives of men who are also on the list. We have then a surplus of 25 married men whose wives are absent from the scene. Why? We have already indicated that in many instances we do not know, though it is possible the wives have simply been slighted and are in reality as pro-nudist as their husbands. This may be true also of the sole married woman who appears on the list without her husband, although in this instance we happen to know that the husband, if not a nudist himself, is not opposed to her interest in the subject. In the cases of some of these extra husbands—nine, to be exact—we are acquainted with the circumstances. The wives of these nine men are not nudists. Most of them, however, while they may disapprove, have consented to their husbands practising nudity in mixed company. A few of these women believe in nudism theoretically though not for themselves personally. A couple of them merely tolerate their husbands' activities, and only two or three are so violently antagonistic as to constrain their mates from lending anything more than moral support to the movement.

Most clubs refuse to accept a married person without at least the written consent of the husband or wife. Applications from married men whose wives do not wish to join are fairly common; an application from a married woman whose husband is unwilling to join is practically unknown. There may be nudistically inclined wives with anti-nudist husbands; but if so, they have not yet asserted their nudistic independence. Nor have we heard of a husband seeking admission to a nudist group who would not take his wife along if she wanted to go. Apparently there is no feeling among the men that such a place is not fit for their womenfolk. Where married women have become nudists, their husbands have sometimes done considerable proselytizing. One hears less frequently of wives converting their husbands. It is only fair here to point out, however, that most of the women were not actually more sceptical about the theories than were their husbands, but pressure was required to screw up their courage to the point of putting the theories into practice—and, many a husband who dragged a reluctant wife to the nudist field has been pestered thereafter by her insistence on returning, in or out of season.

After all allowances have been made for the unreliability of our figures regarding the sexes, there remains a balance in favour of the men. Possibly there is justification for concluding that women in this country are less receptive to nudism than men are, that the former are at least more loath to share in its activities. There is no warrant, however, for concluding that nudism is inherently unfeminine, or that American women in particular are unfitted for it, since once they have taken the plunge, they are whole-heartedly fervent and faithful nudists. The statistics also indicate a definite preponderance of the married over the unmarried in the case of both men and women. Even assuming that the entire 39 dark horses among the men are bachelors—which is hardly likely—there are more married than single males. This of course is as it should be in a group of people all over eighteen and with an average age of between thirty and forty. There would be reason for suspecting the nudists of some sort of peculiarity if the majority of this group had been unmarried. If anything else is demonstrated, it is that practically all the women and a large proportion of the men, being accompanied by their lawful spouses, are in no way radical in their family life. Our composite nudist is apparently a conservative in regard to marriage.

Now what is the standing of this nudist, economically and socially? Again our information is incomplete. Some nudists are willing to bare their souls as well as their bodies and confide everything about themselves save the secret of where and how they earn their living. This reticence can be understood without disparaging their modes of livelihood. It is probably not that they are ashamed of their callings, but that they fear lest their callings be ashamed of them. Many feel too that their economic positions—none too stable at best these dark days—would be jeopardized if the news of their nudism reached their employers, or their clientele, as the case may be. Nevertheless, we do know the vocations of 105 of our 142 men. Our statistics for the women are scantier. Of the ten unmarried ladies, the occupations, if any, of six are a mystery. We have businesses or professions—every one of them different, by the way—for only thirteen women, eight of whom are married. We also know that a large number of the married women are simply that old-fashioned thing known, for want of a better term, as a housewife, with economic and social standing largely dependent on their husbands. Hence, unpleasant as it may be to fervent feminists, the vocations of the men have the chief significance, though as a sop to the champions of women's rights we shall list first the professions of our thirteen women.

We find an advertising writer, an antique-shop owner, a commercial artist, a journalist, an attorney, a professional musician, a social worker, a statistician, a stylist (specializing in sport clothes!), a kindergarten teacher, a teacher of music, a teacher of physical education, and a writer. Arranging the occupations of the men in their order of frequency, we have the following tabulation:

Teachers	15	Office employes	9
College professors	10	(Clerks, etc.)	
College instructors	3	Physicians	8
Secondary school	2	M. D.'s	7
Writers	11	Osteopaths	1
Authors	7	Bankers and economists	8
Journalists	4	(Executives or de-	

[95]

partmental heads of		Advertising men	2
banks, investment		American Consuls	2
houses, and stock ex-		Insurance agents	2
change, etc.)		Optometrists	2
Industrial Engineers	6	Real estate agents	2
College students	5	Retail merchants	2
Lawyers	4	Salesmen	2
Practising attorneys	2	Architects	1
Judges	1	Artists	1
Law students	1	Chiropractors	1
Industrial Scientists	4	Clergymen	1
(Geologists, chemists,		Educational executives	1
metallurgists)		Government officials	1
Business and factory owners	4	Inventors	1
Managers	3	Librarians	1
(Business and industrial)		Pharmacists	1
Statisticians	3	Travel Agents	1
		Typographical designers	1

Some of these classifications may be a bit rough, but they should give an idea of the general nature of the nudists' everyday pursuits. Occupations of course do not tell the whole story; there are both sheep and goats in the best of them. As there is a great gulf between the scholastic requirements for a professor of biology or philosophy and a professor of salesmanship or home economics, it might be well to add that our college teachers are found in the departments of biology, English (2), engineering (2), fine arts, geology, government, physics, and psychology. There may be just as much range in the professional possibilities of some of the other gentlemen we have lumped together in one category, but further analysis is almost impossible. We should mention, however, that scattered among six categories are ten men sufficiently eminent to be in *Who's Who*.

The most striking feature about this list is its decidedly middle-class composition. It is almost strictly limited to the professions, the intellectual pursuits, and the larger businesses or industries. The small tradesman is sparsely represented, and manual labour is conspicuous for its absence. Even the minor employes are of the "white collar" type. Nor are our nudists on the loftiest rungs of the social ladder, the eminence occupied by the wealthy leisure class. Possibly some of those who have made a mystery of their occupations belong on the dizzy heights with the people who live on unearned incomes, but it is scarcely likely that many are in that situation; at the present time, it is more likely that they are among the involuntarily unemployed. Two of the women in our group, both of whom live in large cities but not in the metropolis, are described by friends as being "social leaders," which may indicate some affluence in the family. But while we have no way of estimating the exact financial rating of our nudists, it is obviously modest. The professions most numerously represented are not particularly lucrative; yet they have social respectability and esteem, if not overwhelming prestige. Practically all of them require a certain amount of education or specialized training. Hence we can say that our composite nudist has a small or modest income but a good standing in the community.

But, because our typical American nudist belongs to the middle class, one should not leap to the conclusion that nudism is essentially a bourgeois doctrine. Germany, with its huge proletarian movement and its aristocratic nudist clubs, has demonstrated the fallacy of any such assumption. There are other explanations for the preponderance of the bourgeoisie in our American group. In the first place, had we included in our portrait the entire membership of the American League for Physical Culture in New York with its democratic standards and low economic requirements, labour would be considerably better represented. Furthermore, a new idea such as nudism is slower to reach the proletariate, since the latter reads less and is less well informed both of new theories and what is actually taking place abroad. When nudism invades the radio and the movies—which censorship makes a harder conquest than the comparatively free printed page—then we too may have a proletarian movement. We may have one too soon, in fact, and of the wrong kind, if the Macfadden publications champion the cause. As for "high society," it may already have its nudists, but since this is the class with facilities at hand for "going starko," it does not need to join organizations for the purpose. The wealthy can go naked on their estates or yachts, or in their existing clubs, and the rest of us need be none the wiser.

The astonishing revelation is the appearance at the head of our list of professors and literary men—particularly the professors. Writers of course are traditionally unconventional. Professors too are in many respects abnormal; they are quaint, unrealistic people who devote themselves to dusty details of knowledge that are frequently of no practical value, and who slave for very little money without even the hope of someday making a financial killing. But in the realm of moral conduct, they can scarcely be accused of being a radical or Bohemian class. The very word "academic" connotes tradition and reaction. The professor who has unconventional ideas—outside of the more abstruse and innocuous domains of learning—is usually careful, for good reason, not to mention them. Complete freedom of speech, to say nothing of action, is comparatively rare in the academic world. The instructor is subject to the control not merely of deans and colleagues, of alumni, trustees, and legislators, but of parents who rise in wrath if the sound principles of their children are contaminated by dangerous preachments. Nowhere is moral behaviour more strictly censored, nowhere is Mrs. Grundy more potent, than in the small college community. If anyone believes that professors as a class promulgate advanced ideas in regard to the mores, particularly the sexual mores, let him ask the students. He will be informed that "Profs" are hopeless stick-in-the-muds—Mid-Victorian mud at that. It is not to be expected that these guardians of young morals should dare to appear as public champions of nakedness. Nevertheless, an extraordinarily large number have privately expressed their sympathy for it, and not a few are sneaking off to nudist clubs when assured their secret vice will not be bruited about. As a matter of fact, most of our two hundred are in the same boat. Doctor, lawyer, merchant, chief—it is only the rare individual with an established reputation (or with none to lose) who feels free to risk public confession of his naked peccadillos.

The professional status of our nudist being what it is, he presumably is educated. It is not surprising to find a large proportion of college graduates, and even holders of advanced degrees, among our two hundred. Just what the percentage of college men and women may be, we do not know, for by no means all who have undoubtedly passed through the portals of our institutions of higher education have mentioned the fact. We cannot say how many B.A.'s M.A.'s and Ph.D.'s are on our list—not that it matters greatly. A little concrete evidence regarding the official education of these strange birds, the American nudists, might serve nevertheless to convert some of the sceptics who suspect them of either moronic mentality or abysmal ignorance. Although impossible to undertake their defence systematically by offering a complete record of both academic degrees and class marks, and by giving them mental tests to determine their exact I.Q., we can say in their favour that a large number are known to have gone to college. The institutions they have attended are varied, but those most frequently mentioned are of unassailable standing, and some are pronouncedly conservative. The liberal arts colleges and universities that have our nudists among their alumni include Harvard, Princeton, Yale, Columbia, Cornell, Johns Hopkins, Stanford, Smith, Amherst, Brown, Dartmouth, Williams, McGill, Northwestern, the Universities of Alabama, Chicago, Georgia, Illinois, Kansas, Nebraska, Pennsylvania, Virginia, Wisconsin, and Ohio State. Also many technical schools have nudist graduates; the Harvard and Columbia Law Schools,

Massachusetts Institute of Technology, Armour Institute, and, strangely enough, Union Theological Seminary are among the guilty. Foreign universities, specifically several German Universities, Oxford, London, and even Robert College in Constantinople, have done their bit in producing nudists. Perhaps the source of the nudist dementia is over-education!

A peculiar circumstance—though of doubtful significance —is that the institution claimed as Alma Mater by more nudists than any other is Harvard. Nine of our group—and this does not include those who attended Harvard Law School— have declared themselves sons of Harvard, whereas no more than four have attributed their education to any other one institution. This may be accidental. Perhaps Harvard men are simply prouder of their college than the alumni of humbler schools, and more inclined to talk about their Alma Mater, though Yale and Princeton men are scarcely prone to be ashamed of their university. If the adversaries of the naked heresy wish to attack it at its source, they might begin with Harvard—but we fear they would accomplish little by limiting their onslaughts to that seat of learning.

Naturally our nudist could be well educated and intelligent, perfectly respectable and respected too, and yet be a crank on certain subjects such as hygiene, philosophy, or morality. A complete portrait of a nudist should indicate something of his opinions, prejudices, and turn of mind—whether or not he is a type naturally susceptible to freakish ideas, and his nudism merely a reflection or extension of an erratic mental quirk. Consequently, it is worth while to pry into his opinions on our social organization, our conventions regarding sex and religion particularly, and even questions of physical health, diet, and such apparently personal matters as his attitude toward liquor and tobacco. We do not mean to insinuate that a diet crank, a social rebel, or a violent prohibitionist may not be perfectly sane and estimable, or that the holding of unconventional or unpopular views necessarily renders anyone suspect. In fact deviations from the norm as frequently indicate superior as inferior intelligence. But if the nudists should invariably prove to be extremists of one kind or another, the inevitable implication would be that nudism is not a catholic thing appealing to people of diverse creeds and temperaments, but at best an esoteric doctrine unsuited to the wholly normal and moderate, the mine-run of humanity.

If this were to be determined scientifically—after the mental tests had proved the nudists' intelligence was not conspicuously subnormal—they should be made to fill out questionnaires on their beliefs and prejudices. Perhaps the social psychologists will do a little research in this unexplored field some day and, by figures on the nudists' opinions on Russia, armaments, the League of Nations, prohibition, the tariff, unemployment insurance, government ownership, God, and the Bible, establish the correlation between nudism and mental attitudes. If so, religious attitudes would be the most significant, since nakedness, the body, and sex have for so long been made religious concerns. It *is* inconsistent to be a strict Fundamentalist and a nudist, but humanity is nothing if not inconsistent. Probably our social psychologist would discover a few hardshell Baptist nudists. We already have a number of good Catholic ones for him.

Religiously our group is heterodox enough. There are three or four good Catholics on our list. There are half a dozen who put themselves down as belonging to the Jewish religion, although it is likely that in a number of cases this is an indication of race rather than of religious belief. Most of the Protestant creeds are represented, both by Church members in good standing and nominal Protestants who are not greatly concerned with religious duties. Of the sects specifically mentioned, the balance is in favour of the more liberal ones—Unitarians, Congregationalists, and modernist Presbyterians rather than Methodists or Baptists. The number of Episcopalians is large, due in part no doubt to the quantity of Eastern nudists

—New Yorkers and New Englanders. There are three Protestant ex-clergymen (only one appears on our classified list because the other two are listed under the occupations in which they are now engaged), and two of the non-clergymen have degrees from Union Theological Seminary. Apparently there are more people from religious families than there are people religious themselves, but this is merely a sign of the times. Several who disclaim church affiliations speak of being sons of missionaries or daughters of ministers. One mentions with feeling his bringing up in a Southern Presbyterian manse. We have discovered no members of the more exotic religious cults. In short, our nudists are nothing out of the ordinary way of godliness, and nudism seems not to have attracted the cultishly inclined.

As the application blanks for membership in the American League for Physical Culture ask for information regarding religion, fuller religious statistics are available for the League members than for our miscellaneous group. We have been permitted to consult 111 of these questionnaires, of which 41 were filled out by women and 70 by men. The religious classifications are as follows: 38 no religion (either the question was not answered, or "none" was definitely stated); 27 Protestant (no sect indicated); 14 Roman Catholic; 12 Lutheran; 8 Episcopalian; 6 Hebrew; 2 Unitarian; 2 Theosophist (man and wife); 1 Ex-Baptist; 1 Hindu (an East Indian). The percentage of Catholics is higher here than for our own list, due largely to the presence of many South Germans (48 being either German or Austrian in origin). The German extraction of so many of the 111 League members accounts also for the large number of Lutherans. The Episcopalian quota is relatively about the same as for our miscellaneous list, but we have no explanation to offer for the fact that no other Protestant denominations, except Unitarian and Baptist, are so much as mentioned.

Political nonconformists are likewise inconspicuous in our

two-hundred group. There is at least one out-and-out Communist and a considerable number of Socialists, but the majority either declare themselves to be Republicans or Democrats, or are independents, of liberal though scarcely radical tendencies. That many should be liberal is natural. While the espousal of nudism is not infrequently combined with extreme conservatism in other fields, it usually betokens a certain amount of open-mindedness and the ability to think independently on a few subjects. Nevertheless, the hue of the nudist movement cannot conceivably be called an alarming red.

Though unacquainted with the fancies and foibles of all of our two hundred, we know a large proportion of them well enough to be sure that as a whole they are remarkably free from any sort of fanaticism. There is little trace of excessive back-to-naturism among them. Some few have diet theories, but not even all of these are strictly vegetarian. Such statements as "the sun is the greatest healer of disease that man could turn to, provided of course he keep a natural diet" are exceptional rather than the rule. There is one practising naturopath (not listed among the physicians), and another man writes that his interest in nudism is "from the naturist angle." He is an anti-tobacconist but, unlike the true fanatic, has sufficient sense of proportion to perceive that he might be charged with prejudice. "I was really much prejudiced by the cigar," he writes of another nudist, "because I'm an extremist, being a total vegetarian except when it comes to tobacco." On the other hand, we find men who welcome nudism hoping to be able to discuss it over a good pipe.

Vegetarians are also in a minority among the 111 League members for which we have statistics, although there are more than in our miscellaneous group. The League members are divided as follows: 85 non-vegetarian; 20 vegetarian; 5 "practically vegetarian"; and 1 non-committal. Strangely enough not all the vegetarians are abstainers from alcohol or tobacco —which would indicate that they are not strict "naturists."

The status of alcohol and tobacco is similar. From our own personal acquaintance with American nudists we can say that while some smoke to excess we do not know of any drunkards among them, although more would probably accept an occasional drink than would refuse it; alcoholic beverages are never served on the nudist field to our knowledge, but we have heard of them being served in the homes of the nudists. However, for definite figures on the matter, we must resort again to the records of the American League, since we lack data on too many of our two-hundred group. On the alcohol question we find the following information in the 111 available questionnaires: 41 drink; 61 do not; and 9 do not commit themselves. As for tobacco: 59 smoke; 46 do not; and 6 do not say. (One of the non-drinkers adds that he is not opposed to the use of alcohol.) Eight who drink do not smoke, and 24 who smoke do not drink. The question in regard to drinking is most often qualified by some such statement as "a little," "moderately," or "wine and beer." Many smokers also explain that they are moderate, but one says he smokes "consistently," another "regularly," and a third "perhaps too much." Nobody claims he drinks too much. Probably the average nudist feels it would be better for him to eschew both alcohol and nicotine; but, health being no religion with him, he is unwilling to sacrifice his pleasures for the physical benefits of total abstinence. At the same time he is not inconsistent in going naked for health's sake, since the practice is a positive pleasure.

Having pledged ourselves to present an unidealized portrait, we frankly admit the presence of a few cranks. But out of our two hundred, they do not amount to more than a dozen—a couple of out-and-out naturists, perhaps as many political or social extremists, one mystic whose nudism is somewhat utopian, two with theories on sex that might be termed "peculiar" (though if they err it is in the direction of idealism rather than sensuality or promiscuity), and two or three who are a little sexually pathological. However, we do not know of one actual pervert. Our pathological cases are very mild and harmless. Invariably they are older men who might be said to be suffering from the complexes of repression—from the traditional puritanic and prurient attitude toward sex. They are the victims of a shamefaced and nasty curiosity at worst —which, if annoying, is not dangerous to the healthy minded. The "nuttiest" of our nudists are not candidates for the penitentiary or insane asylum.

As for what Mr. Mencken calls the "striated muscle fetish," here again our nudist is a moderate. Sports and exercises, it is true, flourish in nudist parks, but they are distinctly amateurish. Their chief incentive is the sheer joy of exercising without clothes. The desire for improving physical defects, of which the nudist has been made conscious by his bodily unmasking, is a stimulus; but for the most part he plays ball or swims or tries gymnastic stunts for the fun of it, not as a duty. He aspires to be no lumpy-muscled strong man; his physical ideal, limiting itself to a fairly healthy body and a more or less symmetrical contour, is something short of macfaddenism. He is no more a muscle-worshipper than is the man or woman who seizes every opportunity for knocking around a golf or tennis ball. Insatiable athletes occasionally do appear on the nudist fields, but they usually find little emulation or serious competition. It is the exceptions who have been drawn to nudism by early feats of prowess in college stadiums or by an indefatigable desire for physical activity. More numerous are those who make such confessions as "I am not an athlete nor athletically inclined," or "my interest in nudism isn't primarily athletic," or "I am no athlete, but devote myself to tennis with execrable performance and vast enthusiasm," or who even describe themselves as "gifted with athletic ineptitude."

The dearth of gladiators or amazons in the naked paradises may inspire fears for the æsthetic consequences. In fact, our average nudist is probably pretty average as to physique, but that is no real cause for alarm. The ordinary modern body is something less than perfect, but as a rule its defects have compensations in beautiful features; few physiques are wholly bad. The general effect, even of the unathletic, is inoffensive save to those who persist in believing the body to be intrinsically and inevitably ugly. Few of our nudists could qualify for Mr. Ziegfeld's chorus, but there is enough youth and beauty and grace to leaven the mass.

Lest this composite description still be vague and lacking in individuality, we take the liberty of quoting a couple of specific and typical self-portraits. The first is one of the younger nudists: "I am 28 years old, white, nominally Christian, and as good a citizen as the average, I suppose. The same applies to my wife except that she is younger. I attended Harvard. . . . So far as we know neither of us number Mayflower passengers among our ancestors—but the stock is good old Yankee all the way back. My hobbies are numerous and varied, ranging from fishing to writing verse, and including the stock market. . . . I seem to have left my morals out of this. They are really nothing to go into ecstasies over—as a matter of fact I don't doubt that some folks would think they are absolutely rotten. Personally I think they are a pretty good kind to have. You know, they don't interpret the *can-can* as an æsthetic dance, but manage to keep well up on the curb-stone when the exhibition is truly æsthetic. I'm sure they'd know how to conduct themselves in a nudist park."

Now for a picture of an older nudist—to which we might add that he is distinguished in his profession, a college man, and the father of a family: "I have to confess to fifty years of age, a figure scarcely athletic, and the ordinary Puritan hesitancies—at least in a crowd. (My ancestors came to New England in 1636, and three hundred years of inhibitions and hypocrisies are not easily overcome.) Also I am not primarily athletic. But I have lived out of doors a good deal, and have worked with my hands and my body always. I have always been interested in handicrafts. I have been a Socialist ever since I first voted. I smoke too much, drink when there is anything to drink, and have a sound constitution."

In spite of the difficulties of self-portraiture (expressed by still another nudist when he wrote, "I don't know just how one goes about proving that one is not a sensualist, reformer, or other prurient-minded person but merely an ordinary respectable citizen") these are obviously not the sort of people one would hesitate to meet. It is difficult to be more concrete in describing the composite American nudist than to state that he is nothing more nor less than the average middle-class American. He may be pictured as a college teacher living in New England, about thirty-five years old, married, of American ancestry and Puritan upbringing. This description of course would fit only a comparative few of the actual nudists in every detail. It would be equally true and appropriate to imagine him as a Wall Street broker or a banking economist in New York City. But in any case, his ideas on politics and religion, and his habits of living are in no way exceptional for his class. He is probably only nominally religious and a Republican, a Democrat, or a mild liberal. He leads a respectable existence, perhaps taking a drink now and then but eschewing a wild life. He is no health fanatic and no athlete, but he likes the outdoors and enjoys certain sports. In short, he is anything but the crude, crazy, or disreputable person some people imagine him to be.

PART TWO

THE RECEPTION

ͮͯ͟ͰͱͲͳʹ͵Ͷͷ (decorative border)

VII

WHAT THE NEIGHBOURS THINK

THE FUTURE OF NUDISM IN AMERICA DEPENDS JUST AS much on public opinion as on the convictions of the nudists themselves—in fact more so, since the nudists are in a minority. If sentiment outside of the relatively small number who practise nakedness is universally hostile, certainly the spread of the movement will be slow and arduous. There is no doubt that the spirit of the times is more propitious than formerly. In the first place, the sudden popularity of sun-bathing has made easy the acceptance of nakedness for health. In fact few of the opponents of nudity venture to attack the health arguments. When nudism came to America, it was not private nakedness as an hygienic measure but simply communal nakedness that violated the mores. Conventional standards of decency and prudishness were the chief obstacles—outside of the official and legal bars erected by such standards. Since convention and public opinion are the source of law, and the statutes, necessarily lagging behind changes in modes of thought, are frequently nullified in practice long before they are erased from the books, public sentiment is more fundamental and significant than the penal code. Unless opinion gives some support to the anti-nudity laws, their enforcement will be no more effective than that of the Volstead act.

Nudism Comes to America

In this matter of prudery toward nakedness, the wear and tear on all our moral codes in recent years favours the nudists. It is needless to point out that the aura of mystery, shame, and opprobrium surrounding the body, and particularly its sexual characteristics and functions, has been considerably dissipated; that the flesh has gained in respectability with the weakening of the "old-time" religion which branded it sinful; and that our conventions and morals are being subjected to a questioning and revaluation which make for leniency toward new heresies. While most of those who have presented their views on nudism recently are theorizing without the benefit of experience, and the difference in the attitudes of the theorists and the practitioners of nudity must not be forgotten, it is scarcely surprising to find in the press relatively few violent diatribes against nakedness. There have been several editorials on nudism and considerable comment—serious as well as humorous—by the various "columnists." A cross-section of opinion is also available in the numerous reviews published throughout the country in 1931 of recent books on the movement, for most reviewers, as a result of the novelty and controversial nature of the subject, have devoted themselves to discussing nudism rather than the book they were ostensibly reviewing.

Leaving aside for the time being the purely humorous treatments of the subject, as well as the comments motivated by commercial considerations, we have some fifty articles from daily newspapers or journals of opinion in which the writers disclose their views on the practice of nudity. Of these only a dozen are definitely anti-nudist, as against sixteen who are equally pro-nudist and many more who, though striving to avoid a direct expression of personal opinion, have so faithfully presented the chief nudist arguments without raising any objections that they may be considered fairly sympathetic, or at least tolerant. A few remain whose attitude may be described as mixed—that is, they accept the most important nudist claims but see various disadvantages to the practice.

What the Neighbours Think

Once more we discover the futility of predicting who will favour and who oppose nudism. A logical guess would be that the pro-nudist articles appeared in the *Nation*, the *New Republic*, and the *American Mercury*, and the anti-nudist articles in the Kentucky and Kansas papers. Instead, we find among our anti-nudists such incongruous company as H. L. Mencken alongside of Arthur Brisbane; the *Nation's* "Drifter" hobnobbing, as it were, with Karl K. Kitchen; and T. S. Matthews in the *New Republic* aligned with the anonymous reviewer in the *New Yorker* and Rose C. Feld in the New York *Times*. The pro-nudists are equally miscellaneous, including for instance Stuart Chase, Dr. Frankwood E. Williams, Dr. William J. Robinson, C. Hartley Grattan, Bruce Calvert, Samuel Lipshutz (Philadelphia *Record*), and the Prophetstown (Illinois) *Echo*, while sympathetic—or at least impartial—accounts show up in such unlikely spots as the Lexington (Kentucky) *Leader*, the Chattanooga (Tennessee) *News*, and the Kansas City *Star*. Those of mixed sentiments, who are receptive to the idea but who have some reservations, comprise, to mention the most prominent, Elsie McCormick, Lorine Pruette, Harry Hansen, Isabel Paterson, McAlister Coleman, and Laurence Stallings.

The tolerant, if not entirely favourable, views of the public as reflected in the press are not belied by those of the close neighbours of nudist camps. We have already shown how the community last summer condoned the activities on the farm of the American League for Physical Culture, and that on neither occasion when the League fell into the toils of the law was the arrest the result of outraged morality, the complaints in both cases being motivated by purely personal animus. A nudist disgruntled at being kept out of a nudist camp can scarcely be called an opponent of the practice. We have also mentioned the indifference of the neighbours to the naked swimmers in the "Hill" lake. Rumour of what was going on eventually reached the nearest village, some five miles away, but no one sent the constable. Moreover, some of the club members, listening to talk in the stores and streets of the town about the nudists on the Hill, heard the gossips comment: "I understand they are very nice people." The typical attitude of the dwellers in the vicinity seemed to be that "it's all right for those who like it."

Whatever the private opinions of nudism, published opinion is not only open-minded but, in view of the number and variety of people who have taken pains to consider it exhaustively and thoughtfully, may be said to be definitely interested. Nudism has not been dismissed by our professional critics as too trivial or too dull for discussion. Whether or not they believe it ever likely to assume significant proportions in America, they have found it offers ample scope for argument and speculation, weighing and evaluating nakedness itself and turning a prophetic eye on the possible effects of a nudist conquest of America. When it comes to interesting people in actual participation in nudist activities, that of course is a different matter. While some ardent nudists have found it fairly easy to convert their friends, others complain that they find "no one, or almost no one, definitely interested," or that they "have not had much success." This, however, does not mean their friends refuse to talk about the theories.

There is no lack of curiosity about nudism, as the tabloids are well aware. To be sure, much of the curiosity is scarcely a serious interest, and the curious are mere spying Fishermen. When the tale of the Carmel nudists was broadcast last November, the managers of the Monterey airport reported a sudden rush of passengers who wanted to fly over Carmel and fly low, despite the fact that none of them had seen anything up to that time. Duncan Aikman, after describing in the Baltimore *Sun* for July 19, 1931, the spread of naked sunbathing in California, added that "The chief peril . . . is the Southwest's large but hitherto largely frustrated 'Peeping Tom' element. For these the sunbath cult has created a Roman holiday on an almost incredible scale of lavishness. In consequence, airplane flights, for which patronage had been dropping off for several seasons, are picking up again." In fact the suspected presence of a nudist group in a community cannot fail to attract sightseers if there is any possible way for them to get within view. The urge that moves them springs from the same instinct to which publishers of nudist books cater when they advertise the illustrations rather than the contents. Indeed, the pornographically inclined esteem the former more highly. As T. S. Matthews said in the *New Republic*, the nudist books "are worth the price, if only for their illustrations. And if worst comes to worst, if you live in an ungymnosophic apartment, all cramped up with clothes and closets, you can throw the books away and frame the photographs." Obviously it was not sympathy for the movement that inspired the "gentleman of the clergy" who, according to the *Publishers' Weekly*, was attracted by the display of a nudist book, for he solemnly read the advertising matter, "looked over the book, bought it, and departed with the remark, 'The goings-on in Germany are terrible, aren't they?' " Doubtless he was a potential Fisherman, but being frustrated in his desires he was forced to take his sport vicariously.

Some of the friends and neighbours of the nudists are no more charitable toward the "goings-on" than was the clergyman. "The majority of our friends believe we have gone a bit nutty," wrote one new convert; and another divided the sentiments of his acquaintances as follows: "Some of them think that we are just plain nuts, others think that a house of correction would do us lots of good, and a few are with us one hundred per cent." But more typical than those who consider nudism crazy or criminal are those who, as one man aptly stated, "look askance at it—that sort of one-eyebrow-up supercilious look." This is, indeed, a common attitude of the sophisticate. As he must appear liberal at any cost, he cannot be shocked; so he resorts to sneers or ridicule—*castigat ridendo*

—to dispose of the nudists.

We have spoken before of the avidity with which professional humorists have seized on nudism, of the "wisecracks" of the columnists and the bony or puffy nudes of the cartoonists. We have mentioned *Barely Proper*, the play Tom Cushing devoted to the comedy to be derived from nudism. But as we pointed out, the humour here lies not so much in the intrinsic funniness of nakedness itself as in the conflict of a naked society (the German nudist family) and the conventional, dressed society of today (the young Englishman). Such eminent humorists as Robert Benchley and Corey Ford, however, who travesty nudist literature in full length articles, find comic elements in nudism *per se*. To be sure, in "Among the Prudists," published in *Vanity Fair* (July 1931), Corey Ford, by describing a "prudist movement" in a nudist civilization, has exploited—in reverse, as it were—the humour of just such a relationship as that in *Barely Proper*. This we suspect is the only inherently humorous thing about the nudists— "the incongruity of their relationship to a clothed world," to quote a reviewer in the New York *Evening Post*—and it may account for the fact that Mr. Ford is more successful at being funny than Mr. Benchley. The latter, in "A Day Among the Nudists," in the *Detroit A. C. News* (August 1931), depended for his comic effects on the discomforts endured by his determined German *Nacktkultur* devotees. It is the humour of exaggeration which, carried too far beyond the point of plausibility, ceases to be amusing. Gluyas Williams' illustrations for the article were funnier, for his exaggerations of a certain type of Teutonic physique definitely suggested the reality at the same time as they suggested such unhuman shapes as that of the seal.

But it is not only the professional humorists who are excited to laughter by nudists. It is significant, whether true or not, that the Carmel City Attorney who objected to a nudist colony in the town was reported to have done so not because

MUNICIPAL "TEMPLE OF THE SUN" AT ST. PETERSBURG, FLORIDA, WITH SEPARATE ENCLOSURES FOR MEN AND WOMEN

it would reflect on Carmel's moral purity, but because it would make Carmel "the laughing stock of the nation." May Frank mentioned in the *Oklahoman* the prevalence of this attitude. She reported how, when she announced that she had been reading a nudist book, "Three snickers and four wise-cracks were directed at me. Thereafter I conducted a little experiment, saying that simple sentence quietly here and there. It netted giggles, jokes, and alarm."

A goodly number of the press articles we have seen discover something laughable in nudism. Two—the New York *Evening Post* reviewer who put his finger on the incongruous relationship that makes nudism funny, and McAlister Coleman —directly accused the nudists themselves of having no sense of humour. Mr. Coleman said: "Most nudists we have met have been a particularly humourless crew, like vegetarians and spiritualists." Isabel Paterson found nudism "faintly humorous"; the Boston *Herald* spoke of "the sense of humour that will stir most Americans" in connection with nudism; and William Morris, in the Brooklyn *Standard Union*, declared that "to most of us, making a cult and organizing colonies and evolving philosophies over such things is inexpressibly comic." Laurence Stallings admitted: "It may be just smutty-minded to laugh about this . . . but I confess to having laughed at a photograph of mixed doubles at tennis."

Mr. Stallings may be reassured—nudists will not necessarily suspect him of pruriency. Doubtless, it was nothing more disgraceful than the discrepancy between the photograph and his customary associations that stirred his laughter. He probably associates tennis with flannels and pleated skirts. It is doubtful if Bernard Shaw (according to Frank Harris's last book) or the Cambridge students who tried naked tennis on the courts of Pembroke College would find it so comic. A photograph of a mixed doubles clad in swallow-tailed coats and evening gowns would be ever so much more laughable. Mr. Stallings probably would not be overcome with mirth at the sight of a ballroom full of people in fashionable dress; yet we suspect that modern dress clothes, if we could view them as objectively as the people of the year 2032 may be able to do, are intrinsically more comic than bare bodies.

T. S. Matthews—the "literary editor" of *Time*, no less— writing in the *New Republic*, perceived practically nothing about nudism that was not excrutiatingly funny. "Are you aware," he chortled, "O bundled-up, chafed, sweated, and probably respectably clothed reader, that at this moment there exist in Germany, that home of humourless causes, societies of earnest people banded together for the purpose of going naked?" He derided the "nordic respectability," the "general air of good clean fun" of the European nudists, but he was most entertained by Maurice Parmelee's term "gymnosophy." "Perhaps he is right," remarked Mr. Matthews, "there *is* something rather bare about 'nudism,'" and he proceeded to cite with glee the "gymnosophic prophet," "the pure gymnosophic spirit," "gymnosophic colonies," "gymnosophic apartment houses," "gymnosophic servants," "gymnosophic superintendents," and "gymnosophic" factories and marriages.

Charles B. Coates predicted in the Montclair *Times* that "nudism would be much less likely to go aground in this country because of the efforts of John S. Sumner than because of the ridicule of, say, Arthur 'Bugs' Baer." *Don Quixote* may have ended the vogue of the romance of chivalry—though there is a possibility the latter was already moribund—but institutions have survived the uproarious laughter engendered by the satirists. Medicine persists, and with some of the identical foibles, despite Molière; and all the ridicule directed at the "horseless carriage" delayed not a whit our motor age. Was Henry Ford's career seriously impeded by the "Lizzy" jokes? Surely nudism has at least a fighting chance of outliving the wit of "Bugs" Baer.

On the other side of the picture is a reviewer, Hazel L. Sherrick in the *Town Crier*, who specifically took exception to the attitude that nudism must needs be treated as a joke. She quoted the *New Yorker's* supercilious remark that the only reason for reading a nudist book would be curiosity because it is "tremendously serious." "Who wouldn't be curious," she countered, "about nudist colonies where men, women, and children play together *au naturel?* And why not a serious account? We have had news stories aplenty exaggerating the practice of nudism and poking fun at the various possibilities."

It is not astonishing to discover in America still another attitude toward nudism—one that may be described as "commercial," or "economic," since it considers the question from the point of view of the clothing industries and business in general. Naturally most of the alarm expressed is facetious; surely the textile industries are not yet greatly worried over the threat of nakedness. But it is noteworthy that so many people, whether soberly or humorously, have been concerned with the possible effect of the new movement on industry. *Advertising and Selling* took the matter seriously enough to obtain for its August 1931 issue an article on what nudism would mean to business, which occasioned comment in other trade journals, such as *Retailing*. The *Merchandise Manager* in July had printed a photograph of a bewildered business man frowning over a copy of *Among the Nudists* and titled it "Bad news—sad news—for the ready-to-wear merchandise manager," and the Chicago *Daily News* headed an announcement of the same book, "Bad News for Textiles." The *Shoe and Leather Reporter* last May, while asserting that nudism "has not progressed on our side of the Atlantic beyond the low comedy mark," wondered what American industry would do to meet the menace of the nudist tide should it rise higher. "As we understand it," the *Reporter* continued, "shoes were one of the first articles of apparel to go into discard." Of course this is a misunderstanding, for shoes are the last to be discarded and persist, at least in the form of sandals, on most nudist feet. But under this misapprehension, the *Shoe and Leather Reporter* concluded with the suggestion "of a specific prohibitive tariff of 500% on nudes and nudism."

Corey Ford extracted some fun from this economic aspect of the nudist movement by prefacing his article on the "Prudists" with the statement: "Mr. Riddell, it may be added, is heavily subsidized by the Clothing Manufacturers of America, the Pants Pressers' Union, and the Organized Guild of Mitten Workers." McAlister Coleman, with the workers' interests rather than the manufacturers' profits in mind, also asked: "What will happen to our comrades in the Amalgamated Clothing Workers Union and the International Garment Workers Union?" We are no less anxious than Mr. Coleman that these workers should be protected, but we see the possibility of nudism—that is, nakedness for recreation, sport, and the hours of ease—becoming accepted without destroying the livelihood of the clothing workers. Continual and universal nakedness under modern living conditions is not only impossible but undesirable. A virtually clothesless society is not inconceivable in some dim Utopian age when our cities have been rebuilt and our huddled populations dispersed; but so good a Socialist as Comrade Coleman need not be told that in some such perfect society, the workers of the world might be independent of the demand for clothes.

May Frank, in Oklahoma, quite logically thought first of the cotton farmers, who "are having enough trouble as it is." Next she foresaw bankruptcy for the clothing manufacturers. But on the other hand, she perceived prosperity for certain commercial specialists: "Makers of bags will become captains of industry and get write-ups in the *American Magazine*— for everyone will have to have a pouch in which to carry his checkbook and cigarettes. Cold cream producers will prosper, for women who now doctor only areas that show will, with so much territory to free from blemishes, go in for creams in a big way." In the light of all this, perhaps the clothing clerk

What the Neighbours Think

feared being fired for disloyalty more than shocking anyone when, after failing to sell pyjamas to a nudist, he whispered confidentially: "You sleep in the raw? So do I."

Not all the objections made to nudity are, it must be admitted, so little in earnest or so irrelevant as those of the humorists and the protectors of industry. There are people who are sincerely shocked, and who oppose the movement for the sake of decency. Remarkably enough, only three of the twelve opponents of nakedness among the journalists and magazine writers professed to be shocked. But perhaps this is not remarkable after all, since they belong to a sophisticated class, consciously broad-minded. Four others disputed the "moral" arguments of the nudists, either on the grounds that the nudists' psychological theories are wrong, or because their psychology is right but morality is wrong. Prudery they disclaimed in any case. The three who were shocked, however, are Karl K. Kitchen—for whom nudism violated "standards of taste and decency"—John G. Neihardt of the St. Louis *Post-Dispatch*, and Mrs. Florence Fisher Parry of the Pittsburgh *Press*.

Mr. Neihardt considered "all this as only another symptom of the prevalent exhibitionist mania that has so largely determined the character of contemporary literature. . . . We have forgotten so much of human experience during late years that to favour any form of reticence is to seem narrow minded and reactionary. Sun on the skin is a good thing, truly, but a false rationalization of a determining motive can never be good for anyone concerned." Mrs. Parry, still more old-fashioned, did not even bother with the terminology of the modern psychologists. "It appears to me," she remarked, "that the human body is not really important enough to celebrate, at least outside of the confines of a sonnet form or artist's frame"—thus disparaging poetry and painting along with the human body. "Indeed," she appended to her denigration of nudism, "I was actually depressed to find that our own

[121]

Nudism Comes to America

John Kane had felt the necessity to exhibit his first nude in his Junior League Exhibition. I am of the strong suspicion that it caused him no end of agonizing embarrassment, what with his simple bringing up and all. And I'm sure that Mrs. Kane had her own opinion about it." Without knowing anything about "our John's" bringing up, anyone acquainted with the sentiments of artists in general might suspect that if he suffered agony from his nude, it was due to indignation at views such as Mrs. Parry's, rather than to embarrassment. And Mrs. Parry might possibly be surprised at the insouciance of Mrs. Kane.

Rose Feld, in the New York *Times,* was one of those who felt that the psychological benefits of nudity were falsely deduced. The ease with which the nudists have overcome their inhibitions, she attributed to "mass psychology," although if this were the case they should suffer twinges of remorse—which they certainly do not—as soon as they had an opportunity for sober and solitary reflection. Miss Feld insisted, nevertheless, that "nudism when practised in crowds has no basis in depths of the pure and simple . . . but touches shallower waters." She failed to say whether nudism in groups of three or four was any purer or deeper. The three other critics who objected to the nudist pretensions to morality protested not because nudity is immoral but because it is not erotically stimulating. B. S., of the Winston-Salem (North Carolina) *Journal,* pronounced nudist arguments "the most unattractive to be found." "Nudity doubtless destroys obscenity," he conceded, but he insisted: "Obscenity is the life of sex, it has been affirmed again and again. And even if one will not accept the phallic theory, how can it be consistently maintained that to strip sex of its most alluring suggestions is to nurture a higher æsthetics? To remove our clothes would certainly not be immoral. But it would be a step toward the 'higher pruddery' [*sic*]."

Of course this all depends on what one means by obscenity.

What the Neighbours Think

What many people call "obscenity" is indeed the life of sex; but lewdness, the filthy and sly attitude connoted by the word "obscene," is not. Obscenity is after all a state of mind and not a fact or an object. What may be obscene to one person or civilization may be pure, healthy, and natural to another. The obscenity destroyed by nakedness is merely a prurient mental attitude, and it is to belittle sex to insist that such a pruriency is essential to either its existence or its enjoyment. B. S. further weakens his own case by calling a frank, unsuggestive nude photograph "provocative." If he were consistent, such a photograph would be unalluring.

Ray Kimbell, in the *Industrial Democrat*, the Louisiana labour weekly, agreed with B. S. "We should be fools," he declared, "to deny ourselves the sweet pleasure of anticipation the wearing of clothes affords us. Why rob ourselves of delightful expectation? When all the world goes naked, sex will lose its fascination and become a banal thing, and the greatest charm of life will have perished." As a refutation of both B. S. and Mr. Kimbell, the analogy that has been made between the effects of the prohibition of alcohol and that of nakedness is excellent. Prohibition probably endows drinking with certain charms wanting in lands where it is legal and open, but surely B. S. would not contend that the absence of prohibition strips liquor of all, or even its greatest, attractions. Frenchmen and Germans are not insensible to the appeal of wine, beer, and even stronger drink; they enjoy their cafés no less than we do our speakeasies. But they are undoubtedly more particular and selective in their drinking than are Americans. And so with the nudists. They are more discriminating in sexual matters than those artificially stimulated by the mystery of tabooed nakedness, but they do not lose interest in sex. The sex instinct after all is more fundamental and universal in the human race than even the desire for alcoholic beverages, and it takes more than frankness to destroy it.

The *Nation's* Drifter also delivered the ultimatum that he

would not join the nudists until the moral arguments were changed, for purity would "rob the world of all variety and interest." Over-ardent advocates of nakedness are as much to blame for this fear as the Drifter himself, but no anæsthetizing of sex instincts is claimed or desired by the reasonable nudist. As C. Hooper Trask has pointed out, "the disciples of the nudist movement are not mere emasculated ascetics. Sex plays a normal, healthy role in their lives." The Drifter was, after all, intelligent enough not to believe that nakedness would result in excessive purity: "As for a person who is unconscious of the difference between men and women, the Drifter hopes he may never meet one. Fortunately, he never expects to, even though he, too, should visit every nudist colony in the whole world."

Lorine Pruette, Harry Hansen, and Isabel Paterson—each of whom saw advantages in nudism but also some drawbacks —were a bit sceptical, in a mild way, about this matter. Miss Pruette believed "a movement which is engaging the serious attention of many persons in Europe" deserves consideration, but she felt that it "will have several serious questions to meet." She was not very specific, but she mentioned the fact that "Stekel has recently disapproved of the cult of family nakedness which has been adopted by many young couples who seek to prevent the development of shame and prurient curiosity in their children." Mr. Hansen thought "the theory that nudism lessens desire is not yet fully proved," because the advanced age of many of the nudists invalidates their testimony. Miss Paterson found that, "The rising generation has been so freely exposed to the open spaces that some of the younger set can take them or let them alone when it comes to clothes," and she pronounced this "a healthy and happy state of mind." But it is, she feared, one that cannot last beyond extreme youth. The argument that the psychological effects of civilized modesty are harmful, she believed "breaks down as long as clothes must be worn at any time. Modesty will resume its sway the moment the least garment is put on." Doubtless modesty does return with the resumption of clothes in so far as the observance of conventions of decency constitutes modesty. But once nudity has become commonplace as a result even of occasional practice, the prudish, shamefaced view of nakedness, the usual concomitant of that convention, does not return.

However, the great majority of published opinions support the psychological claims of nudism. Those who have acquitted the nudists of moral turpitude or false rationalization are in fact too numerous to quote, but the following statements are representative of a quantity of others:

Stuart Chase (The *Nation*): "Unsegregated nakedness in large doses is undoubtedly the best medicine conceivable for persons suffering from dirty minds, perverse desires, and snooping complexes."

C. Hartley Grattan (The *Thinker*): "The nudists do make a contribution to the dissipation of sexual prurience."

Bruce Calvert (The *Open Road*): "I believe it to be a movement for greater cleanliness of mind and body, for morality, a higher ethical and spiritual life."

Samuel Lipshutz (Philadelphia *Record*): "Here also is purity and innocence, and health, and something so Grecian as to be very precious. . . . It doesn't take a lot of idealism to convince one that the awesome qualities of that word [nakedness] are due to something rotten in the way folks drag themselves up."

Charles B. Coates (Montclair, N. J., *Times*): "We can't see anything wrong with nudism whether practised individually or in droves. . . . It is really a poor target for reformers and prudes."

The Chicago *Post*: "The movement has nothing at all to do with any trend of human conduct that could be called libidinous."

May Frank predicted that the prurient "won't get a kick

out of these unself-conscious naked ones playing handball, swimming, taking exercises, for pornography depends on sug-gestiveness." She longed to see people "stop insulting Mother Nature by looking on the human body as immoral, obscene, and material for hilarious humour," and she was very specific in prophesying the improvement in mental cleanliness that would follow the adoption of nudism. "Jokesters whose main stock in trade is choice thighs and breasts," she said, "will have to invent new subject matter. Novelists who depend on breathtaking accounts of what their heroes feel when they see women's bodies will have to adopt a new technique. Comic artists who depend on women's underclothes for a living will have to enroll in business college. Newspapers which display legs on their front pages will have to clean out their morgues. College humour magazines will die. . . . We'll have no more Peeping Toms. Exhibitionists will have to get a new psycho-logical quirk."

This last statement shows more psychological insight than do those which accuse the nudists of being exhibitionists. Ex-hibitionism can be a source of erotic pleasure only in a clothed civilization; the same psychological quirk in a naked society would be forced to take the form of displaying the body decked in coverings. Even such experts on pornography as the writers in the tabloids have failed to find the erotic in nudism. Hear Emile Gauvreau, in the *Daily Mirror*: "The itch to go nude is by no means symptomatic of a diseased mind. It is a natural, healthy instinct." And Milo Hastings in the *Evening Graphic* declared nudity "disappointing to the seekers of erotic thrills . . . the shock of nudity is all in the anticipation, and the pleasure of a good coat of all-over tan is something entirely different than the prude's idea." Walter Winchell himself de-tected the paradox in the conduct of the police who arrested a nudist club in the heart of the Times Square burlesque district.

The opinions cited are typical of the press commentators as a whole—more typical than the moral and psychological objections. But do not leap to the conclusion that America is therefore safe for nakedness. The *literati* as a class are unusually liberal, and there is no doubt that less articulate classes would offer more opposition. The lack of anything like an organized drive against nudism cannot be taken as an indication that none will materialize, for no movement is actively opposed until it begins to loom large. It may be that we ourselves are doing nudism a disservice by demonstrating that it has already gained a little foothold in our land and that it is beginning to expand. We feel, however, that even now there is too much essential strength in the American interest for the Comstockians to nip its bud. There may have to be martyrs to the cause, though we do not advocate unnecessary martyrdom—nudists going out of their way to be crucified or insisting on crucifying someone else in the fashion of some American Communists.

Sermons are not yet being preached against nudism, but it is reasonable to suppose that religious Fundamentalists will denounce the doctrine as soon as it seems to be a menace. Such people as one S. S. W. Hammers, of Gettysburg, Pennsylvania, the good Baptist author of an amazing pamphlet on "Nudity," are hardly nudist prospects—even though the nudity in Mr. Hammers' broadside is only the partial nakedness of modern bathing suits and fashionable women's dress. Extreme as his opinion is, it cannot be disregarded for it is representative of much of the mental outlook in the Bible Belt. The bathing suit, Mr. Hammers generously conceded, is not objectionable in the water, but on the beach "It suggests evil thoughts, and is therefore immoral." As for the undress of modern women, "There is no other one crime at this hour that is sweeping souls on to perdition at a swifter rate. . . . Woman's dress is destroying her and leading her victims to Hell." And he upbraided the sects that take the ban off such sins—all equally deadly—as "dancing, card playing and other gambling . . . theatre, movie-going, public mixed bathing, displaying nude beach swimming hole 'beauties' and athletic nakedness," and permitting "women to wear men's apparel and cut off their hair."

Mr. Hammers would doubtless agree with the pious gentleman in Missouri who wrote thus damningly of a woman nudist: "That lady you quote as describing her first experience ought to convince any sound minded person of the damnableness of the stinking filthy thing [nudism]. . . . Now she is as dead as Hell can make her so far as shame and morality is concerned. And we might add also, so far as respectable society is concerned. Not one inch of her lost ground can she ever regain, for she has defied the very Spirit of God, the power in her soul that gave her that peculiar feeling of adversity, that deep sense of shame which her selfish determination to follow off after a wild and foolish philosophy murdered in cold blood."

Nor will nudism be welcomed by the Pope, who could not receive Gandhi because of his "improper" costume. *Time,* for July 14, 1930, quoted His Holiness as pronouncing nudism "a sad aberration"—and, authentic or not, the quotation is plausible. Even one of our most liberal and broadminded Protestant clergymen, who is known as a "radical" in politics and religion and even in the field of sexual questions, was bitterly opposed to young men playing tennis without shirts in a secluded country camp. On the other hand, there are Protestant clergymen in the American nudist movement, and even Catholic priests in France who approve it. An English clergyman, the Rev. J. C. Hardwick, former Chaplain of Ripon Hall, wrote very favourably on nudism in the Manchester *Evening News,* saying among other things that "It makes for physical health, and it undoubtedly contributes to a sane outlook in matters of sex. . . . Nudism would flush out people's minds as a rush of water flushes a sewer." Of the biblical viewpoint, he remarked that "Some Fundamentalists will declare that it is against the divine Will that men should abandon their clothes. But if it is impious to be naked, why were not human beings created wearing skirts and trousers?" Yet the religious attitude that despises the body is prone to colour the devouts' emotional responses to nakedness, intellectually emancipated though they may be in other respects.

Many nudists have found some of their enlightened friends expressing doubts as to the morality of the practice. "Most of them," one man wrote of his associates, "feared that the intermingling of the sexes would lead to promiscuous sex life." Another stated that the Americans with whom he travelled in Germany "thought that places such as Klingberg and Egestorf must be places where sexual orgies took place. They actually refused to go with me and try *Nacktkultur* lest they become perverts." A psychologist cited, "as illustrating how prejudices instilled in early childhood can persist even when we realize their senselessness," a middle-aged teacher in a boys' school who "said he could never get used to seeing the boys working and practising in the gymnasium unclothed." Bruce Calvert has described how, when he lectured on nudism at the big Spiritualist camp at Lily Dale, New York, "Many left the auditorium. One lady was heard to say as she flounced out in high dudgeon: 'He's a dangerous man. He ought not to be permitted on this platform.' " Others, however, applauded, and Mr. Calvert has been invited to lecture there again.

The prospects for the nudists seem gloomy when, as happened last summer, a girl goes to jail for being unable to pay the fine for letting a shoulder strap slip at Coney Island, and when other girls are haled into court for wearing shorts on the boardwalk. Commenting on the tale of the Carmel nudists, an editorial in the Boston *Herald* expressed the opinion that "Although a visitor to our gaudier bathing resorts might not believe it, we are still a very moral country. The naked body is pretty well confined to boys' camps, the Broadway stage, L Street, and the art museums. . . . Californians may delight in a pretty 'figger' in a one-piece bathing suit, but the absence of all clothes shocks their sensibilities." The writer, after

Nudism Comes to America

contrasting conditions in Germany, added: "But Germany is a long way from Carmel, Cal.!" And indeed naked sun-bathers are frequently reminded of the distance from Germany. Last summer, Judge Francis Allegretti of Chicago fined 31 boys and men ten dollars apiece for sunning themselves on the 12th Street Island in Lake Michigan and threatened to make it a hundred dollars if they were caught again. It is not astonishing to find the Baptist Mr. Hammers giving "Three cheers and a tiger for Judge Allegretti" for his moral handling of another case. In St. Petersburg, Florida, the "West Coast Cultural League" in December 1930 complained of "indecent exposure" on the beaches and asked for special investigators to prevent promiscuous sun-bathing, although the Chief of Police denied that there was any sun-bathing outside the municipal solarium and similar, but private, institutions.

The inanimate nudes of art, though vastly more respectable than they used to be, still find an occasional Puritan pursuing them with a fig-leaf. But the rash Puritan, though he may succeed in imposing his draperies, is apt to stir up unpleasant publicity and find himself the target of the gibes and raucous laughter of the public and press. Such was the case when the Boston City Fathers spent a thousand dollars for granite ribbons for two brazenly bare youths on the city shield adorning a new public library. The press throughout the country grasped with glee the opportunity for another fling at Boston's moral mentors. And John S. Sumner, on protesting at Tintoretto's Susannah performing her ablutions in the window of a New York art gallery, set off such a hullabaloo in the staid *Times* that the President of the New York Society for the Suppression of Vice was forced to write a letter to the Editor in defence of its Secretary and in protest at the "attempt to discredit the society." But a few days thereafter the editorial writers were equally severe with the customs officials who refused to admit, as obscene, the nude etchings by Whistler and Zorn, on the peculiar grounds that they would be unobjec-

[130]

tionable in an art gallery but not as commercial articles. The customs authorities, in fact, debar the European nudist literature, although equally inflammable nudist publications are now appearing in this country without restraint—an anomaly by no means restricted to the United States, for the German nudist periodical, *Lachendes Leben,* was confiscated in Cuba last summer during the very period when a Cuban magazine was publishing *Among the Nudists* serially, with illustrations.

The belief is common that nudism in America will arouse the hostility of many such organizations as the Florida West Coast Cultural League and the New York Society for the Suppression of Vice. Stuart Chase has predicted that "Any movement for health and morality such as this will be greeted with violent, uproarious opposition from every nationally advertised organization, from the Ku Klux Klan to the Daughters of the American Revolution. Its supporters will be ostracized, branded, and stoned." And "Doubtless," said Laurence Stallings, "the wowsers are already fashioning periscopes and consulting evidence tables." That nudism cannot be public and legal in America but will have to be bootlegged for a long time to come is a common opinion. "Nearly every one of our more intelligent acquaintances seems to practise sun-bathing as a sort of secret vice," wrote Roi Partridge, the American etcher, and "The next step in this land of peculiar taboos is to gain the public right to be ashamed only of shame." But much pessimism exists with regard to any immediate progress in this direction.

"The spirit of Puritanism," "the difficulties that beset an advocate of so 'daring' a thing as nudism," "the erotic interpretations that so many people place on the matter" worry many nudists—for one may believe the taboos of the neighbours ridiculous, yet be forced to respect them. "Professional obligations" and the fear of losing jobs, all too precarious nowadays, demand a little caution in going counter to prejudices. In a small community it is only too easy to acquire a damaging reputation, if not for outright immorality, for eccentricity. As one of the academic nudists pointed out, unfortunate taboos bind us in more trivial matters than nakedness; he would sometimes like to trot along the street instead of walking, but if he did so—unless he seemed to be heading for the railroad station or a fire—he would soon have the reputation of "queer" in the little college town. Many others, taking a look at their neighbours, doubt that respectability will soon be bestowed on nakedness. From Wisconsin a woman wrote: "Now I am living on Main Street of a small village where all the people are highly conventional and proper. If nudism depends upon their approval, I fear it will have to wait long." A Philadelphian considered his native city a poor starting point for the movement. "I beg you to remember," he reminded us, "that Philadelphia proudly boasts more churches per unit of population than any other city in *the world*. We don't even have baseball on Sunday." From the Southwest have come complaints of Fundamentalists who disapprove even of shorts. And a Canadian lawyer, who wrote that "our people have very much the same inhibitions and prohibitions," predicted that "it will take a considerable time before a sufficient body of public opinion will react in favour of the movement so as to bring the legislatures of this country to the opinion that it should be legalized."

The isolated nudist without the means for establishing a sun park for himself is frequently discouraged by the difficulties of obtaining even a little bootlegged sun under the nose of shockable neighbours. A professor at a large western university reported that a small group of students and instructors—men only—had formed the habit of sun-bathing in shorts on the athletic field, but that they dared not dispense with the trunks for fear of interference by the authorities. This anecdote from a New Englander is an indication of how public opinion harries the would-be nudist: "I paid a visit to a stretch of rocky coast, determined to peel down and get a dose of air and sun-

shine. I had no sooner stripped than, lo, there came the sound of feminine voices. My first impulse was to cover up, my second to be nonchalant and remain naked, but finally reason told me to put on at least my track pants."

But there is a reverse to the picture. Actually more of the press writers who ventured to prophesy the future of nakedness in America discerned auspicious signs than omens of disaster. Samuel Lipshutz was the most sanguine. To the question "Is it possible in America?" he replied: "Of course. . . . One of those inevitable things." Elsie McCormick believed "we might justifiably wonder if we are moving toward a costumeless society." The Chicago *Post* forecast from the "preliminary splashes" of nudism "not a shower but a steady downpour." And the Boston *Herald*—casting no doubt a reminiscent glance at the Watch and Ward Society—remarked that "it is a changing world," and that "the experiment is not wholly unknown in America." May Frank is the canny seer. "It isn't beyond my thinking that nudism will be acceptable—say in the year 2030," was her cautious prediction, though she proceeded to note evidence of much swifter changes in the status of exposure in the past. "I've heard Our Family Philosopher tell," she recounted, "how Old Man Park 'ran down' Mollie Phelps because she made a Sunday go-to-meeting dress that didn't drag on the ground, and how he direly prophesied, 'If it goes on it won't be ten years before we'll be seeing a woman's ankle.' "

And there are portents more tangible than the auguries of the oracular critics of nudism. For instance, there is the tolerance of New Yorkers for the naked boys and men—not all youngsters by any means—who disport themselves in the Hudson in the vicinity of 113th Street, the Columbia University district. On this tolerance an editorial in the *World-Telegram* last July commented thus favourably: "The bathers are all more sun-bathers than water-bathers. They strut vainly in full view in the 'altogether.' The well-to-do apartment dwellers note the unconventional goings-on and never call a cop. Women with their perambulators, students, lovers sitting on the park benches or lounging upon the sloping greensward likewise note the stark skin in the distant sunlight and instead of blushing possibly envy the nudists their comfort. It is a civilized town we live in." Moreover, Judge Ross C. Hall, in a Chicago Criminal Court, according to a United Press dispatch of February 1931, dismissed the case against a young lady, her boy friend and her mother, arrested because one August day the young woman had undressed in her backyard and the young man had turned the hose on her. The Judge even censured the police "for not minding their own business."

Rex Beach, in an interview in the *World-Telegram*, July 2, 1931, declared that "America's wealthy families are becoming a class of sun-worshippers, following the summer from one smart resort to another . . . in a fashion that almost presages an era of nakedness." If he is right, and wealth and fashion are on the side of sun-worship, it can count on considerable prestige and security. Writing in the Baltimore *Sun* last July, Duncan Aikman found nude sun-bathing in southern California had passed "the health crank and popular cult stages," that in fact the region appeared to be "fast heading toward habitual nudity." He reported few if any objections, provided there was rigid sex segregation, but there were alarms from traditionalists who perceived too much leniency in such matters and who feared for American morality. "On the other hand," he said, "moral and hygiene innovators burble over the growing popularity of exposure in all its features. Though a little less liberal on some points of thought and conduct than other metropolitan areas in the United States, they anticipate that Los Angeles and its suburbs may yet . . . teach Americans to lay by their ancient body pruderies and become as civilized in their attitude toward complete epidermal frankness as the Japanese or the Russians."

It is propitious for nudism that in a number of instances

where sun-bathers have shocked the community, the latter has been reluctant, or powerless, to inflict any severe penalty on the offenders. Isabel Paterson mentioned a club where members exercise unclothed across the Hudson from New York. The rural community is slightly scandalized and the sheriff not sure what to do about it, but nothing has been done. Last June a delightful story from Easthampton, Massachusetts, appeared in the Boston *Post* concerning six feminine nudists who frolicked in the Loudville Pond. This shocked the farmers and kept the boys away from the swimming hole. When complaints resulted, a local policeman tried to deal with them, but the situation was too much for his modesty. He ran away. The State police were next given the job, and a trooper sped out on his motorcycle. But the lecture he attempted to deliver to the mermaids was ruined when they rushed from the water and charged him with sticks and stones. He fled, and presumably the district despaired of saving Loudville Pond from profanation. At Santa Barbara, California, the complaint of an indignant lady that she could see boys bathing naked through opera glasses led to the discovery of an old ordinance permitting nude bathing between the hours of 7 P. M. and 7 A. M., and the inhabitants are reported to have availed themselves of it immediately.

The decided trend of censorship, according to Morris Ernst, is away from sex—which of course includes nakedness—and in the direction of crime news. This is all to the good for the nudists, mild people not apt to be involved in murders, racketeering, and gang warfare. Even the zealous Mr. Sumner has ruefully admitted that "the courts are increasingly liberal in their attitude towards pictures. The same is true with nudity on the stage." Naturally this was deplorable, and Mr. Sumner went on to say: "Personally, I believe that the more liberal attitude of the courts since 1910 has had its share in the loose living, immorality, and crime which is such a feature of present day life." So nakedness, after all, may find itself enmeshed

in the drive on crime. Perhaps there would be no Al Capones
today if the courts had kept our fig-leaves clamped on! The
New York *Herald-Tribune,* however, scarcely an organ of
radicalism, was rude enough to assert that some people believe
Mr. Sumner's view to be "simple poppycock," and that convictions under the obscenity statutes are of "almost negligible effect upon the actual morals of the people."

Many individuals in all sections of America have perceived
that "our country is not so Anglo-Saxon as we sometimes
think" and surmise that when city fathers are beginning to
recognize the virtues of the sun with municipal solaria, the
next generation may go much further. A Bostonian "honestly"
believed that "the time is coming when the youth of this country will start a nudist movement," and that "such organizations as the Watch and Ward Society are fast becoming
unpopular." An Eastern scientist was "convinced that the attitude of tolerance is growing especially in this part of the
country and in California." He recalled "the rather sudden
change of attitude from a strict taboo of sexual and other
topics to somewhat free discussion of them; and some similar
change may take place regarding clothing." A Middle Western physician thought it "inevitable that there will soon spring
up small groups throughout this country which, in spite of
criticism and perhaps ridicule, will be formed to enjoy the new
physical freedom." A lawyer was sufficiently optimistic in Alabama to declare: "It would seem that with the right approach
and the use of a great deal of tact a trail might be blazed even
in America for the sunlight-way." A Californian wrote that,
"Being old enough to have witnessed the terrible upheavals
in American conventionalism within the last forty years, the
overnight changes in its code, I am not sure that America will
be many years older before this movement becomes recognized
and sanctioned." A Canadian reported "progress," and one of
his compatriots had "no great fear for the ultimate success of
nudism."

What the Neighbours Think

Striking a balance between the optimistic prophets of a nudist era and the Cassandras who warn of puritanism, and taking into consideration both the Sumnerites and the liberals, it is reasonable to conclude that nudism will still have to face moral opposition, but that the forces of prudery are not so great as they used to be and are constantly diminishing. Even now, the favourable signs are at least as conspicuous as the threats, and public opinion in all likelihood will tend less and less in the future to attack nudity on moral grounds. It should not be forgotten, however, that the opponents of nakedness do not always base their objections on moral grounds. Among our press critics, more than twice as many have protested for æsthetic as for moral reasons. The æsthetes, by the way, do not include any famous artists—who unaccountably persist in seeing beauty in the body, even the distorted modern kind—but those who have raised æsthetic objections number among them such ill-assorted figures as Arthur Brisbane, McAlister Coleman, the *Nation's* Drifter, Harry Hansen, T. S. Matthews, Corey Ford, and Mrs. Florence Parry.

Mrs. Parry's opinion, in view of her remarks about the unimportance of the body, and the obvious shock she suffered from the nude at the Junior League Exhibit, can be dismissed at once as not inspired by abstract considerations of pure beauty but coloured by a subjective emotion—plain, old-fashioned prudery. While Rose C. Feld in the New York *Times* was more consciously broad-minded than Mrs. Parry and employed scientific arguments to make out her case against nakedness, the fact that she attacked nudism on so many different grounds and for such tenuous and extraordinary reasons lays her open to the suspicion of rationalizing what was an instinctive repulsion—a repulsion based on a strong, though unconscious, association of nudity with evil. Her statement that the human form "except in rare instances is not divine, and human suffering is sufficiently great without additional pain" can be accepted on the face of it as an objective æsthetic judgment; it is invalidated only by the obvious straining in all her other arguments to justify her stand.

The others who expressed æsthetic objections—ranging from McAlister Coleman's mild wish that "there should be a little mystery left in the world," to the *New Yorker's* strong assertion that nudity is "pretty damned ugly, especially in crowds," and the Drifter's threat that if there were a successful nudist revolution he "for one would not care to stay in the world a day longer"—are less vulnerable to the charge of prudery. There is also the extenuating fact that most of them are not over-serious, a number of them in fact belonging to the ranks of the professional humorists. Yet it is not unlikely that some of the clowning cloaked serious beliefs, and that the humorists in presenting the anti-nudist arguments in facetious guise were convinced none the less of their soundness. Corey Ford stated that one of the chief motives of the Prudists was æsthetic: "Beauty, they held was the first concern of everyone; and the beautiful body, with its soft curves and perfect proportions, was the rarest gift of God. In fact, after viewing the exposed bodies which the nudists displayed, the new cult came to the conclusion that this gift of God was so *very* rare that the cause of beauty would best be served by putting on as many clothes as possible. In some cases, they even recommended a mask and long, false whiskers." Mr. Ford was perspicacious in putting a beauty plank in the Prudist platform; for beauty, if not the aim, is a chief claim of prudery.

The majority of the æsthetic protesters were content to dismiss the question with the assertion that the ordinary body is not much to look at. Harry Hansen was more specific, declaring that "there is nothing very attractive in the average nude man or woman after the age of thirty." No one will disagree that youth is generally superior to age in a physical way, but Mr. Hansen seems to have put his beauty line unduly low. Nowadays, at least, when athletic habits are prevalent among both men and women, and women are more apt to escape the ravages of excessive child-bearing and poor maternity care, there are plenty of people in their thirties, and even much older, whose physiques can stand comparison with the teens and twenties. The mother of several children who has the body of a slender girl, the man of sixty with the figure of an athletic boy—we have seen both—are doubtless exceptional. But Mr. Hansen would have to raise his age limit to at least forty for his strictures to be true. It is a fact that, unless abused by unhygienic habits, the body ages less rapidly than the face, escaping the fine wrinkles etched by changing facial expressions. May Frank also was definite in her protest. "I don't hanker," she explained, "to see corns, bunions, swaybacks, varicose veins and fatty lumps." Leaving aside the question of the frequency of these afflictions, it is pertinent to note that most of them are clothes-made deformities, and that they may be expected to decline if the practice of nudity becomes widespread.

Significantly enough, none of those who insisted on the ugliness of the human figure have, so far as can be ascertained, visited a nudist camp. Stuart Chase is the only experienced nudist who has expressed himself on the æsthetic question, and he took the moderate stand that some bodies "are worth observing and some are not—and by and large the males stand up better than the females in this entirely casual survey." A number of the others admittedly founded their conclusions on observations in locker rooms (Harry Hansen), public beaches (Miss Feld), and Turkish baths (Arthur Brisbane), or the photographs in nudist books (T. S. Matthews). In defence of the human body, it might be alleged that locker rooms frequented largely by middle-aged golfers, and Turkish baths patronized by gentlemen who need to reduce their girths, are perhaps not typical, since the youth and beauty of the land are not proportionately represented. The illustrations supplied Mr. Matthews with his information that some of the nudists have "tremendous behinds and downcast bellies." The pictures, however, are of German nudists, and national pride might be permitted to boast that this style of figure may be less common in America. But photographs of even German nudists do not always offend the artistic eye of the critics. The Boston *Herald* reviewer, insinuating that they have been unfairly selected, stated such pictures give the impression "that all the nudists are young and beautiful and that the old and scrawny, the fat and flabby, apparently have no interest in the movement." The *Warwick Lorgnette* (Philadelphia) pronounced the movement, judged "by the many photographs of brown, healthy bodies . . . all to the good." Granting that such photographs are selected and are not representative of the average, such testimony does indicate that even contemporary bodies are sometimes lovely, a thing the extreme æsthetes refuse to concede.

Most of the æsthetic objectors—Corey Ford, the *New Yorker*, the Drifter, McAlister Coleman, T. S. Matthews, Harry Hansen—are obviously in the sophisticated or liberal camps. They are people who would protest, and perhaps kick and scream, at a charge of Puritanism or narrow-mindedness. Yet a careful study of the reactions of our liberal friends inclines us to think that Samuel Lipshutz put his finger on the reason why so many liberals are convinced that nakedness is unbearably ugly. Mr. Lipshutz mentioned nudism to a dozen people, and he said: "Each looked shocked, then realized that he must remain liberal at any cost, and finally announced, 'Well, it must be ugly—all those fat people.' This is known as liberalism saving itself by gross tonnage." The *New Yorker, et al.* cannot be shocked, but they can be amused or outraged in the name of beauty. Rationally of course they are convinced that there is nothing wicked or shameful in nakedness, but it is barely possible that subconsciously they are suffering an emotional hangover from an earlier association of nudity and sin.

We would not contend that modern men and women are

built like Greek gods, but we—and even some of the press commentators—find reassurance in the fact that dispensing with clothes will help rather than hinder the attainment of physical symmetry. George Currie pointed out in the Brooklyn *Eagle* that the sports of the German nudists might be a corrective for neglected figures, and Isabel Paterson believed it "highly probable that the scanty fashions in clothes which have prevailed for some years have improved the average of feminine grace." She added that "If there is no disguise left we may have to become beautiful whether we like it or not." Even some theoretical nudists feel that the physical imperfections of humanity are not insurmountable obstacles, but that nakedness, by distributing the attention ordinarily focused on the face, often discloses beauty that would otherwise be hidden. Far from shying at the æsthetic drawbacks to nudity, a distinguished psychologist has declared that æsthetic considerations are among the chief things that attracted him to nudism. "I see no reason," he asserted, "why a woman with a beautiful face should have such an advantage over one whose beauty lay elsewhere." But for those who insist there is no beauty elsewhere, comfort there is none save that the nudists are not plotting the revolution feared by the Drifter and his sensitive colleagues that would force him to gaze on their unlovely physiques.

The critics of nudism, perhaps as a result of fictitious newspaper stories of nudist parades or of a confusion with the Doukhobors, are subject to wholly baseless fears of having nakedness thrust upon them. The nudists are driven again and again to explain that what they wish is privacy for their naked gatherings, and above all the assurance that the privacy will not be disturbed by either inquisitive Fishermen or interfering policemen. C. Hartley Grattan was well aware of this. "We need not fear," he reassured us, "that we shall see nudists on Fifth Avenue. If they appear in America, they will appear as they do in Europe, in isolated places for the purposes of gymnastics." But Corey Ford expressed the popular notion in relating the imaginary history of the first nudist colony in America thus: "Like its continental predecessors, it was characterized by a tactful modesty and an evident desire to shun all publicity; and consequently its members gathered inconspicuously at high noon in Macy's window." Other critics feared that they would not only have to gaze on unlovely sights but be forced to uncover themselves willy-nilly. McAlister Coleman, who seems to have encountered such fanaticism, related how, "Whenever I fell in with a bunch of them [nudists], they immediately suggested going in swimming *à la* Adam and Eve, and if I feebly suggested that a bathing suit might not come amiss in a swimming pool in plain sight of the main road, I was pooh-poohed as a sissy." Isabel Paterson, after pronouncing Stuart Chase's sun-worship "smug," expressed the fear "that pretty soon they'll demand a law, or at least create a convention, compelling people like us to endure sunstroke every summer." Every movement has its extremists, but nudism does not necessarily entail strong arm tactics. The "smug" Stuart Chase stated what is probably the attitude of most nudists, and certainly that of the present writers, in saying: "It ought to be anybody's privilege to strip or not as he or she pleases, so long as he does not leave his clothes on every hickory limb. . . . Bathing costumes on all but the most public beaches should be optional."

The health advantages of nakedness are the ones that suffer least from the scepticism of the press and the public—as a result no doubt of the general belief in the good of sunbaths. The modest Mr. Kitchen did suggest that "abbreviated costumes could be worn without sacrificing any of the beneficial effects," but on the other hand C. Hartley Grattan contradicted him by asserting that "the sun has a definite and measurable therapeutic value and that it works best when the whole body is exposed to it. Partial nudity does not turn the trick." Only two of the fifty or so writers were so rash as to attack the whole principle of the healthfulness of bodily exposure. Rose Feld was one of them. She advanced as proof of the harmlessness of clothes the primitives tribes of Africa whose "pictures as brought back by anthropologists and explorers do not show bodies of unusual beauty or grace or strength," and who are "neither healthier, because of the mode of living, nor do they live longer."

Whether or not the savage is healthier or more beautiful than clothed races we shall leave to the anthropologists, for in any case it is irrelevant. Too many elements besides nakedness enter into the question of the savage's health—climate, diet, sanitation, and personal hygiene, for instance. The only way to prove anything by the dress or undress of the savages is to compare the health of the same race, with the same habits, in the same environment, naked and clothed. Most testimony indicates that tropical peoples were physiologically better off in their naked state than after civilization dressed them up. Elsie McCormick asserted—and considerable scientific evidence bears her out—that "the missionaries' Mother Hubbards were more deadly to the natives of the South Sea Islands than all the rum and whiskey ever brought in by unregenerate traders." Miss Feld said later that the savage's undress was a matter of "meeting his environment"—which would indicate that in his environment, at least, he is better off without clothes.

But the grand attack on the healthfulness of nudity was made by the doughty H. L. Mencken, who loudly thwacked his drum of alarm in the June 1931 *American Mercury*. "Putting a civilized man into the broiling sunlight, especially with his clothes off, is a foul assault upon both his spiritual and civic dignity and his physical well-being," he banged, thumbing his nose in the direction of the physiologists. "The fact is that, to the higher varieties of civilized man, sunlight is often injurious," dinned Mr. Mencken, "and their natural inclination to keep out of it is sound in instinct. If it were beneficial, then farmers would be healthier than city men, which they are surely not. Man has apparently sought the shade since his earliest days on earth, and all of his anthropoid ancestors seem to have been forest dwellers."

Mr. Mencken ignored the fact that many other contributing factors besides sunlight and open air affect the farmer's health. Nor should it be forgotten that though he works in the fields in the sun, he generally wears a most unhygienic costume for the purpose. His example is as inconclusive as that of the naked savage tribes. Mencken also inconsequentially lumped together the over-development of college football with his thunderous attack on heliotherapy and sun-bathing. His editorial in fact was entitled "The Striated Muscle Fetish," though the striated muscles are not involved in sun-bathing, according to the scientists, save by an indirect reflex action. Football, in any case, certainly has nothing to do with nudist activities or ideals. A sport so murderous that it requires the completest and heaviest wrappings worn outside of the arctic is not for sun-lovers, who no more long to don a football uniform for their exercise than to put on a deep-sea diving suit when they go swimming. Mr. Mencken made much of the susceptibility to illness of the highly trained football player, without realizing that this in itself is an excellent nudist argument. Might not the damage come from violent exercise in a hampering and unhygienic costume that shuts in the heat and sweat of the body and creates an artificial and injurious atmosphere? The athletic ideal of the nudist is the Greek athlete, who realized that exercise naked in the sun was more beneficial than exercise clothed, and whose empirical conclusion has been confirmed by modern science.

But one would scarcely expect Mr. Mencken—Germanophile though he be—to embrace the German revival of the Greek gospel. After all, the natural instinct of the Baltimore prophet is for the sunless cavern of a Rathskeller. One may be a sun-worshipper and yet descend at times to the smoky gloom of a Weinstube; even Stuart Chase, who claims to have been born with the love of sun in his blood, has been seen in Rathskellers. But the sun-worshipper will emerge into the light to dissolve his *Bierbauch*, while Herr Mencken stays with his stein, submerged in the murky depths. He was never one to feel uncomfortable at being alone in his opinions. His beer will not be embittered by the knowledge that all the other critics take the healthfulness of nudity for granted, and that even B. S., from North Carolina, who could find nothing too harsh to say about the unattractiveness of the other nudist claims, asserted that "it would be difficult to inveigh against this argument."

The critics are on the whole less disturbed by any possible health mania on the part of the nudists than by the distrust of organizations and a fear of cults. The headline writers who persist in calling it "the nudist cult" are to blame rather than anything cultish in the behaviour of the nudists themselves. But T. S. Matthews classified nudism "among the modern legion of cults"—for which he had an ingenious economic explanation—and William Morris took the stand in the Brooklyn *Standard Union* that the nudist movement is being unnecessarily fanatic about something all right in its way but not worthy of being made into an issue. According to him: "In America, the men and women who cared to expose themselves exposed themselves, and that was all. But not so in Germany, Russia, Austria, and other countries. . . . One must have company and form a cult and enlist members and write books and make a philosophy of it."

If exposing oneself were such an easy matter as Mr. Morris believes, there would be no necessity for an organized movement or for nudist propaganda. One could take nakedness or leave it, and worry not at all about what the neighbours think. But so long as the neighbours can use not only social pressure but the force of the law to curb nudity, propagandizing is essential, *not* to gain converts but tolerance, and so long as inviolable privacy is a *sine qua non* to nakedness, organizing is the only way most people can secure it. Mr. Morris himself seemed almost to detect the objection to his argument and to attempt to forestall it by admitting "that in America, to hope to be able to get a glass of beer one must either be a lawbreaker or member of a movement." But he insisted: "One does not have to join a cult to eat raw fruit or to go hatless." Note that he carefully avoided saying "or to go naked," though the implication is that stripping is in a class with vegetarianism and hatlessness. Unfortunately most of us find it just as hard to go naked as to get a glass of beer without breaking the law or joining a movement. Stuart Chase has as strong a distaste for organization as any of the other critics, and he does not even see "why stripping needs be a social pursuit." But such is his tolerance and his ability to view the other side of the question that he conceded the need for organizations to secure facilities for the nakedness of the less privileged classes, and he suggested—somewhat facetiously to be sure—that his lack of appreciation for sunning himself in company at the municipal solarium at St. Petersburg may have been due to the fact that "the city fathers segregated the sexes rigorously." Doubting that he himself would ever be an habitué of "air parks," he nevertheless expressed the wish to see them "all over this great Republic." There were others who absolved nudism of cultishness. The Chicago *Post* reviewer asserted very sanely that "it is not a cult—unless one calls any gymnastic or swimming association a cult," and Adelin Hohlfeld in the Madison, Wisconsin, *State Journal*, perceived that in America those who wish the benefits of nudity must "seek them in solitary boredom, performing a tedious duty for the sake of health," while they order things better in Germany by combining them "with comradeship and recreation."

There has also been some hedging at nudism on the ground of impracticability and discomfort—a thoroughly irrelevant objection based on a fallacious assumption that nudists are fanatics determined to go bare and unprotected anywhere and everywhere. The Drifter was among those who thus went astray. He explained that he himself is a devout sun-worshipper, but that this very fact keeps him from being a nudist. "The reason for a sunbath is, or should be relaxation. Being a nudist, on the other hand, strikes the Drifter as one of the most uncomfortable, unrelaxing pursuits in life. He is not speaking just now of moral considerations and martyrdom. He is speaking of physical discomfort." In specifying these discomforts he disclosed that he conceived of nudists as maniacs who insist in their nakedness on reclining on stubble, sleeping on fir boughs without blankets, and sitting on wicker furniture and plush that "can prickle a fiendish prickle." It did not occur to the Drifter that the nudist might be sane enough, when he wished to treat his skin to light and air while sitting or lying on rough or prickly surfaces, to take along a blanket.

May Frank likewise saw a menace to bare bodies in "our sharp cornered chairs, prickly couch covers and present climate," and Corey Ford's Prudists advocated clothes as desirable "from the standpoint of comfort (as when stubbing the toe on a gravel-walk, for example, or sitting down suddenly on a horsehair sofa)." Of course not all of the "practical reasons" of the Prudists can be taken seriously since they include such points in the favour of trousers as "something to fasten suspenders to" or "to roll up, as in wading" and "to determine the sex of the wearer"—nor are Robert Benchley's dogged nudists who endure insects, stubble, cold and rain to be taken literally. Yet there is a very real, though erroneous, belief that nudists submit to all sorts of physical torture and mental ennui for the sake of an ideal. Those who have not tried nudism often imagine it to be, if not a positively painful ordeal, at least a dull and joyless duty. The prudish Mrs. Parry announced: "My observation has been that all cultists [again the assumption of a cult] are about the most self-conscious people on earth, and I am of the mind that the nudists, sweating

under the instinctive strain of walking about bare-naked, are
no doubt the most insufferably self-conscious of all." And
strangely like this was the comment of the unprudish *New
Yorker:* "The trouble with nudity . . . is: what are you going to do with it when you've got it? It still seems more of a
burden, even to the most determined cultists, than the heaviest
outfit of winter clothing, and the only way the burden can be
lightened apparently is by keeping constantly in motion."

To anyone who has experienced the natural and happy
sensation of walking around outdoors without his or her
clothes, even under the eyes of observers, provided the latter
are equally unhampered by bodily draperies and old-fashioned
mental furnishings—to anyone who has watched the free and
unself-conscious movements of other unclad men and women
—it is hard to understand what on earth Mrs. Parry and the
New Yorker were talking about. But, after all, their attitude
is comprehensible if one remembers that they were speculating
about something remote from their experience and absolutely
contrary to all the conventions, habits, and thought-moulds of
everyday life. Habit can make the most artificial things seem
natural and, conversely, the most natural appear artificial. The
"strain of walking about bare-naked" and the "burden" of
nudity exist only in the imagination of those who have not
broken with the clothed habit and thought. The actual break
is a strain and burden—in anticipation. In realization, it is
nothing but the simple act of taking off one's clothes in company—more arduous perhaps than the same act performed in
the privacy of the bedroom, though not everlasting. There
may be a fleeting, momentary awkwardness, but with the
sartorial shell vanish the burden and the strain. One is surprised to discover that he feels, not like a fish out of water, but
like a creature that for the first time has found its natural element. The physical activity with which Corey Ford and the
New Yorker twitted the nudists is not nearly so unremitting
as they would have us believe, for nudists bask as well as

bound. Nor is it an effort to lighten a burden or dispel any self-consciousness. It is merely the expression of the sense of freedom, the reaction to the stimulus of sun and wind on the skin, the overflow of liberated animal spirits, and no more forced or self-conscious than the impulse of children to run and play and shout.

Some of the critics indeed—those who know what it is to swim without swimming suits or sun-bathe without sun suits —glimpsed the pagan joys of nakedness. Bruce Calvert, who lived a naked hermit on the dunes for years, knew "the unspeakable delight of exposing the whole body, unclothed to the sun, air, wind, and weather." To those who have never experienced it, he had the message "that you have something coming to you; and that if you once try it, you will never forget the joy of it, and you will be converts forever." George Currie too remembered "that swimming in the altogether in the waters of the Minnetonka was beyond all comparison with swimming in a hotel pool in a bathing suit. Part of the exhilaration came from the sylvan scenery. Most came from the glowing smoothness of water gliding over skin." Adelin Hohlfeld was another who found the sheer delight the most attractive argument for nakedness. "Imagine," she wrote, "being able to plunge carelessly into cool water in broad daylight quite naked, to lie afterward on the warm sands, to run through sunlit woods with the soft air blowing on bare, tingling skin, to play games with no garments to become sticky and irritating with perspiration, to walk in the rain without being hampered by soggy, clinging clothing or steaming mackintoshes."

Infinitely varied—from horror and disgust, through amusement to tolerance and even enthusiasm—are the expressions with which the non-participants have greeted the nudist movement. It would be an interminable task to run through the whole gamut of the hopes and fears, the facetious and serious speculations to which it has given rise. A naked civilization is a fertile field for fantasy, and the writers have hazarded light

guesses on all of its aspects. Laurence Stallings saw the Legislature of the State of Nevada "going into a huddle" prepara-
tory to acquiring, in addition to the divorce and gambling
monopoly, the monopoly on nudity. Elsie McCormick imagined
the citizen "followed by a small boy with a wheelbarrow containing his keys, address book, and the letters he forgot to
mail." And the *Warwick Lorgnette* of Philadelphia inquired if
we will "develop a Neolithic hairy hide and be mistaken for
our Airedale pup?" May Frank wondered about certain classics
in an age unable to comprehend Lady Godiva and the bathing
Susannah. A more serious effect on the social order was seen by
several—a threat or a promise according to whether or not one
believes the lower classes should be kept in their places. No
longer could people be classified by tailor-made suits and
Chanel gowns. "With velvet, ermine, and tall hats eliminated,"
according to Elsie McCormick, "princes and potentates would
have nothing to sustain their dignity. If they appeared as their
unprepossessing selves, there would probably be ominous snickers from the strong-muscled proletariate."

But the hope of Stuart Chase that the movement will come,
"fight for its life (not too solemnly either), and win"; the
wish of the unconverted, such as Lorine Pruette and Elsie Mc-
Cormick, that nudism will not make us nude but will teach us
to wear fewer and more comfortable clothes; the remark C.
Hartley Grattan attributed to a friend that "If they don't
mind, I don't see why anyone else should"—these all reflect in
varying degrees the prevailing tolerance of the critics. None
of the objections they have raised are over-important; most of
them are trivial or irrelevant. The general public, containing
many elements violently opposed to nakedness, is less broad-
minded as a whole than the ladies and gentlemen of the press.
Nevertheless, throughout America tolerance for infractions of
convention and even of the moral code has been increasing
during the last decade, and the sin of nakedness is not so
heinous as it used to be. The austerer forms of religion, which

What the Neighbours Think

were the greatest barrier to the respectability of nudity, are
so effectively weakened that there is little likelihood of their
immediate repair. The tide is away from prudery and in the
direction of even greater freedom for the epidermis. Ebbs of
course at times set in suddenly and without warning, but there
is yet no indication that the tide has begun to turn.

VIII

WHAT THE PHYSICIANS THINK

(1) Of Sun, Air, and Bare Skin

WHILE THE BASES OF NUDISM ARE AS MUCH PSYCHOLOGI-
cal as physiological and its adherents swayed relatively little by
the desire for improved health, the physical benefits of nakedness, we have seen, are the ones most generally accepted by
the public. In Europe, particularly in France, the ardent champions of the movement include a large number of distinguished
physicians. The lay public in America, being addicted to sunbaths and having fully accepted the gospel of ultraviolet rays
and vitamins—even though not always clear as to just what
those rays are, or how they perform their miracles—is apt to
take it for granted that medical science and health authorities
in this country will likewise welcome the cause of nakedness,
though perhaps with reservations regarding unsegregated nudity. But even a superficial study of the annals of medical societies and the publications and utterances of our scientists will
temper any such sanguine view, and a talk with the average
medical practitioner will be a positive disillusionment.

There will be found plenty of testimony, it is true, in favour
of ultraviolet rays and vitamin D, but the rays are considered
chiefly as a treatment for specific diseases. If advocated as a
preventive measure, it is usually for infants threatened with
rickets, and even here the attention is centred rather on cod-

[152]

liver oil, or the concentrated form of irradiated ergosterol. The practice of nakedness, except for the purpose of absorbing ultraviolet rays, has received scant notice, as has the whole matter of clothing in relation to the health. Heliotherapy in this country—that is, the therapeutic use of the natural sunlight in its whole spectrum—has had less attention than the therapeutic use of artificial light, limited usually to the ultraviolet rays and including shorter wave lengths than those to be found in natural sunlight.

"A survey of recent medical literature," Dr. Edgar Mayer, of Saranac Lake, wrote in his *Clinical Application of Sunlight and Artificial Radiation*, "discloses a steadily increasing interest in the possibilities of phototherapy." Yet Dr. Mayer's book, published in 1926, was the first comprehensive survey of the whole subject of phototherapy by an American physician, and none has been published since. The only medical material previously available in this country had been articles in the scientific journals dealing with isolated experiments and special phases. M. Luckiesh and A. J. Pacini, of the research department of the General Electric Company, had published as early as 1925 their *Light and Health*, discussing many of the physiological effects of light and collating and making available the results of many different experiments. In any bibliography of the subject, it must have a prominent place, as must Luckiesh's subsequent work on *Artificial Sunlight*, but neither book was written primarily from the physician's viewpoint. The work of Luckiesh and Pacini, like the recent synthetic production of vitamin D, is characteristic of much of the scientific research in America in having a commercial backing and motivation. But Dr. Mayer's book is so exhaustive that, until further research and experimentation have extended the knowledge of the subject, there is no need for other works to supplement it except on specialized aspects, such as *Ultraviolet Light and Vitamin D in Nutrition*, by Katharine Blunt and Ruth Cowan, published in 1930. Dr.

Mayer's book of course is highly technical; and about the only American work intended primarily for the general reader is *Sunrays and Health,* by R. Millar and the chemist E. E. Free (1929). However, during the last five or six years there has been no dearth of material on ultraviolet radiation published in both scientific journals and general periodicals. Under the heading "ultraviolet rays" in the Reader's Guide to Periodical Literature, there are long lists of articles, and though the majority appeared in such mediums as the *American Journal of Public Health, Hygeia, Science,* and the *Scientific Monthly,* there are listed such miscellaneous periodicals as the *Saturday Evening Post, Collier's, Outlook, Survey, Forum, Harper's, Current History, Literary Digest, Good Housekeeping,* and *Ladies Home Journal.*

There is no American Rollier, but nevertheless heliotherapy is now being employed in many sanitaria in this country for the treatment of tuberculosis, pulmonary as well as surgical. Dr. Horace LoGrasso, of the J. N. Adam Memorial Hospital at Perrysburg, New York, a disciple of Rollier, was the pioneer in the scientific use of heliotherapy on an extensive scale in America, and his work is becoming increasingly renowned. Other outstanding examples are Dr. F. M. Pottenger, who uses heliotherapy with marked success in his sanitarium at Monrovia, California; Dr. Clark L. Hyde, of East Akron, Ohio —also a disciple of Rollier—who has developed an excellent sunlight hospital; and the Desert Sanitarium at Tucson, Arizona. Dr. John Harvey Kellogg, of Battle Creek, was among the first in this country to realize the value of solar and air exposure, as well as to use the carbon-arc and incandescent lamp clinically. In 1930 he opened a sanitarium at Miami Springs, Florida, presumably to utilize some of the famous Florida sun.

Miami as a matter of fact is in a fair way of making the most of its solar advantages (though this will not be fully achieved until the city becomes less prudish about exposure on the beaches). Heliotherapy is an important feature of the St. Francis Hospital, where a solarium was installed and equipped by Dr. Joseph H. Adams for use in conjunction with the Joseph H. Adams Foundation for Sun Ray Research. In 1929, this Foundation set out, under the directorship of O. J. Sieplein, of the Chemistry Department of the University of Miami, to study the Florida sunshine scientifically—and no doubt to demonstrate in a big way the benefits of the Miami sun in particular. The hours of sunshine, the amount of ultraviolet energy, temperatures, humidity, and the like, are carefully recorded in an observatory at Miami Beach, and the therapeutic experiments are carried out at the St. Francis Hospital. The ultraviolet radiation has been found to compare favourably with that of Alpine sun. This is ground enough for the Miami Chamber of Commerce to feel "safe in saying that the ultraviolet radiation in the sun is at least ten per cent more efficient here than anywhere else in the world with the probable exception of the Island of Sumatra and some equatorial regions inaccessible to the white man." One wonders why they except Sumatra, unless because it is far enough away to discourage Americans in quest of ultraviolet. But although the Chamber of Commerce ballyhoo may well be discounted, the Sun Ray Research is doing valuable work. Dr. C. W. Saleeby, the British campaigner for sunshine, after remarking that the greatest surgical "show" of North America was the Mayo clinic, and the greatest surgical "show" of Europe was Rollier's clinic, "where surgery has been abolished," expressed astonishment "that no American has found out this open secret and made fame and fortune for himself, years ago, in California." Perhaps this secret is at last on its way to exploitation by Americans.

The employment of heliotherapy and ultraviolet irradiation is not of course being limited to tuberculosis in its various forms. They have also been used in this country in the treatment of anæmia, certain skin diseases, fractures, hyperæsthetic rhinitis when accompanied by calcium deficiency (all conditions in fact characterized by inadequate calcium supply), tetany, and even burns or scalds. Although ultraviolet rays are considered a specific only for rickets and certain bone diseases, and less essential to adults than children (except when unusually large quantities of calcium and phosphorus must be retained, as during pregnancy, or when fractures are healing), there is an increasing realization that the effect of light is not limited to the chemistry of the blood. It is believed to act on the nervous and glandular systems to an extent not yet fully determined. American scientists have noted also the mental stimulation resulting from exposure to light—a factor stressed by Rollier. Blunt and Cowan state that "the psychic influences and general effects upon the nervous system must not be passed over in discussing the effect of irradiation." And Luckiesh says: "The brilliant sun overwhelms depression. . . . Sunless days are the suicide days." Consequently some attention has been given to ultraviolet radiation as an aid to building up the general health of those weakened by illness or undernourishment, or the crippled whose condition deprives them of a normal amount of sunlight.

The foundations for heliotherapy were laid down by the French and first developed systematically on a large scale by Rollier in Switzerland, but American scientists have had an important share in widening knowledge of the properties of ultraviolet rays. Dr. Janet Clark, of Johns Hopkins, for instance, has done significant research in the action of light on the content of white blood cells. But the field to which Americans have most notably contributed is the study of ultraviolet rays and vitamin D in relation to rickets. Huldschinsky in Berlin and an Englishwoman, Dr. Chick, working at the Child Clinic in Vienna, had already demonstrated that ultraviolet rays could heal rickets, but it remained for the Americans to work out scientifically the whys and the wherefores, and to show the relationship between ultraviolet light and vitamin D.

What the Physicians Think

Dr. Alfred F. Hess and his colleagues in New York proved in 1922 that sunlight increases the phosphorus and calcium in the blood of infants, and that rickets accompanies their deficiency. The chemist, Harry Steenbock, of the University of Wisconsin, in 1924 produced vitamin D, the antirachitic vitamin, in food products by irradiation. Although the clinical use of ultraviolet light has been successful in curing rickets in this country, vitamin D in its various forms is probably more widely employed. In fact, Dr. Henry J. Gerstenberger, of the Babies' and Children's Hospital in Cleveland, opposed the general establishment by public health departments of ultraviolet ray clinics, on the grounds that such clinics are expensive; that rickets, not present in those over three years old, is the only disease specifically cured by ultraviolet rays; and that even rickets are "as satisfactorily prevented and cured by the use of the more economic and old-fashioned cod-liver oil or by the ingestion of small doses of the modern irradiated ergosterol."

Not only is the action of irradiated ergosterol—now produced commercially according to the Steenbock method—quicker than that of light, but vitamins in general, and D in particular, seem to be more attractive to the American public than even the magic ultraviolet rays, which in turn are far more interesting than commonplace sunlight. Commercially, vitamin D is a gold mine. It is worthy of front page newspaper stories, as when it was isolated in the fall of 1931 in Germany, Holland, and England simultaneously, and again when announced at the meeting of the American Association for the Advancement of Science, December 29, 1931, that Drs. Charles E. Bills and Francis G. McDonald, of the research laboratory of Mead, Johnson and Company had produced vitamin D in ergosterol synthetically without irradiation. In fact, the latter occasion was deemed of sufficient importance for an editorial in the New York *Times*. As a result of the Steenbock discovery, we are all familiar with the virtues of irradiated breads and cereals, acclaimed as they are in newspaper advertisements and on billboards. When advertising takes up science, one may expect strange miracles; hence we have irradiated cigarettes and beauty creams, although it taxes the imagination to understand the physiological benefits of vitamin D absorbed in tobacco smoke.

But the publicity given ultraviolet rays and the antirachitic vitamin, while lending itself to quackery, has had a decidedly beneficial effect. The common knowledge of the efficacy of sun and vitamin D in preventing rickets, and the consequent dosing of infants with cod-liver oil and toasting of them as a matter of course, has resulted in a decrease in the frequency of the disease. Drs. E. T. Wyman and C. A. Weymuller wrote that whereas five years before, 95 per cent of the children brought to the out-patient department of the Boston Children's Hospital had active or healed rickets, they were having in 1927 "considerable difficulty in finding a sufficient number of babies with severe rickets" for their study. This decrease, they said, "can be due only to widespread adoption of antirachitic measures which has resulted from public health propaganda and the recognition on the part of the general practitioner of the specificity of cod-liver oil and sunshine." It is noteworthy that the Chairman of the 1927 meeting of the Section of Diseases of Children of the conservative American Medical Association stated in his address: "In order to prevent rickets, the administration of cod-liver oil or the exposure of the child to the actinic rays should begin early—in our opinion not later than the beginning of the second week of life."

Closely related to the question of ultraviolet radiation is that of special window glasses permeable by the ultraviolet rays of the sun's spectrum—a field as commercially interesting as vitamin D, and incidentally as susceptible to quackery. For one thing, there is considerable variation in the amount of ultraviolet transmitted by the different types of glass; all of them are subject to deterioration in this respect, and of course unless the window receives light containing ultraviolet rays, it is no help to have glass that will let them through. Experiments made with windows of special glass reached by direct sunlight indicate, however, that ultraviolet rays can penetrate them in large enough quantities to prevent or heal rickets in even the latitudes of New York and Boston.

This type of glass has been widely recommended, not only for hospitals and sanitaria, but for schools, houses, and offices. The *Scientific American* made an investigation of this subject in 1929, sending out a questionnaire to a large number of medical and other scientific authorities. Opinion as to the value of such glasses was divided, but the great majority of those unfavourable to their use, except for people who could not obtain enough outdoor sunlight, belonged in the category of those who had done the most experimentation in the field—for instance, Professor Harry Steenbock, Dr. Janet Clark, Dr. A. F. Hess, M. Luckiesh, Dr. Brian O'Brien (Dr. LoGrasso's co-worker)—and practically all of them questioned its use except for windows receiving direct sunlight. An opinion particularly of interest to nudists was that of Dr. W. H. Eddy, of Columbia University. Dr. Eddy wrote: "I have objected to the installation of glasses in schoolrooms, as in the case of Bronxville, as a waste of money. Clothed children sitting away from windows would get little ultraviolet, regardless of the windows used. I believe the Vitaglass panes have a valuable use where persons can undergo exposure on the nude skin. . . . My own feeling is that schools and office buildings would invest their money more efficiently by equipping solaria, preferably with sky lighting and sexes segregated, so that the needy cases could lie exposed for certain periods of the day to the full effect of the sun with as little clothing as possible. I do see a place in homes and apartments for these glasses to permit mothers to save some hours of perambulation with the baby."

Even if such glass is limited to solaria, as most of the experts recommend, it is likely that its use will increase tremendously, for the trend is certainly in the direction of solaria. The most striking example is the municipal solarium opened last fall at L Street in South Boston, with its profusion of fused quartz glass. Boston, in order to preserve its municipal modesty, wastes some of these expensive ultraviolet rays, for although only men are admitted, "trunks or some other suitable cover must be worn." The other ambitious municipal solarium in the United States, the "Temple of the Sun" opened at St. Petersburg, Florida, in February 1930, required no outlay for quartz glass, but $20,000 was spent building and equipping it. Women as well as men are provided for at St. Petersburg, as the roofless structure is divided down the middle by a high wall separating the sexes. One can only bask at L Street, but the Temple of the Sun has a volley ball court in each division, as well as other gymnasium equipment, and an athletic director for each sex, who gives calisthenics if desired. In spite of these luxuries, it is cheaper than L Street, for twenty-five cents admits one to the Temple for the entire day while the same sum procures only two hours in the Boston solarium. Also the Temple of the Sun is less prudish. One's quarter includes a "silly little apron" (to quote the publicity department of the Chamber of Commerce), but apparently it is not obligatory. The same spokesman of the Chamber of Commerce described some of the sun-worshippers as "nude and others, for some mysterious reason, wear a small 'fore and aft' apron about a foot square"—an observation corroborated by a photograph of the men's corral.

Strictly speaking, neither of these solaria belong in the domain of health measures, for neither is under the administration of a health department. The L Street institution is under the authority of the Park Department, and the Temple of the Sun owes its origin to the request of a "sun-bathers" club, an informal organization of winter visitors. However, the demand for sunning facilities by both the L Street Brownies and the St. Petersburg hibernants would probably not have cul-

minated in municipal action were not people generally convinced of the healthfulness of sun-bathing. The demand in
Florida, incidentally, is almost unlimited; despite the low
charge, the Temple is making a profit, and the overflow has
taken to secluded spots on the beach. St. Petersburg's Chamber
of Commerce states that during the winter of 1930–1931 there
were also some 250 "individual private solaria" in the city,
most of which were set up on vacant lots and rented by the
hour. These contrivances are probably on the order of the
Sunshine Bath Cabinet advertised by Wanamaker's in New
York last summer (at $135) for city roofs. Having high canvas
walls, and being about as spacious as a bathtub, it was admirably adapted to stewing the bather in his own juice, but the
advertising writer ingeniously made even this feature a selling
point. Quoth he: ". . . the skin remains moist with perspiration and obviates burning and blistering."

In Miami Beach, these "special tent arrangements on lawns
and lots" are frequent, and there are many roof solaria on
hotels, apartment houses, and bathing casinos. The Chamber
of Commerce there, however, does not believe in government
in the sun-bathing business, as it explains the absence of a
municipal solarium thus: "Since so many people make a business of sun-bathing, we do not think that the City has any
right to go into a similar business in competition with them."
The St. Petersburg Chamber of Commerce spokesman referred
leniently to "the beginning of what might be termed a nudist
cult" on the "remote beach and nearby key," but the Miami
Chamber states righteously: "We have an ordinance against
indecent exposure of the human body, and for the sake of common decency find it necessary to rigidly enforce the ordinance."

According to an Associated Press dispatch, the individual
tent solaria were introduced at Savannah Beach, Georgia, last
summer. But more amazing is the information given us by the
Mayor of Savannah Beach that the Women's Society of the
First Baptist Church contemplated putting in a solarium at the

Beach, though "for some reason" they did not do so. Perhaps the good ladies discovered that sunbaths are of little avail if taken fully clothed. Apparently the Mayor was favourable to the idea, for he said: "I believe it probably would have been considerably used by persons suffering from rheumatism and other ailments likely to be improved by sunbaths."

More directly in line with medical concern for sun-bathing are the efforts being made in some quarters to supply school children with actinic rays. The state of California requires by law that every boy and girl have an hour of physical education daily which is spent out of doors, and, in the high schools at least, the boys are allowed to wear only shorts, "usually rolled up as far as possible and down as far as possible" according to one of our correspondents. In Oakland, another correspondent informed us, one can see every day boys up to the age of sixteen or eighteen nude to the waist—"the yard filled with them on a busy street corner." At the University of Chicago Nursery School, according to Blunt and Cowan, mercury quartz lamps are being used. Six children are exposed at a time, and "the teacher gives exercises or games to each little naked group." "Previous irradiation experiments at the school," they say, "involved treatment of one child at a time, with no better results, less fun for the children, and much more labour for the adults." Whether or not fig-leaves are required or the sexes segregated for the exposure is unstated, but in any case the practice is more in keeping with nudist doctrines than individual irradiation, since it combines the light-bathing with exercises and companionable recreation. The *Ladies Home Journal,* in the issue of October 1931, in which was published an article by Paul de Kruif on the work of Rollier and LoGrasso, editorially advocated arranging school hours to "give the growing little ones full benefit of the sun in the middle of each day throughout the winter," and suggested that readers take up the matter with their local school boards.

There is even indication that health authorities in educational institutions perceive benefits in ultraviolet light for others than growing children. At Cornell University, in the fall of 1929, a solarium equipped with mercury tubes and carbon-arc lamps was installed on the top floor of the Old Armory, under the direction of Dr. Dean F. Smiley, Medical Adviser to men. The solarium was open to all male students for a fee of four dollars for six months. According to *School and Society* for November 1929, arrangements for women were to be made later. A number of college athletic departments have for some time been making use of ultraviolet rays to build bigger and better athletes. Luckiesh and Pacini in 1925 stated that Alonzo Stagg's trainer at the University of Chicago was giving every member of the athletic squad daily exposure under a mercury arc during the winter months, and a similar practice was being followed with the Army athletes at West Point. Tests indicated that the toasted athletes had greater muscular strength and endurance—and did better class work than the unirradiated athletes. Last October, Dr. Pacini wrote that he found the practice of irradiating college athletes had since increased. Experiments have also been made in supplying industrial and office workers with ultraviolet rays.

The attention of public health authorities to the shutting out of light by city smoke and dust is another indication of the concern for sunlight. Last fall the committee on public relations of the New York Academy of Medicine, which made a study of the atmosphere of New York City at the request of Health Commissioner Shirley W. Wynne, announced that smoke and soot were depriving the population of from 21 to 50 per cent of the light rays and urged "aroused public opinion and courageous court action" to remedy conditions. Millar and Free assert that, "Except in the clearest days of summer a man could lie on the roof of a Manhattan skyscraper naked to the noon sun for days on end without acquiring visible sunburn or tan." They see little hope of city air ever being purified, as much of the contamination—the dust kicked up by

the crowds, and gases from automobile exhausts, for instance
—is inevitable, but they predict an increasing concern for
light radiation. "Before long," they prophesy, "we may expect
all metropolitan newspapers to include, as the London *Times*
does already, a light radiation report along with the daily
weather forecast."

The New York City Health Department deemed sunlight
of sufficient value to distribute last spring a pamphlet by the
Commissioner of Health on "Why You Need the Summer
Sun." "The ultraviolet rays of the sun," he stated, "have been
found not only to make ill persons well, but to keep well
persons well. . . . They help restore a jaded appetite, induce
resistance to disease, aid in the cure of anæmia and rickets in
children, and counteract sleeplessness." Rollier's work was cited
as an example of the medical use of sunlight, and the importance of the skin in regulating health was stressed. "The
skin is the natural clothing of the body," was the almost
heretical assertion of Dr. Wynne, who added: "Under the influence of light and air the skin can recover the full power to
fulfil its many functions."

The recognition by the American medical profession of the
importance of sunlight to the general health and its possibilities
in building up resistance to disease is growing. Preventive
medicine in general and a conception of personal hygiene are
comparatively new things in our civilization. In reality, as
Dr. C. E. A. Winslow, of Yale, has pointed out, they are very
old, going back to the Greeks and falling into disrepute only
with the rise of Christianity. According to Dr. Winslow, "We
are not today preoccupied merely, or even primarily, with
keeping out dangerous germs. We are even more interested
in building up the resistance of the human body itself by
the development of habits of healthy living." This preoccupa-
tion with building up bodily resistance is still chiefly that of
public health officials rather than of practising physicians. The
prevailing specialization of medical practitioners, by tending

to limit their horizon to one or the other particular organ
or disease, militates against interest in the general health. Preventive medicine remains a sort of bastard child of medical
science, viewed by the practitioner with something of the disapproval and alarm with which legitimate monarchs used to
eye their illegitimate brothers.

Yet there are traces of a broader view of phototherapy in
the American medical profession, as witness this citation by
Blunt and Cowan from "the cautious *Journal of the American
Medical Association*": "After irradiation, general improvement of health has been observed in many cases. It may be
attended by increase in appetite, gain in weight, improved
sleep, or less well defined signs." Dr. Henry J. Gerstenberger,
who opposed the establishment of ultraviolet ray public
health clinics, believes nevertheless in the value of ultraviolet
light. He said in fact: "I come to this conclusion in the face
of my own conviction, based upon clinical experience, that
the exposure to ultraviolet rays, properly managed, is of value
not only to infants but to children and adults during the
winter months in those parts of the country where climatic
conditions make impossible an adequate exposure of the individual's skin to ultraviolet rays."

A remarkable plea for sunshine was presented in a paper
on "Environment, Health, and Disease" read by Professor A.
Bachem of the University of Illinois Medical School, at the
annual meeting of the American Physical Therapy Association
in 1930, and published in *Physical Therapeutics* for April
1931. His general thesis was that civilization, by creating an
unnatural environment, depriving us of light, air and exercise, and subjecting us to unholy din, is responsible for many if
not the majority of our diseases. He recommended a more exact
study of environment as a potential cause of disease and predicted that such a study "may even bring prophylaxis into a
more dominant place in the future than therapy occupies at
the present time." Dr. Bachem himself has performed

extensive research on the penetration and distribution of light in the skin, which he summarized before considering the physiological effects and chemical changes produced by irradiation. The action of light, he concluded, might be of great value in preventing disease, but he regretted that, "Although some of the facts are well established and are known to the medical profession and to the public, very little use is made of the value of light by the general public." He advised sunlight particularly for children; his own, a girl of five and a boy of one, play either nude on a secluded porch or in sun suits in the garden. When they go to Europe, "they play in the nude on the beach as all the other children do." In winter they play under a sun-arc lamp in the house. "I have noticed," he said, "that they are more active and content than while wearing heavy dresses, they look well tanned, never have had any sunburn, and never were sick for more than twenty-four hours."

The popularizers of irradiation, Luckiesh and Pacini, and Millar and Free, stress the harmfulness of the indoor life that has made us "sun-dodgers," but they do not agree on what is the ideal source for the essential light—a moot question with the medical profession as well as the public. So much emphasis has been placed on ultraviolet rays that many people assume them to be the only ones that matter, and jump to the conclusion that the more of them the better. The Council on Physical Therapy of the American Medical Association, however, sees grave danger in the sale of ultraviolet lamps to the public, and in 1927 resolved that the sale, or advertising for sale, directly to the public of ultraviolet generators was "detrimental to public welfare," and declared "inadmissible for inclusion in its list of accepted devices for physical therapy apparatus manufactured by a firm whose policy is in this matter detrimental to public welfare." Dr. Bachem also stated in his address before the Physical Therapy Association that "the prophylactic use of [carbon-arc or mercury-vapour] lamps in private homes should not be encouraged." He believed preferable the lamps that contain infrared, visible, and ultraviolet rays in something approximating their proportions in natural sunlight, and that have none of the extremely short ultraviolet rays absent from the solar spectrum.

Luckiesh and Pacini, who have been working on just such lamps for the General Electric Company, favour a lighting system that will contain a quantity of ultraviolet, but not enough for there to be any danger of over-exposure or injury to unprotected eyes. They consider such lighting to be a necessity in view of our indoor life, the dependence of ultraviolet radiation on variable seasons and weather, and in smoky cities the almost complete dearth of ultraviolet radiation even on clear days. Owing to their professional connections, their marked leaning toward artificial light is open to suspicion. They doubtless have sound scientific grounds for their conclusions, but the latter would be more convincing if reached by scientists independent of the product and profits of the General Electric Company.

Millar and Free incline toward natural sunlight. "The old Greeks and Romans had the ideal method of getting their ultraviolet energy," they assert. "Lying naked under the blue sky is still the simplest and most effective way to insure for ourselves all the benefits of sunlight. . . . While it is true that the ultraviolet rays are probably the most essential ones, the visible and infrared waves may play their parts in the total effect. . . . And of these different rays the mixture best suited to us is the one found in sunlight. No artificial lamp has yet been invented that quite matches that combination." They conclude: "For maximum value, a sunbath must be taken outdoors. In other words, we must take an *airbath* at the same time. Under proper conditions this easily doubles the worth of sunlight alone."

Although there is no such ardent American champion of the value of air on the body as Sir Leonard Hill in England, many of our scientists do realize the important part played by the free circulation of air in stimulating the vasomotor reflexes and improving metabolism and the muscular tone of the body. Benjamin Franklin's compatriots are beginning to justify scientifically his empiric faith in tonic airbaths, although the question of how much of the benefit is due to light and how much to air is not yet settled. Mayer notes that, "One of the gratifying effects of exposure to air and sun is the prevention of muscular atrophy. The physical development and relatively firm musculature of patients who have been in bed for years is surprising." This is indeed one of the most striking features observed in Rollier's patients—that wasted cripples, mere skin and bones, develop well-rounded and muscular contours while bedridden or even held inactive by apparatus. Mayer apparently considers light an important factor in this development, for he remarks that, "It is most marked in the pigmented patients."

The circulation of air on the body, however, is known to have a definite effect on the metabolism and heat regulation. Dr. C. E. A. Winslow, of the Yale School of Public Health, has given much attention to the question of air and ventilation. He states: "It will be obvious that the hygiene of ventilation and the hygiene of clothing are closely interrelated, since both are primarily concerned with the regulation of heat loss from the body. . . . As in the case of air conditions, the main essential in the selection of clothing is to guard against chill on the one hand, and to avoid on the other the debilitating effect of heat and uniformity—in other words to keep the blood-vessels of the skin stimulated by moderately cool and moving air." Dr. Edgar Mayer considers at length the role of clothing in disease, stating: "Civilized community life, forcing the adoption of protective covering of some form of clothing, has brought about a diminished activity of the skin, which may have an important bearing on the increase of infection." He also observes that, "The advantage gained by outdoor life from an increase of metabolism can be neutralized by over-clothing." So-called sunstroke, he explains, is usually heatstroke, the result of overheating the body when it is surrounded by stagnant, moist air which does not permit perspiration to evaporate. Even burning sun on the naked body is less apt to result in a stroke than when hot air is held stationary by clothes. "Strong sunbaths," he says, "do not raise the body temperature to any considerable extent in normal man, because in this instance other regulating mechanisms are brought into activity."

A physician, Dr. Walter B. James, was quoted in the *Saturday Evening Post* last fall as saying: "I think the development of women has come largely by discarding their clothing. A father will come to me with a cold and sore throat and pull off clothes like a human onion; they would fill a bushel basket. But his daughter's would go in a quart measure." Blunt and Cowan, commenting on the physical superiority of the contemporary college girl to the one of earlier generations, attribute it in part to her "looser, lighter, more sensible dress." They point out that in northern latitudes in the winter ordinary dress allows little light to penetrate the skin, and that finding enough antirachitic value in winter sunshine for rats "does not prove that human beings, with all their clothing and their short exposures to light, can get much help."

The unhygienic nature of our clothing was one of the chief evils attacked in Dr. Bachem's condemnation of civilized environment. He too spoke of the interference of dress with the evaporation of sweat and hence with the regulation of body temperatures, and observed that moreover it leads to excessive sweating, less acid than normal. A moist skin, lacking acidity and shut off from light, is more easily infected. "Under our garments," he stated, "we are practically always living in a tropical climate. In summer this becomes entirely unbearable and many heat prostrations and fatalities occur during heat waves." He believed that there were "two ways by which an improvement in our dress could be made; either it should be more porous and consist possibly of one layer, so as to permit evaporation and irradiation radically; or it should be worn very loosely with no obstruction at waist or neck, in order to allow tangential circulation from feet to head and permit evaporation. Men's dress as it is is the worst that ever could be designed."

This paper was discussed by a widely known physician, Dr. Curran Pope, of Louisville, Kentucky. If proof were needed that Dr. Bachem's ideas are radical, we have Dr. Pope's comment that the paper "has opened up to me a new world of thought and has certainly clarified matters regarding the very, very dense and unexplained things with which I come in daily contact." With the strictures on men's dress, Dr. Pope heartily agreed, declaring he often envied the modern woman whose clothing admits light and air and has wiped out "tuberculosis of the pelvic organs practically completely." He prophesied that if this continued, women would be the dominant sex.

Millar and Free are fully aware of the evils of dress, observing that the skin "seems to resent our strange treatment of it, which consists either of hiding it like something shameful or displaying it like a gaudy ornament, whereas it is in reality a hard-working, self-respecting area that deserves a free and dignified position in our life." They optimistically predict that, "Undoubtedly the time is coming when, for purely æsthetic reasons, men will rebel against the uniform that fashion compels them to wear . . . and they will start all over again where Adam left off." Eloquently they describe modern men as "more upholstered than chairs, harnessed like beasts of burden—all buckles and buttons, with necks confined by halters, legs encased in flapping cloth tubes."

It is a hopeful sign that the United States Bureau of Standards has become interested in the problem of the transmission of light through textiles and has tested a number of different fabrics for penetration by ultraviolet rays. But there is scant likelihood that the publication of the findings would affect in any way the selection of materials for men's clothing. The scientific foundations have indeed been laid for liberating humanity from its sartorial prison, but comparatively few prisoners are making strenuous efforts to get out, and fewer of their medical keepers—who have it in their power to help them to freedom—are actively assisting them in a jail delivery. "It is really surprising," was the sage comment of Dr. Bachem, "to see how much we know scientifically and how little we are doing practically to make use of it, in spite of suffering by our obstinacy." As another physician has remarked, "Therapeutically, as a curative and corrective measure, the medical profession has accepted, but has not generally utilized, the natural forces found in sunlight and atmosphere."

(2) Of Nudism

That the medical profession in America is not making full practical use of its knowledge is confirmed by the reaction of physicians to the direct question of nakedness. They do know scientifically the benefits of light and air to the body now "cabined, cribbed, confined"; some medical practitioners even appreciate the harmfulness of ordinary dress. But the physicians are not publicly acclaiming the nudist movement as an hygienic blessing. Most of them have ignored it, and those who have expressed approval—even where they have gone so far as to participate in nudist activities—have usually done so only to avowed nudists and under the seal of secrecy.

But the physician is not therefore to be unqualifiedly condemned; there are extenuating circumstances. He is dependent for his standing and his livelihood on the esteem of the community, and he must be as above suspicion as Cæsar's wife. A hint of immorality is more ruinous to physicians than to almost any other class of professional men with the exception possibly of teachers and clergymen; and nakedness is unfortunately associated with immorality in the public mind, if not in that of the physician himself. Poultney Bigelow was perhaps unduly hard on the medical profession when he said: "Doctors are the creatures of those who buy their drugs or follow their counsel. They dare not openly advocate any remedy until the wave of popularity floods it—and themselves—into public favour." Economic necessity has made the doctor "the creature" of the public. A Western physician, who declared that "from the health point of view, all physicians should encourage nudism," and that the mental effect of the practice "makes it of prime importance to mankind," confessed that he and many of his colleagues are timid about having their names used in connection with nudism, because "we are still forced to conform to public taste in order to make a living."

As to the charge of indifference if not actual opposition to nudism on the part of physicians, we have already indicated that the medical practitioner, as a result of specialization, is prone to be apathetic toward questions of general hygiene and disease prevention. Furthermore, conservatism is almost a *sine qua non* of medicine—and with some justification, since human lives are not proper material for rash experimentation. Moreover, the practice of nakedness for hygienic reasons is suspect on another account. Anything savouring of naturopathy is in bad odour with the orthodox members of the profession. Because charlatans, as well as sincere but ignorant cranks, have dangerously exploited natural methods of healing, the utilization of light and air as hygienic measures may, to the regular physician, smack of quackery. "As far as I know," wrote a New York doctor, "most medical men, if they have heard of the nudist movement, think of it as just one more health fad." Indeed, excessive claims for nakedness as a health panacea will very quickly place nudism among "the medical follies" that so arouse the editor of the *Journal of the American Medical Association*, Dr. Morris Fishbein.

In order to ascertain more accurately the attitude of American physicians when actually confronted with the question of nudism, we sent out a brief questionnaire to a number of medical men and one woman, mostly practitioners but including a few academic physiologists—a small list chosen more or less at random, some because their reputations would give their opinions particular weight, some because they had done work in heliotherapy that would especially qualify them to speak on the subject, and others merely because we happened to have personal contacts with them. As the list was small at the outset, and was further reduced by the fact that a number did not reply, the results prove little. But they are probably representative. At least the men who expressed opinions vary widely in interests, celebrity, and geographical distribution, and include not only metropolitan physicians and academic men, but doctors in small towns. The questions we asked them were as follows:

A) Do you believe sunlight is hygienically (as well as therapeutically) desirable for the human body?

B) Do you believe the free circulation of air on the body is beneficial?

C) Do you believe there are health benefits to be derived from total exposure of the body to these elements?

D) Do you see any advantages, moral or psychological (educational, æsthetic or other), to the practice of total nudity (for sunbaths, outdoor exercises, games, etc.) by both sexes in common, as demanded by nudist theory? If so, what? Any objections (aside from legal ones and public disapproval)?

We also asked them whether they had any objections to being quoted on the subject, and rather surprisingly eighteen out of the twenty-four who filled out the questionnaire (or 75 per cent) were unafraid to have their names used. However, those willing to be quoted included a number of eminent men whose reputations are too well established to be affected by damaging admissions, and seven of the eighteen were distinctly unfavourable to mixed nudity—an attitude unlikely to injure their professional standing. On the other hand, perhaps too much significance should not be attached to the unfavourableness of their views in connection with their willingness to be quoted, since one of those who did not wish his name mentioned was unfavourable to nudism, and another of them answered question D) only with interrogation points—scarcely compromising. A large number of those who answered the questionnaire developed their views in extended supplementary statements, giving us the benefit not only of their conclusions but of the reasons on which they were based.

Five of those who did not fill out the questionnaire wrote to explain why they did not do so. These explanations in themselves are illuminating. Dr. G. W. Crile, of Cleveland, said that, not having given the matter any consideration, he did not believe anything he might say would be of value. A physician on the faculty of a medical school also claimed to have "no well considered opinions on the subject," although he added that "for reasons which are more or less vague in my mind, I am not in favour of nudism." Dr. Morris Fishbein declined on the plea that he simply did not have time to answer all the questionnaires sent him. Dr. Edgar Mayer referred us to his book for his views. This work, from which we have drawn heavily, gives a clear indication of its author's opinions of the specific values of sun and air and of the deleterious effects of clothing. Nevertheless, we should have liked his ideas on the mental and moral aspects of mixed nakedness—a question naturally untouched in the *Clinical Application of Sunlight and Artificial Radiation.*

The most remarkable refusal was that of Dr. William J. Robinson, of the *Critic and Guide,* who wrote: "As you know, I am sympathetic to the nudist movement, but I do not consider it at the present time of paramount importance. There are more important questions confronting humanity today. The nudist movement will not help the question of unemployment, of graft, of gangsterism, nor will it tell us if the salvation of the world is to be looked for in the U.S.S.R. or in Western Capitalism." True enough! It is also true that a cure for cancer would do nothing to solve these undoubtedly vital problems, but would Dr. Robinson oppose all attention to finding such a cure on the ground that these other questions are more pressing? Man's economic ills are perhaps more grievous today than his physical or mental afflictions; yet is seems unnecessary to neglect either for the sake of remedying the other.

When we sent out the questionnaire, a Middle Western physician forecast the results thus: "As a whole the profession will answer 'yes' on questions A), B), and C) [regarding the health aspects] and be non-committal on D), partly because of a lack of first hand information and experience and partly because the obstacles seem insurmountable. There are some to whom the terms 'nudist' and 'cult' are objectionable, carrying the opprobrium of eccentricity. Physicians as a class may be fairly progressive in thought but conservative in action. They will consequently agree to the hygienic benefits of nudism but shy at any departure from the conventional."

The first part of this prophecy was borne out. None answered the first two questions—relating to sunlight and air—in the negative, but six believed total exposure of the body to be unnecessary for health. (Two of these nevertheless saw possible psychological benefits in nudism; one was doubtful, perceiving both advantages and disadvantages; and the other three opposed nudism.) On D)—nakedness in common—they were less non-committal than was expected, the only really evasive reply being that of the New York physician who answered with a question mark. A few of the others hesitated to make categorical pronouncements, on the ground that they had not given the subject sufficient thought, or that they lacked personal experience; but they indicated at any rate whether or not they were inclined to favour or oppose the idea. Fewer than one might suppose "shied at any departure from the conventional," only eight registering definite disapproval against one who eluded the question, one who was undecided, and fourteen who favoured nudism or gave it the benefit of the doubt.

The question of whether sunlight is beneficial was usually answered by a simple affirmative, although some made qualifications. Three warned against over-exposure. Dr. Ira S. Wile, the well-known pediatrist, answered: "Yes, with necessary variations to meet individual needs in terms of health, comfort, and safety." In a supplementary statement he remarked: "The fact that some sun-bathing may be advantageous does not mean that sun-bathing may not be dangerous for some people." Dr. N. Worth Brown, of the Toledo Clinic, was quite specific, stating that there is "adequate scientific basis for the use of sunlight in the prevention of tuberculosis, respiratory infections of all kinds, and the endocrine disturbances to which we in America are particularly liable." Dr. Walter J. Meek, head of the Department of Physiology and Assistant Dean of the University of Wisconsin Medical School, brought up the question of rays other than ultraviolet: "As you know, the evidence for the beneficial effects of the ultraviolet rays of the spectrum is quite convincing. Recently an international authority told me that he thought there was good reason for believing that the red and infrared rays were also of importance physiologically. If so, your arguments for exposure may be doubled, since the winter sun still has its red rays."

Most of the answers regarding the value of air were also unqualified. However, Dr. Joseph E. Raycroft, Director of Physical Education and Professor of Hygiene at Princeton University, modified his statement thus: "I think that free circulation of air on the body is beneficial if the air temperature is not so low as to involve an excessive loss of heat from the body by radiation." Dr. Ira S. Wile answered: "Yes, with proper reservations for temperature, humidity, and the recognition that free circulation may be secured without nudism." A few others were specific as to the benefits of air. Dr. Robert

What the Physicians Think

L. Dickinson, of the New York Academy of Medicine, and one of the most eminent gynecologists in the country, answered: "Yes, in whatever climates and seasons that this is possible. At present male costume covers or confines in the maximal fashion those very areas with the most sweat glands and capacities for evil odours." Dr. Brown said: "I believe also that the exposure of the body to air in motion has a definite tonic value, perhaps almost as much as sunlight itself." Dr. Meek was more specific and technical: "The stimulating effect of fresh circulating air may be strongly emphasized. It reflexly keeps the skeletal muscles in better tonus and the vasomotors in good condition. It is a marked and desirable stimulus to the nervous, muscular, and circulatory systems."

To the question of whether there are health advantages in total exposure of the body, two—Dr. Richard L. Sutton, a dermatologist, and Dr. Ralph Major, both of Kansas City— merely answered in the negative. Dr. Harvey J. Kellogg, of Battle Creek, said: "Yes, with the understanding that the small covering required by modesty is not omitted." (Does he mean to imply that the omission of this covering endangers the health?) Dr. Wile answered: "Yes, again with numerous reservations including the belief that there are no greater health benefits to be derived from exposure of the genitals." In his supplementary statement he said further: "There is necessity, however, for recognizing distinctions between exposure of the larger surface of the body and complete exposure of the body. To make a plea, for example, for a larger ventilation of the skin because of the healthful values of radiant energy and solar rays is not tantamount to calling for complete exposure of genital organs. To use exercises, games, and sunbaths when completely unclothed except for loin cloths cannot be differentiated in any way, from the health standpoint, from similar practices with the clothing removed. If one considers the physical side alone, there is no great necessity for complete nudism." Dr. Stanley D. Giffin, of Toledo, Ohio, believed:

"For physical health *total* nudity is certainly not necessary."
Dr. Meek elaborated the same idea: "Although an excellent
and interesting case for the valuable effects of air and sun on
the body can be made, it does not follow that total exposure is
necessary. The scanty covering which now suffices to placate
Mrs. Grundy, in all probability, still allows a sufficiency of sun
and air. . . . I do not believe that to secure full benefit of air
and sunshine, it is necessary to remove the last vestiges of clothing. The savage with his breech clout certainly gets all the air
circulation and sunshine he needs for physiological and therapeutic purposes."

The others—including Dr. Alfred F. Hess, whose work we
have mentioned as one of the greatest American contributions
to the study of ultraviolet rays in rickets, Dr. Joseph F. Collins,
author of *The Doctor Looks at . . .* series, and Dr. Robert
Briffault, the famous anthropologist as well as a physician—answered in the affirmative without giving an opinion as to
whether or not exposure of every inch of skin was essential.
A few, however, developed the question at some length. Dr.
Dickinson replied: "Yes, the example of our women's clothes
as compared with those of men is enough argument for further
progress in health along this line." A Middle Western physician who does not wish his name mentioned wrote: "I have
become very enthusiastic over exposure of the body, having
practised such exposure for several years." And a California
practitioner, also desiring anonymity, stated: "The value of
sunlight and air to the skin as an hygienic and therapeutic
agent is conceded by all medical men." Dr. N. Worth Brown
listed the benefits thus: "1. As a prophylactic, by increasing resistance to infections, particularly those of the upper respiratory tract. 2. Therapeutically in certain chronic infections, in
some disorders of the circulation, and in many functional de-
rangements. 3. In the establishment and maintenance of a
normal endocrine balance."

Dr. L. Mason Lyons, of Kansas City, answered as follows:

What the Physicians Think

"Exercises in the nude have many hundredfold the advantages of exercises in light clothing, as the latter have over exercises fully clad. . . . Most of us who have become civilized have also become 'softies.' Our endurance and our resistance are both low. The practice of nudism will undoubtedly increase our stamina and, more important, our resistance. Acclimating the body to free exposure should do away with a thousand and one minor illnesses that we Americans have fallen prey to, among them all the upper respiratory infections, the sinus troubles, the common colds, etc. It is impossible for me to conceive of people who indulge in nudism from childhood contracting pulmonary tuberculosis. Similarly, I believe that such things as infantile paralysis, meningitis, diphtheria, and pneumonia can be largely eliminated by increasing the vigour of the body to the point where a casual exposure to an infection would find the person entirely immune." Dr. J. H. Toomey, of New York, after warning against over-exposure or exposure where an abnormal condition is a contra-indication, said: "I don't think that the benefits to be derived from such exposure can be attributed to any one element, such as light, but that the combined effect of all the elements, as they occur in nature, is responsible. I would especially emphasize the value of the variety of influences exerted by these elements as compared to the uniformity of effect that our bodies, sheltered by clothing and housing, have been accustomed to endure. It is really remarkable how much the body has been able to tolerate of the harness that civilization has imposed upon it."

The reply of Dr. F. M. Pottenger, of Monrovia, California, merits quotation *in toto* as his experience with heliotherapy in the Pottenger Sanitorium for diseases of the chest gives it particular weight. He wrote: "I will say that if health and strength alone were to be considered, there is no doubt but that the practice of nudity would be beneficial. I advise my patients who are suffering from tuberculosis to use as little covering as possible, and for a portion of each day, while lying in their beds, to throw off the covers and lie in the nude. The effect of this is to improve the general tone of the body. It is quite a stimulant to metabolism; it improves the condition of the skin, and through the cutaneous sensory nerves doubtless influences the physiologic activities of the body. It is impossible for anyone to say just what value comes from this practice, but I base my use of it on the general principle that anything that will improve the general tone of the individual will aid in making him stronger, and consequently improve his powers of resisting his disease. As patients get better, and the disease becomes inactive, I use sunbaths, the patient being placed in the sun, wearing only a pair of shorts. I have had some of my male patients take their walks up in the mountains back of the sanatorium with their bodies bare to the waist. I think this method is preferable to taking sun treatments while lying down. The exercise itself has a tendency to aid the elimination from the body." (Dr. Pottenger's observation on the value of combining exercise with sun-bathing is particularly interesting from the nudist viewpoint.)

Thus far the questions considered are obviously those on which medical men and physiologists can speak with the most authority; they are the ones to decide whether nudity is of any avail physiologically. Judging from their statements, the American physician does see therapeutic and prophylactic benefits in exposing the body to light and air. But as one can take advantage of these elements either alone or with the sexes segregated, establishing the healthfulness of nudity does not automatically establish the validity of nudism. The crux of the matter is the psychological effect, and the touchstone of nudist approval by the medical men is their response to question D)—on which they must speak as amateurs. Psychiatrists of course can give an opinion as professionals. For this reason, we are considering the psychiatrists separately, in Chapter X, and have limited our present list to practitioners dealing with physical, rather than mental ailments. Hence the opinions of

What the Physicians Think

D. Ira S. Wile on the mental aspects of nudity will be found in Chapter X, since he, though primarily a pediatrist whose general medical background entitles him to speak as an expert on the physiological question, is also a psychiatrist interested in mental hygiene, and it is presumably as a psychiatrist that he has answered the questions regarding the mental effects.

It is neither astonishing nor inconsistent that some of the physicians who strongly endorsed nakedness as an hygienic measure objected to mixed nakedness quite as strongly, or that those who favoured nudism did so primarily on psychological grounds. In view of their professional conservatism and the fact that they are necessarily subject to the same traditional morality and conventions as the public at large, the surprising thing is to find so many taking the unconventional stand. Only eight, as we have said, decisively condemned mixed nudity. Some of the others, it is true, perceived objections, or were not willing to commit themselves too forcibly, but they were on the whole inclined to believe that advantages might outweigh possible drawbacks.

It was characteristic of those opposed to nakedness in common to make no definite explanation of their objections; they stated categorically that they disapproved and let it go at that. They may have assumed the objections were obvious to all right-minded people. Dr. Hess, for instance, when asked whether he saw any advantages in mixed nudity, simply replied "no." Dr. Pottenger stated only: "The practice of nudity by both sexes, in common, I believe would be very unfortunate." The retort of Dr. Richard L. Sutton, the Kansas City dermatologist, was the most crushing. After asserting he saw no advantages, he wrote under the question of objections: "Yes, I consider it asinine." This admits of no argument! His fellow townsman, Dr. Ralph Major, was almost as final but slightly less cryptic, perceiving no advantages but "on the contrary, disadvantages," because "any fad brings definite disadvantages as a sequence."

[181]

Nudism Comes to America

Dr. Joseph F. Collins looked at nudism and saw no benefits. The only objection he mentioned was æsthetic, but he implied there were others, his words being, "One of my objections is that the human body, especially the female human body, is so damned ugly, and only one man in twenty after fifty is fit to be looked at." One physician who saw a preponderance of disadvantages, and who preferred to remain anonymous, said: "I personally have never been in a nudist camp or compound and freely admit I am unqualified to answer your question directly. However, I do not think the mass of people are educated sufficiently to tolerate the freedom demanded by your premise." He also believed that people with physical defects would not wish to participate in nudist activities. Dr. John Harvey Kellogg's objection was strictly moral: "Modesty and a decent sense of propriety demand concealment of certain portions of the body." Dr. Joseph E. Raycroft, of Princeton, likewise saw no advantages and his objections were specific: "1. Physical: the ordinary adolescent or adult male requires protection and support of genitals during vigorous games and contests entirely apart from the clothing function of such supports. 2. Emotional: sudden and profound changes in age-old customs or 'mores' that are practically universal in one form or another among all grades of civilization are likely to be accompanied by undesirable defence reactions that border on exhibitionism, which in its marked form is a pathological state. The emotional disturbance suffered by a savage who has lost his 'gee-string,' which is clothing reduced to a symbol, is an illustration of the kind of thing I have in mind."

Perhaps because their sports are usually co-educational and not the most strenuous forms of athletic competition, such as intercollegiate sports or the Olympic games, nudists do not feel the need of the support Dr. Raycroft mentions, and we know of none who has suffered from the lack of it. As for his second point, the break with age-old custom is so much easier than the non-nudist imagines, and the clothesless state seems so natural to anyone who has tried it, that the alleged emotional disturbance simply does not exist. The savage's distress over his lost gee-string is not comparable to the feeling of the civilized man who has deliberately abandoned his clothes, for the latter is capable of regarding his clothes rationally while the savage cannot contemplate his garment objectively in the light of reason. The savage's attitude toward a custom is tangled with superstition; to violate a taboo is either to incur the wrath of supernatural powers or to lay himself open to the magic of an enemy. For the civilized man to suffer anything like the same emotional upset, it would be necessary for nudism to be forced on him when he is not mentally prepared for it, and compulsion is certainly no part of the nudist program.

Almost as many and some of the identical objections were raised by those favouring nudism; these men, however, considered them minor and not insoluble problems. Dr. N. Worth Brown made one of the same points as the anonymous physician cited: "Because of physical imperfections or peculiarities many individuals will remain disinterested and still further reduce the number who might be physically benefited by nudism." The other two obstacles he perceived were: "1. The apparent necessity for secrecy by individuals and groups engaging in nudist practices. The thought of locked doors, high walls, private parks, etc. is distasteful. 2. The habits of conventional behaviour will limit the practice of nudism to a relatively small number of people." The first of these points is indeed a serious handicap; the only remedy is to eliminate the necessity by education. Dr. Brown inclined to the opinion that at this stage it might be well to encourage a modified form of nudism (with a minimum of clothing, but less than is commonly worn for sports and outdoor occupations), leaving pure nudism for the "more philosophical."

Dr. Toomey also believed nudism must be selective. The objections, he said, arose from "human imperfections" and not from "anything inherently wrong in the practice." "The state of nudity," he continued, "is possibly an ideal condition of existence for which the average individual of our civilization is unadapted. . . . And human nature in the nude is often enough perverse and offensive, and entirely out of harmony with the constructive aims of the practice of nudity. But while the practice of nudity may be regarded as objectionable because it reveals too realistically the defects of the human body and human nature, it should not be forgotten that the artificial life of modern civilization is largely the cause of these defects."

Dr. W. S. McCann, of the University of Rochester Medical School, suggested that the "menstrual period in women might introduce difficulties, chiefly æsthetic." This difficulty of course is solved by partial clothing, such as "shorts." Dr. L. Mason Lyons brought up the question of the "oversexed," whom he defined as "those for whom delectable female nudity will always evoke a physiological response," and yet who might be attracted to a nudist group for wholly proper reasons. Dr. Lyons remarked: "One doesn't have to join a nudist group for sex adventure. My impression is that such a group is the *wrong* place to go." But Dr. Lyons was not sure that "rigid mental self-control" would entirely solve the difficulty, although he believed "that *eventually* familiarity would make for a decrease in the urge." Perhaps the "oversexed" have never gained admission to a nudist group—though that seems improbable— but we have never known of anyone unable to control his sexual impulses, nor indeed anyone who had to exert "rigid" mental discipline to do so. We have known any number of virile men who in advance feared such a struggle, if not defeat, but they were always surprised at the actuality.

A New York physician, who for obvious reasons does not wish his name to be used, but who was attracted to nudism by "a loathing of humbug," believed "nudism will lead, quite naturally, to free love." Not, however, that this "jolly sex-expression in an ideal setting" was to his mind an objection;

[184]

what he objected to was the "affectation of innocence" to which he is "not enough of a cold-blooded reptile" to subscribe. Alas for him, we must state that nudism does not lead to free love in the sense of promiscuity, nor does it intensify sex urges. On the other hand, as we have reiterated, neither does it obliterate sex interest or capacity. Nudists too are anything but cold-blooded reptiles, and we doubt they affect to be.

Among those willing to concede possible advantages in mixed nakedness as practised by the nudists, only a couple were as indefinite as the objectors tended to be. One, a Middle Western physician, also anonymous, said: "I really have not given much thought to this phase of the subject and would hardly be able to give an opinion in this regard. Just off-hand I really do not see any real reason why there may not be some advantages. I can see no real objections." Somewhat the same attitude was expressed by Dr. Stanley D. Giffin, of Toledo: "After all, is it not an individual question, and when one is shading sixty years, should he seek to influence custom for those sixteen years and beyond? For physical health, *total* nudity is certainly not necessary, but as for moral or psychological advantages—I don't know! Possibly if approached gradually it might work."

Four of the physicians believed nudism might be profitable in stimulating people to overcome physical defects. Dr. Robert L. Dickinson expressed this idea most forcibly: "As a near-artist, I can conceive of nothing that would make for avoidance of pot-bellies and other acquired deformities as nudity would. As a physician, I can conceive of nothing that would so improve posture." Dr. L. Mason Lyons too was specific: "Exposure of the body to public view must create a pride in the perfect body and a shame for the imperfect one, therefore a person who has carelessly allowed himself to become overweight would use every means to take off the excess poundage. Similarly a painfully thin person would endeavour to *add* weight. A person with skin blemishes would find some means

[185]

to eradicate them. Necessarily nudism would call for more frequent bathing which, by the way, is a crying need." The other two who believed it would make for physical improvement were Dr. William S. McCann, of the University of Rochester, and Dr. N. Worth Brown.

The contribution of nudist practices to the sex education of the young was mentioned several times. Dr. McCann said: "If one were accustomed to it from childhood, there would be no morbid curiosity and less lewd thinking and looking." It should, thought Dr. Brown, "lead to a clearer understanding during childhood of the physical characteristics of men and women, and simplify the problem of sex education." Dr. Lyons, after expressing his doubts concerning the "oversexed," added: "But for those youngsters educated in nudism, the matter [sex] becomes a simple one. Sex loses its mystery, the human body its false allure, and a return to a healthy mixed companionship would be possible." A New York physician who does not desire to be identified, "Would stress the psychological advantages of nudism in the growing child in an endeavour to make the sex problem a less difficult one for a normal mental hygiene." Dr. Toomey likewise thought "the experience should under proper conditions exert a corrective effect upon the modern child."

The whole matter of a less prudish and prurient attitude toward sex, for adults as well as children—the question of mental health—was the one to which it was generally felt nudism could make the greatest contribution. Dr. Dickinson's remarks, in view of their pertinence as well as the writer's eminence, are unusually interesting. They were: "The practice, if gradually developed, would be certainly as free from excitation of sex responses as the present silk stocking is to most people, or the exposed body is to artists and doctors. It would do away with the mystery about anatomy that is, because of the covering, sexually exciting. Anyone who has visited the tropics knows that where nakedness is a matter of course it loses all sensual connotations. The exposures of sex organs are practically only these: 1. nipples, 2. female pubic hair, 3. male genitals. Habituation removes from sight of these all sexual excitation. . . . As a specialist on diseases of women, in practice nearly half a century, one is conversant with the skirt to the heel, Jaeger wool underclothes from neck to foot in winter, the bathing suit with arms, the assertion that 'no nice woman has any anatomy between her neck and her ankles,' vs. the one-piece bathing suit that is not suggestive to youth but only to grey hairs, the present unconsciousness with free exposure, [and] the inevitableness of frank and complete nakedness wherever it is suitable."

Dr. Walter J. Meek, of the University of Wisconsin, stated that "the question of removing the last rag must be settled on other grounds, i.e., psychologically, morally, or æsthetically." He said further: "In this field I am entirely out of my line, although I have a few thoughts on the matter. Certainly self-consciousness of person, which is usually sexual in the final analysis, militates against natural, straightforward behaviour toward our fellows. The American aversion to mentioning or discussing the simplest facts of waste metabolism or reproduction is harmful. . . . Its very artificiality increases the possibilities of erotic stimulation. A sense of shame over natural functions can hardly be a good thing. The very function itself may become distorted or perverted. Whether the practice of nudism might help combat this situation is to me the most interesting question involved." In conformity with these premises, he suggested as possible advantages to be derived from nudism: "It may reduce our prudishness. It may reduce the erotic stimuli which ordinarily come from even slight variations in our clothing. It might therefore make for self-control and less self-consciousness." Dr. N. Worth Brown similarly prefaced his statements with the remark that his experience was too limited for anything but theoretical deductions. Regarding sexual relations, he thought nudism might possibly: "1. Develop a keener sense of moral responsibility and establish mutual confidence between the sexes. 2. Promote a more natural and sincere companionship between men and women. 3. Eliminate the accentuation of sexual characteristics by artificial means and inhibit sensuous impulses associated with physical concealment."

Robert Briffault's statements on this question will be discussed with those of other social scientists in Chapter XI, since Dr. Briffault is celebrated primarily as an anthropologist. Dr. Milton H. Erickson, of the Worcester State Hospital, suggested that "commonsense attitude on moral questions [is] a greater possibility [than physical benefits]." Dr. L. Mason Lyons said that "the two outstanding benefits to be derived from the mental aspects of nudism [are]: First, the peace of mind that it should bring; and second, the discarding of the false sex ideas." Dr. Edmund Lissack, of Concordia, Missouri, answered the question thus: "Yes—great advantages. In the practice of nudity in common, sex plays no role. Nakedness is not shameful or erotically stimulating." Dr. Toomey believed nudism should "have a wholesome effect upon the instincts . . . provided the members of a practising group are selected in accordance with some standard of qualification." Our anonymous California physician had much to say on the subject, but space permits us to quote only representative selections. He pointed out: "Where nudity is practised in a solitary way or limited to one's family, there is a great benefit from the air, sunlight, and the sense of physical freedom—freedom from the restraint of clothes—but this falls short of the benefit to be derived when this same nudity is practised freely in the presence of others. . . . No doubt the greatest psychic effect is obtained as a result of freeing the mind from restraints of years of prudish accumulations. . . . Nudity will dissipate morbid curiosity, erotic irritability. . . . Civilization may be charged with many offences, but perhaps the greatest offence against health has been due to the induction of the sense of sin in the exposure of the human body." He referred to the fact that many cases of sexual deflection are accompanied by extreme prudishness in regard to bodily exposure, and suggested that there is "a distinct relationship between the sexual deflection" and the attitude toward nakedness.

Two physicians, Dr. Lyons and Dr. Toomey, perceived a possible eugenic effect—young people practising nudism might be more selective in mating and tend to set a high physical standard for their mates. Dr. Lyons was the most versatile of all in descrying possible advantages in nudism. He saw a likelihood of its eliminating venereal disease: "One so afflicted would not be a nudist and nudists would be unlikely to expose the bodies of which they are so proud to the possibility of the ravages of such an illness." Class consciousness, he felt, would be abolished with the class distinctions in dress. Moreover, mental peace would result because: "When one drops his clothing, one would properly drop all petty harrassments, the little unessential worries which we have delighted to inflict ourselves with."

Assuming the attitudes of the physicians we have quoted to have some significance, we perceive that while the American medical profession is not yet battling for nudism in the market-place, it does not present a united wall of opposition. Some of its members at least actually detect possible benefits in the movement. Dr. Dickinson, in replying to the questionnaire, stated that he did so willingly because of "the physical-moral importance of the issue." Would it be rash to predict that as knowledge of nudism grows the realization of its "physical-moral importance" might increase among the men of medical science?

unnnu

IX

WHAT THE PSYCHOLOGISTS
THINK

IF THE QUESTION OF NUDISM WAS TO BE SETTLED LARGELY on psychological grounds, it seemed only reasonable to put it up to the professional psychologists. Yet it is an error to assume that because the contemporary American physician is qualified to give expert testimony on the physiological effects of nakedness, the American psychologist is equally qualified to pass on its psychological effects. We state this without any reflection on the psychologist, because the physician—owing to recent scientific discoveries—has had an opportunity to study and observe the action of light and air on the body, whereas the psychologist with few exceptions has had no chance to observe the effect of mixed nudity on the mind. He is reduced therefore to theorizing, and since psychology has been divorced from philosophy and become an experimental science, hypothetical reasoning is an inadequate basis for psychological deductions. The psychologist himself is the first to admit that his opinion of nudism is an opinion and not a scientific conclusion. A large number of the academic psychologists whom we approached declined to express their views for this very reason, and some of those who ventured an opinion pointed out that it was simply a guess that should carry no special weight.

Our psychological questionnaire was sent to a list of nearly

ninety of the leading academic psychologists—an objectively
selected group of members of the American Psychological Association, many of them officers or former officers. Half of these
replied, though sixteen only to explain why they were unwilling to express an opinion. The reasons they gave for declining were, like those of the physicians, revealing. Twelve
of them plead want of knowledge, claiming they were "not
sufficiently informed" or "too ignorant." A number felt that
the only valid opinion would be one based on observation of a
practising group over a considerable period of time. And one
prominent Easterner asked: "Why not consult those who *know*
about the movement? The mere fact that a man is a psychologist gives him no right to an opinion." A similar consciousness of inadequate grounds for an opinion was found
among those who filled out the questionnaire; they repeatedly
warned us that their views were purely theoretical. Still another evidence of hesitancy to make *ex cathedra* pronouncements is that the stand of four out of the twenty-seven replies was undecided, the writers perceiving both advantages
and disadvantages and declining to hazard even a guess as
to whether the ultimate result would be fortunate or unfortunate. Several others saw good and bad possibilities in almost
equal proportions, though they did venture at least a tentative
decision in favour of one or the other. The psychologists undoubtedly have the ability to see both sides of a question! It
will be remembered that while a few of the physicians hesitated
to make their statements too positive, only two were seriously
in doubt as to whether they favoured or opposed nudism.

Greater caution was also displayed by the psychologists in
the matter of the use of their names. Only fifteen of those
expressing opinions (or 55%, as compared with 75% of the
physicians) were willing to be quoted. The explanation might
be found in their academic connections, practically all of them
being college professors. For, despite the efforts of the American Association of University Professors, academic freedom

of speech is decidedly limited. Apparently, however, it was in this case less a fear of being known to favour nudism than of being identified with the subject in any manner, since of the twelve who preferred to remain anonymous, five opposed nudism, three were undecided, and only four were favourable. Most of those with objections to being quoted gave explanations which indicated that the fear of an improper use of the quotation was greater than the fear of nudism itself. This observation is borne out by the fact that half of those who granted permission to use their names did so only provided we quote them *in full* and without alteration. None of the physicians made such a stipulation.

The questionnaire sent to the psychologists was even briefer than that submitted to the medical men, the specific questions as to the effects of light and air on the body being deemed unnecessary. The psychologists were asked only two questions:

A) Do you believe the practice of nudity to be beneficial to civilized man for reasons of health, æsthetic enjoyment, saner moral outlook, or other grounds?

B) Do you see any special advantages (moral, educational, or other) to the practice of nudity by both sexes in common, as demanded by nudist theory? Any objections (aside from legal ones and the disapproval of public opinion)?

Few answered "yes" or "no." Many in fact chose to make an extended comment instead of filling out the questionnaire. Where the questions were filled out, the answers to A) frequently applied equally to B), or vice versa. The majority of the replies cannot be quoted piecemeal, either because the writers have asked to be quoted only in full, or because the form of the statements does not lend itself to "lifting" bits from their context. A few generalizations can be made, but they cannot always be substantiated with specific quotations without citing at the same time material irrelevant to the point at issue. In general, it can be said that while the numbers of approving and disapproving replies were almost equal, there was a slight balance in favour of an open-minded and tolerant attitude. Eleven of the replies were definitely opposed to nudism, while twelve were favourable, and four open-minded to the point of indecision. Of those whose attitude is classified as unfavourable, five saw no advantages whatever; the other six perceived a few but felt the disadvantages were more serious. Only four of the twelve who were favourable were unaware of possible objections, and one of them hastened to add that he did "not want to pose as an expert," while another said he would "have to observe the effects to say [whether there were any objections]." The others mentioned possible ill effects or unpleasant concomitants of the practice but conceded that these were either negligible or avoidable.

Owing to the need of considering so many statements in their entirety, the only feasible course seems to be to discuss separately each group of replies divided on the basis of whether they are favourable, unfavourable, or non-committal in tone, rather than to take each topic raised—for instance, æsthetics, health, or morality—and discuss all the views on the subject, pro and con, at one time. Frequently the advantages and objections are so neatly balanced and interwoven that any one taken out and considered separately would give a distorted impression of the real intent.

The group of four who avoided committing themselves was composed of three who preferred to remain anonymous (one in the Middle West, one in the Far West, and one in Canada) and Professor R. S. Woodworth of Columbia University. Two of them specifically mentioned the matter of health, the Middle Westerner seeing a possible gain from nudism, and the Far Westerner believing that "the problem of physical health should be given over to the medico." The same two also mentioned æsthetic objections. But the question which all four deemed the most important and developed at greatest length was that of attitudes toward sex. "In purely speculative flights

of imagination," said the Middle Westerner, "I can see possible
advantages in the practice, such as gain in physical health and
freedom from the (hypothetically) harmful effects of repressed curiosity in children; and also possible disadvantages,
such as the opportunity for display afforded to so-called exhibitionists, and also to the much larger class of persons whose
bodies are such that their public display could be nothing but
æsthetically offensive, at least to the eyes of persons brought
up with conventional attitudes toward necessity of dress. . . .
In common with everyone who does not believe this is already
the best possible of worlds, I am glad that experiments in the
practice of nudism are being tried out where they have a chance
of proving themselves successful in the eyes of persons who are
aware of the powerful impact on social life of all attitudes
toward sex problems."

As we have already discussed these points in so many different connections, the only comment that seems called for
now is on the matter of exhibitionism. The practice of the
nudists it seems to us should be, if anything, a damper to exhibitionistic tendencies. The peculiar sexual excitement which
those afflicted with this perversion obtain from displaying
themselves must come in large part from such exposure being
an extraordinary act with a strong emotional effect on the
spectators—who are disturbed, disgusted, or frightened. Surely
the exhibitionist derives no satisfaction when he is unobserved,
as would be precisely the case among nudists to whom all parts
of the body are a commonplace sight. He could neither attract
attention to himself nor upset the beholder by mere nakedness when everybody else was naked.

The Canadian's views were expressed as follows: A) "I feel
that the ideal society would be one in which nudity or non-
nudity would be a matter of indifference. Whether this ideal
can be attained I don't know. The Greeks did it." B) "As society is at present constituted, no, except possibly in intimate
family groups. Until society is educated by other means, I feel

there is grave danger of defeating the ends of sanity in sex matters. I feel rather strongly that until we have a more rational sex education the abuses of nudity are likely to outweigh the good and put back the clock. Those who would be rational about it don't need it; those who need it would abuse it. We should begin by educating the latter, and when this is done the specific practice of nudity won't be necessary."

With this attitude we have considerable sympathy. Tolerance for nudity, rather than compulsory nakedness, is the ideal, and we differ from the psychologist just cited chiefly in believing that this is feasible even in our present society and that the danger of abuse is negligible. In contrast to his views on the sex question, the psychologist from the Far West said: "From what little anthropological reading I have done, I would judge that the degree of nudity has little relation to the aggressiveness of the sex drive or to the degree of freedom in the relation between the sexes. Such matters, the latter especially, seem to be more dependent on the advent of certain peculiar people—witch doctors, priests, and reformers—and on the mores which they help to establish."

This statement is of particular value in connection with the question of sex interest raised by Professor Woodworth, of Columbia, whose complete reply was as follows: "I have no definite opinion as to the value of complete nudity. Such stripping off of clothes as has gone on in the course of the past forty years, especially in bathing, seems to me to have been beneficial. I don't see anything shocking in complete nudity groups as you found them in Germany. I have heard from other visitors as well that the whole situation seems rather matter-of-course after a brief period of adaptation. I have always noticed that as fast as a portion of the body was freely exposed it lost its sexual interest to quite an extent. So I have no doubt that the same would hold good for the whole body.

"The main question raised in my mind was whether the sex interest wasn't being cheated by nudism. I should hate to lose sexual interest in the female body. Then, I couldn't quite see how sex interest could have any freedom in a nudist environment, especially because the male would so patently betray such interest. Certainly a certain amount of covering is a great convenience to a male if he is at all excited by a woman in public or in a social group. I imagine the nudist groups have, by tacit consent, to banish sex interest from their group activities. Perhaps they even have to put on clothes in order to make love."

The anonymous Westerner's anthropological conclusion regarding the sex drive is the correct answer to Professor Woodworth's doubt about sex interest. Nudists have even fallen in love when they met on the nudist field—sufficiently in fact to get married. Physical expression, but not interest, is out of place in their group activities, for nudists—like most people, dressed or undressed—prefer privacy when it comes actually to making love. Flirtation may be a group activity, but lovemaking is not, even in a clothed society.

The second group of eleven, or those definitely opposed to nudism, was in no such quandary. Two or three faltered between various advantages and drawbacks but in the end turned thumbs down, and at least half of them never had a moment's doubt that an unfavourable verdict was required. With this group belongs William McDougall, of Duke University—who, though British strictly speaking, has become a part of the American psychological scene. We did not send him a questionnaire because he had already answered the questions publicly in his article "Should All Taboos be Abolished?" in the Calverton and Schmalhausen symposium, *Sex in Civilization.*

In his essay, Professor McDougall paid nakedness the compliment of rating the taboo against it as the least important of the sexual taboos. "It would seem," he remarked, "that we have gone far towards the abolition of this particular taboo." But he nevertheless offered "valid objections" by way of answering his rhetorical question whether we should complete the process. "First, as a race we are not beautiful enough to make this policy desirable," and secondly, climate forbids. It was on the first count, however, that he dwelt: "If all young women were divinely beautiful, I think that as regards them, the policy might work well. For strangely enough, such is the complex and incurably irrational nature of men, the beauty of woman's form, although it greatly adds to its power to excite the sexual impulse in man, yet in some way evokes a restraining influence. . . . Hence, the free representation of that beauty in art. But unfortunately, few women are beautiful to the required degree." (Perhaps this is the answer to those who fear nudism would destroy sex interest: it won't because women are too ugly!) "But the climatic and æsthetic objections do not stand alone," continued Professor McDougall. "We have no record of a people entirely without the taboo on nakedness, and those who approximate most nearly to such freedom are generally regarded on other grounds as the lowest of the low." (Alas for the Ancient Greeks, the Japanese, and the Scandinavians!) "Does not this universality of the taboo constitute presumptive evidence of positive social value of some kind? The question of the origin and motivation of the practice of clothing has been much discussed, and several rival theories are in the field. I suggest a new one. I suggest that clothing, and more especially the covering of the sex organs, has a symbolic function and value. It symbolizes the fact that men are not free to copulate as animals do, whenever and wherever the impulse is stirred in them. It is the outward and ever present symbol of all the other sex taboos." (Professor McDougall's theory is indeed new—as new as Genesis.)

But the major objections of the psychologists opposed to nudism were "public opinion," the "cultural pattern," and "custom," as related to the sexual mores, although three of them were like Professor McDougall in raising climatic objections. Four also had æsthetic objections. A professor in a Middle Western university spoke with particular feeling on the subject:

"Unadorned people are less beautiful—old women with pendant flaps are *very* unæsthetic." The only woman in the group said: "I have strong objections on æsthetic grounds. . . . How far my æsthetic objection is based on habit I am unable to determine to my satisfaction." One of the men who declined to express his opinion on nudism, did throw in an æsthetic observation which (although he has not been included in our count) properly belongs here: "Most people—men and women both—have such ugly bodies that I very often thank God for clothing. There is about one man in three hundred and about one woman out of a hundred who have beautiful bodies. I think it would be marvelous if they could be persuaded to go without clothes." The other objections—ranging from insects to a personal "horror of participating"—are too diverse for classification. The most original was that of a psychologist in the Far West. "We must keep in mind," he asserted, "that with nudity the possibility of fashion changes does not exist. . . . The changes in the nude condition are obviously few, and I think many would not be satisfied to remain approximately the same year in and year out. This would then mean the adoption of some sort of dress—or ornament—to relieve the sameness. I see no hope for the nudists in this respect, unless nudity is accepted as a 'religion,' and if it is, only then may we expect the sameness of nudity to be satisfactory to the fashion-loving, so-called 'civilized' man."

This objection would be valid only if nakedness were continuous and universal; it does not apply to the nudists' practice of nakedness limited to recreation, sports, and the like. If the monotony palls on the nudist, he can resume his clothes and go back to "civilized" fashions. The sameness might be a problem for a distant nude Utopia, but not for us who live in crowded dirty cities that demand garments for protection.

Advantages of one sort or another were conceded by six of this anti-nudist group. In conformity with the general attitude of the public, the health benefit was mentioned most frequently—by five altogether, including Professors Samuel W. Fernberger, of the University of Pennsylvania, and S. M. Newhall, of Yale. Dr. F. L. Wells, Head Psychologist of the Boston Psychopathic Hospital, suggested that nudity "when culturally acceptable, might lead to physiological benefits through greater care of the body." An anonymous Eastern psychologist had this to say: "I subscribe to exposure of the body under certain conditions for reasons of health, but I do not see that this requires complete nudism except for psychological reasons. Thus, I see no reason why the use of a breech cloth and, in the case of women, breast cloths, should be significantly contrary to the general benefits to be derived from otherwise complete exposure. Of course exercise with the body entirely naked is exhilarating, yet I do not personally feel that complete nudity is essential or even desirable." He felt that nakedness might contribute to a saner attitude toward sex on the part of adults —and then again, that it might not. Perhaps he should have been classified among those undecided, but while he did not state his verdict in so many words, he seemed to feel that the possible benefits are more doubtful than the objections. His opinion in more detail was as follows:

"It seems to me that the nudist movement has both wholesome and unwholesome aspects. . . . It probably symbolizes the modern tendency toward release from restraint and inhibitions and is a response to the current desire for personal and social freedom. Insofar as it represents a tendency toward a saner and franker attitude toward sex, I think that the result should be beneficial. However, I strongly suspect that for at least the present adult population nudism represents a rationalization of inhibited desire. Assuming that these inhibited desires might have been originally induced by a too prudish attitude toward the human body, it would logically follow that the removal of such prudish attitudes might lead toward the lack of such desire in the next generation. On the other hand, it seems to me the movement must be more or less temporary,

[199]

since the tendency of civilization, presumably for good reasons, has been away from nakedness and toward clothing. This tendency I think initially did not represent a moral trend in the sense of native modesty but more probably represented the desire in the first instance for decoration, perhaps in the second instance for physical protection, and now represents merely an established convention. . . .

"With reference to the 'saner moral outlook,' as noted above, I think this [practice] up to a certain point encourages a saner moral outlook since it robs the human body of that type of prurient sexual curiosity which in itself is sexually stimulating. However, I think the attendant risks may be fully as important as the gains. While we have two schools of opinion on this point, we have very little evidence. . . . I very seriously question whether the practice of nudism will go very far toward changing the normal instinctive and acquired sex attitudes which are indeed essential to the preservation of the race. Mankind has always found it advisable, if not necessary, to control these sex attitudes and in our day the use of clothing has come to be viewed as a proper means toward that end. . . . It seems to me that the conflicts which develop in individuals in relation to their sex attitudes arise from religious indoctrination more fundamentally than from any other single source. I personally feel that exposure of the body is only one element in the whole question of sound sex attitudes, at least insofar as these are related to mental hygiene and morals."

This brings us to the heart of the matter—the question of moral effects. The complete statement of Professor S. M. Newhall, of Yale, was as follows: A) "I believe the practice of nudity with sexual segregation and at reasonable temperatures, etc. is beneficial to health." B) "No immediate advantage: I do not feel qualified to judge regarding long-time effects. I guess that the immediate effect would be demoralizing (with both sexes in common) and that the long-time effect would be to further reduce marriage and propagation." The woman previously cited, who is connected with an Eastern institution, considered "mere custom a serious objection" and elaborated this as follows: "I do not believe that the wearing of clothing is conducive to morality or to decency, but it does not follow that it would be more conducive to morality to leave off our clothes suddenly. I should be more interested in a gradual reduction of clothing, such as has been permitted during the past few years. I think we would be better off morally if we had been provided with fur or feathers and if the idea of wearing clothing had never arisen. However, I believe that the habit of wearing clothes is too deeply fixed to be eradicated in a generation."

The anonymous Far Western psychologist who brought up the monotony of the unadorned body answered the questions concerning advantages thus: "None, but neither do I see any special advantages in clothing towards moral or educational improvements." Under objections he said: "None that I know. The main objection is public opinion and such opinion leads to legal restrictions." And he summed up his position: "My general reaction is that neither the nude nor the clothed conditions are necessary for health, morality, or æsthetic enjoyment. Convention has so governed, and still governs most people that they would be affected (mentally) in health, and they would feel a debasement if nudity more than at present became the vogue. On the other hand, less than a generation would suffice to overcome these attitudes to a great extent." Professor Leonard Carmichael, of Brown University, was still more positive concerning the obstacle of public opinion. To the question as to possible benefits, he answered "no," and under objections he said: "Public opinion in this matter is, it seems to me, against 'nudism.' I cannot help believing, although I have no evidence for it, that public opinion in this matter reflects sanity; nudism, mental ill-health."

Professor Edmund S. Conklin, of the University of Oregon, also perceived no advantages and stated: "The disapproval of public opinion I consider a most important and significant objection. Aside from and secondary to that I think there is an æsthetic objection. A really beautiful human figure is rare. Some clothing adds much to the appearance of most people." Dr. Joseph Jastrow, formerly of the University of Wisconsin and now lecturer on psychology at the New School for Social Research, wrote: "My reaction to your question is that clothing is an institution which is part of our civilization. Apart from matters of protection and climatic conditions, it does not seem to me either possible or desirable to take out one factor of our customs and attempt to return to a practice which even in primitive life had a very different place, and which among the Greeks was associated with physical culture and not a social practice."

Of interest where the subject of Greek nudity is concerned is John Erskine's article, "Clothes Didn't Make the Greeks," in the *Mentor World-Traveler* for February 1930. Mr. Erskine believes that the Greek simplicity of dress and attitude toward nudity was "an achievement of their philosophy, the result of discussion and education." He pointed out: "Actually the Greeks progressed from many clothes to few, and from a quite Victorian reticence to a cult of nudity," and that "Only toward the climax of Greek culture was that noble frankness achieved, that worship of the body, which we admire and envy." The Greeks, he said, revered the body as the expression of the soul. That nakedness of women was less common than that of men, except in Sparta, he attributed to the inferior position of women; their bodies were covered because they did not have souls worth expressing. Plato's discussions of nakedness of course indicate that Mr. Erskine is right in believing it was an achievement of philosophy and not an accidental accompaniment of physical culture.

Dr. F. L. Wells of the Boston Psychopathic Hospital was another who stressed the matter of custom. Under A) he wrote: "Scarcely in present cultural situation outside members of

same family; depends essentially on other cultural factors."
Under objections, he listed with climate and insects "the
general cultural pattern." Professor Samuel W. Fernberger,
of the University of Pennsylvania, did not object on the basis
of public opinion, but solely on account of the psychological
consequences which he foresaw. His belief as to the effect of
nudism on the sexual impulses resembled somewhat that of
Professor Newhall, quoted above. The fears of both are answered very soundly, it seems to us, in the letter of Professor
C. A. Ruckmick, reproduced in full at the end of this chapter.
Dr. Fernberger's complete opinion follows:

"I am strongly in favour of exposing the nude body in private for reasons of health and of greater æsthetic enjoyment.
I am strongly in favour of exposing the nude body of the
adults of the family to pre-pubescent children. I am, however,
equally strongly opposed to what I conceive as the primary
function of nudist theory, namely of the practice of nudity
by adults of both sexes in common. Basically I believe that
one is here dealing with an instinctive reaction of great strength
—the perfectly normal reaction for procreation. Social conformity demands that this perfectly normal and useful instinctive reaction must be controlled. Certainly this is true as
society is at present constituted.

"We are dealing, then with an instinctive activity which, for
social conformity, must be controlled but which, for the con-
tinuance of the race, must not be suppressed. The control of
any instinctive activity can only be the result of training, and
this training should begin as early as possible in the life of the
child. Hence, nudity within the family I conceive as a highly
important factor in this training of the children. The child,
by observing his own parents, soon takes for granted the differences in anatomy of the other sex and also soon takes for
granted the changes in anatomy of his or her own sex which
will take place during pubescence. But it seems to me that all
of this must be accomplished before the child has sexually

matured.

"The practice of nudism among large groups of adults would seem to result in one of several aspects. Either the group would be sexually overstimulated but would learn to control the natural instinctive reactions, which can only result in a terrific drain of nervous energy, or it would lead to sexual adaptation so that the normal sexual stimuli would no longer be effective in calling forth the normal instinctive reaction. I am of the opinion that both aspects are harmful in the development of human personality and in the nervous equilibrium of the individual.

"You will realize that I raise no moral objections and that I have not considered the question of public opinion. My objection is solely to the practice of adult nudism in larger groups with the sexes mixed. My objection is purely on account of the possible psychological effects on the participants. I consider these difficulties far outweigh the benefits of health and æsthetic enjoyment which I consider real contributions. But these beneficial aspects can be as well obtained by exposing the body in private as in public."

The fallacy in this argument is probably the assumption that mere sight of the naked body of the opposite sex is a normal sexual stimulus. Certainly it is a strong stimulus when the body is universally covered. There was a time, not so remote, when the sight of a woman's legs was a sexual stimulus, but normal sex interest has not been irreparably damaged by the loss of this excitation. If sex were such a simple matter as to depend on the sight of the naked body, sexual difficulties should have been straightened out long ago. And if clothing were essential to a normal sex life, naked peoples must be decidedly abnormal in this respect. One wonders how humanity managed to survive until clothes were invented to incite it to propagation. In fact, to anyone holding such a view of the importance of clothes, the Biblical version of creation would appear to be the only one tenable.

What the Psychologists Think

The twelve psychologists inclined to favour nudism discerned, as we have said, varied but less serious handicaps. As usual there were æsthetic protests. Some noted the dangers to those not mentally prepared. A psychologist in an Eastern university said that "the initial shock would probably be somewhat painful to many persons," and Professor Howard C. Warren, head of the department of psychology at Princeton, pointed out that nudism "is feasible only in the case of those who are not dominated by the taboo—who are not self-conscious in their nudity." He added: "A majority of my acquaintances would feel decidedly uncomfortable and ashamed to appear naked in such a group, owing to their lifelong acceptance of the notion that exposure of the human body is indecent and immodest." Professor Knight Dunlap, of Johns Hopkins, made the same point in a statement that will be quoted in full below. Professor Lewis W. Terman, of Stanford University, said: "Those who are too steeped in the Victorian attitude toward the human body and its functions to change this point of view are right to leave nudity alone." This brings in the matter of compulsory nakedness, which no nudist except a fanatic would advocate, and which Professor Max E. Meyer, of the University of Missouri, also stressed in his statement given below. The objection that some people are psychologically unfitted for the practice of nakedness, however, is no indictment of nudism, since nudists are not only willing but anxious to exempt them. Professor C. A. Ruckmick, at the start of his letter, which will be reproduced in full, expressed what is actually the nudist feeling about compulsion.

The health benefits were mentioned by five, including Professors Dunlap, Guthrie, and Meyer. One of the anonymous listed it first among the advantages. Another psychologist who preferred not to be mentioned stated: A) "Mostly for 'reasons of health' and 'on other grounds'—that is pride in one's body." B) "Yes, woman's presence would greatly stimulate man's pride in his body. The urge to appear at one's physical best would, I believe, be greatly increased. I should not, for example, feel the urge of reducing my waist line if I were among men; but if women were present—I'd start to reduce it before joining the colony!" Professor Warren wrote: "The relation of nudity to health is for the physician to determine rather than for the psychologist. I have been greatly benefited by sun-bathing, and by open-air exercise in the nude. I can well believe that athletic sports and exercise would be much more effective and beneficial without the hampering effect of clothing; the Greeks discovered this in their 'golden era.' It has long seemed to me a silly practice to don a costume for bathing and swimming—much as though we should put on dark glasses to appraise a picture, or stuff our ears with cotton to enjoy music."

Some of these men appreciated æsthetic advantages, or at least that the æsthetic objection is not a death knell to the practice of nakedness. Such was the view of Dr. Carney Landis, Research Associate in Psychology at the New York Psychiatric Institute. Professor Ruckmick, of the University of Iowa, saw positive æsthetic gains, as did Professor Warren. Dr. Warren's well-considered opinions on this subject were as follows: "The practice of nudity is undoubtedly of æsthetic value, since the human form, in its more perfect types, is an object of beauty. We have long recognized this fact by displaying the nude body in painting and sculpture. But neither a picture nor a statue can equal the beauty of the human figure itself. Furthermore, the human body in action, as in a graceful dance, or in athletic exercise, brings additional elements of æsthetic enjoyment to the spectator. It is true that nudity may frequently accentuate bodily defects; but I am inclined to believe that, except in cases of glaring malformation or injuries, the general effect of an ugly body is no more displeasing unclothed than draped."

The feeling of freedom and joy from nakedness out of doors was specifically mentioned only by Professor Ruckmick. Many nudists consider this one of the strongest arguments for their practice, although the Freudians do not (see Dr. Coriat's statement in the next chapter).

Strangely enough, three of those who looked with approval or tolerance on the practice of nakedness did not even refer to the moral factor or the possible effect on mental hygiene. One answered "yes" without qualification to both questions regarding advantages, and under objections replied: "No—except that the initial shock would probably be somewhat painful to many persons." The second, Professor E. R. Guthrie, of the University of Washington, listed no objections and merely stated: "The practice might result in devoting as much effort to keeping fit as is now devoted to keeping well-dressed. I rather think the æsthetic pleasure would be on the whole reduced by the practice. It is easier to approximate standards of beauty (which are the result of habit) in dress than in figure." Dr. Carney Landis in reality answered the question as to moral effect, but only by implication. His complete statement was this:

"As a psychologist I do not believe that the practice of nudity would particularly affect the life of civilized man one way or another, after a brief period of adaptation. The human being seems able to adjust to all sorts of situations and environments, and after a period of adjustment goes his way accordingly. There is no reason to believe that nudity would have any effect except, perhaps, that of health which might be endangered by exposure in rigorous climates. There are no objections to such practice from a psychological viewpoint other than the legal ones and the disapproval of public opinion and of organized religion. It is possible that certain objections might be offered on an æsthetic basis, but one doubts that such objections would have very much meaning in view of the things which the race has accustomed itself to and which were considered as æsthetic affronts when inaugurated. Psychologically, I believe that the question may be summed up by the phrase, 'It is all what one gets accustomed to.' "

All the rest made at least some reference to the likely effects on our mental conceptions of morality. Professor Max F. Meyer, of the University of Missouri, who without being a nudist believes in tolerance for nudists, stated this sane credo: "I believe in everybody's right to dress and to make himself (herself) thereby more presentable. I believe that society ought to be educated to the point of tolerating those who for the sake of health desire to take sunbaths on the beach unclothed and swim unclothed, and that—to bring about this education —certain bathing places at certain times ought to be opened to the public with this toleration, very gradually extending the practice as opposition from objectors diminishes. Nudity no more than stylishness of dress should be forced on unwilling victims. I am neither a 'nudist' nor a 'dressist.' I believe in tolerance. I believe in educating the public, very gradually since it is not possible in a hurry, to look with 'moral indifference' to styles of dressing and of nudity, *provided* the individual otherwise behaves chastely." (What nudist could want more than that the general public and those in authority should come to this stand!)

One of the anonymous contributors answered A) with the succinct statement: "Yes—health and 'saner moral outlook.' Æsthetic enjoyment in selected cases!" He had no objections. Another, who believed that the presence of the opposite sex would stimulate pride in one's body, said: "The moral outlook would not, I believe, be affected. It is the draped and not the nude figure that is sex appealing." He also said he had "not the slightest" objection. A psychologist who feared the use of his name "in connection with a sensational propaganda" had no objections to nudism, though he did not wish to pose as an expert, and replied thus to A) and B): "Yes. I have not thought much about the practical aspects of the problem, but it seems to me that a great many neurotic inhibitions would be avoided if the social taboo upon the exposure of the human body did not exist."

Dr. Frank N. Freeman, of the University of Chicago, replied as follows: A) "I think there may be advantages, but this guess is based largely on indirect evidence. I think clothing probably promotes self-conscious 'modesty' and is a means of creating curiosity." B) Advantages: "Probably a lessening of morbid interest in sex characteristics." Objections: "I should have to observe the effects to say."

Professor Lewis M. Terman, of Stanford University, replied thus: A) "Yes." B) Advantages: "Yes, besides the moral and educational values it would, in my opinion, contribute greatly to mental hygiene." Objections: "Not under appropriate conditions. Those who are too steeped in the Victorian attitude toward the human body and its functions to change this point of view are right to leave nudity alone. It is my personal belief, however, that the world would be morally cleaner and more sane if all children from the earliest years up were made accustomed to the practice of nudity by the sexes in common."

Professor Knight Dunlap, of Johns Hopkins University, made the following statement: "From the point of view of so-called 'savage' cultures, it would seem plausible that we have something to learn from them in this respect; also modern tentatives in the field of bathing costumes and women's garb generally seem to have had wholly beneficial results in all respects. There may be distinct psychological and consequently moral benefits in the practice of nudity of the sexes together, under conditions which avoid the obvious psychological dangers. This should be approached cautiously, as an important experimental matter. The best methods of trial in America are through the reduction of bathing costumes to simple trunks for both sexes, and a progressive discarding of clothing in early childhood. Sudden changes in body exposure by adults, whose habits of perception, thought, and emotion are fixed, are always productive of bad results, although such results may be temporary. More adverse results occur in the case

of the male only, and because of the sexual emotional morbidity which is characteristic of 'civilized' males." (We feel
that Professor Dunlap's term "sexual emotional morbidity" is
the accurate one for what Professor Fernberger called the "normal instinctive reaction.")

Professor Howard C. Warren, of Princeton, in the *History
of Psychology in Autobiography*, Volume I, published in 1930,
wrote at the conclusion of his autobiographical sketch: "The
Anglo-Saxon taboo against the human body and its functions
appears quite unnatural, especially in a civilization which glori-
fies the nude in statuary and painting. The recent tendency to
abolish many of the Victorian conventions seems to indicate
a healthier attitude of mind in the community." Hence it was
not surprising that Dr. Warren in reply to the questionnaire
expressed himself thus: "As regards the ethical problem, there
is direct evidence that children brought up in frank familiarity
with the bodily differences of the two sexes are spared much
worry and curiosity and 'repression.' It is only through some
odd kink of human mentality that we have come to regard
the natural state of the body as indecent. I believe that the
traditional attitude of concealment and mystery with respect
to the human body, and especially the sex organs, is responsible for much immorality and perversion.

"I know of several families whose children have been
brought up from the start to accept nudity as a matter of
course—with other children of both sexes and with their elders;
the effect has been decidedly helpful, both educationally and
ethically. I can see no objections (except the legal ban and the
social taboo) to the practice of nudity by adults as well as
youthful members of both sexes together, for sports, exercise,
and health. *But* this is feasible only in the case of those who
are not dominated by the taboo—who are not self-conscious
in their nudity."

There remains only the statement of Professor Christian A.
Ruckmick, of the State University of Iowa, to which we have

several times referred. Dr. Ruckmick asked to be quoted in full if his name were used, but his letter is such a sound and convincing expression of what is essentially the attitude of the nudist that we should have wished to do so in any case. In his final paragraph he has answered effectively those who, like Professor Woodworth, Professor Newhall, and Professor Fernberger, fear nudism would detract from sex interest; practising nudists can add little more than the assurance that their experience bears out Dr. Ruckmick, who wrote:

"I am in favour of the underlying principles of nudism but I am as much against implanting my ideas in others as I am in seeking converts to my own philosophy of life. These things have to grow on individuals gradually and should not be thrust on them. Following the suggestion of my own great teacher in psychology, I have from the beginning practised nudism in my family. At our summer resort whenever we are sure that we shall not offend others we have bathed without clothes in the lake at night or when other residents were gone. My children have a perfectly normal understanding of the appearance of the body and its functions. But the most devilish thing that can happen is that nudism should be practised even with a subtle implication of shocking others. That would be sadistic and would undermine the fundamental principles of the whole movement. There is a decency and good taste about such matters as there is in the display of one's affections in public. Furthermore, individuals who are so aggressive as to flaunt their new ideas before an uneducated public must take the consequences.

"Much can be done by open discussion and by gradual transformation of ideas. Already many educated families are bringing up their children in the way that I have mentioned and there has been a change in the attitude of our students in the period of my teaching among both sexes. Men students often swim together without clothes of any kind and girls are less apt to be embarrassed at the exposure of their own bodies

or at the sight of other exposed bodies of their own sex. In
certain restricted groups, as among students of art, there is
not even much comment in sketching or painting from nude
bodies of either sex in mixed classes. In certain experiments
performed in medical laboratories and in some psychological
laboratories, various parts of the body or all of it may be exposed for scientific purposes and in an objective way. Of
course, even under some of these conditions we have to guard
against the attacks of maliciously and sensuous-minded individuals. Even unfounded suspicion can do as much harm. It
is furthermore possible today, as was not possible several dec-
ades ago, to discuss mind and body with students in a perfectly
frank and open manner. All told, I should say there is much
less prudery among members of our younger generation than
there was in previous generations. The idea of partnership in
marriage and the openness of the relationship among men and
women have done much to bring this about.

"The practice of nudism has, to my mind, certain mental
as well as physical advantages. First of all, it removes idle and
suggestive curiosity. It is a well known fact, of course, that
only the partly clothed figure of the opposite sex is sexually
attractive. When the fact of form stares you in the face much
of the glamour wrought by the imagination is removed. I do
not mean to say that many revealed figures thereby lose their
beauty, and I should say in addition that if nudism is not
combined with a certain amount of æsthetic enjoyment it will
lose much of its force. A great many human figures of both
sexes are of course very beautiful and the poetry of life should
not be dissipated by any such practice. I do not think it will.
On the other hand, I think the artistic forms that are por-
trayed in our art museums will be seen more in their artistic
environment and less as manifestations of sex when everyone
can satisfy his curiosity from the early days of life without
going to an art museum. This is true especially of books containing artistic human forms. My point here is that both

science, which tries to understand the human mind and body, and art, which appreciates its form, rhythm, and symmetry, will be advanced through the increasing practice of nudism.

"Of course, one of the greatest achievements will be on the moral plane. Our greatest incentive to crime and malpractices of all sorts is the urge to do the forbidden thing. Wrongly motivated curiosity has been an enormous factor in the process of sexual wrong-doing. If we can cultivate both a reverence for the marvel of the human body and an increasing understanding of its place and function, education will do much to minimize sinful acts.

"There are several disadvantages which may have to be overcome in the practice of nudism. There may be a danger that those individuals who already have strong exhibitionistic tendencies will be the first to advocate the scheme. I hope I am not among them for this reason. As I have said before in connection with sadistic impulses this would undermine the whole scheme and be a contradiction in terms. Persons who honestly believe in nudism should stress the natural features of the situation. It should not lead to embarrassment of themselves or others but rather to the removal of embarrassment. I am violently against the practice if it recruits to its ranks people who already have perverted sexual ideas.

"Another objection might be raised in connection with the sexual function itself. At one time I thought that a too frequent exposure of the body of the opposite sex would lead to the reduction in the attractiveness of the opposite sex in the sexual relation. This argument in itself might be worth discussing because instead of becoming more highly sexed we might become more blasé in such matters. I do not think, however, that there is any real danger here because to a person of proper moral standards the attraction of the other sex involves not only the physical but the mental side, and there will always be a great deal of affection between the two sexes because of permanent differences in both mind and body. We do not have to hide a beautiful vase in a closet in order to appreciate it; the more we look at it, the more we love it. As a matter of fact, the ties that bind the home together may on this account be made stronger because members of the other sex will no longer seem as enticing when the factor of curiosity is removed. As for the experience itself, I can attest, as many others can, to the feeling of freedom and joy experienced while swimming in the water unclothed or the contact with the air about you. This joy, of course, is removed the moment anything occurs which destroys that freedom. I should not wish to be gazed at or to have any remarks made which are derogatory to the feeling of freedom."

The psychologists may have had difficulty in making up their minds about nudism, and may not have agreed when they did, but on the whole they were willing to look at it impartially and listen to all sides of the question. One of them wrote: "I venture to predict that if you send out a similar sheet ten years hence you will find a notable change in favour of nudism." In ten years there should be an opportunity for the first-hand knowledge and observation of nudist groups of which so many of the psychologists have felt the lack, and if they avail themselves of it, this prediction may be realized.

lᴜᴜᴜ

X

WHAT THE PSYCHIATRISTS THINK

SINCE THE JUSTIFICATION FOR NUDISM INVOLVES SO DEEPLY both the physical and mental aspects of life, and so many questions regarding it have to do with matters of sex or related problems and with human conduct in general, it seemed only proper that the psychiatrists, as specialists in these realms, should be heard. Moreover, the psychoanalysts, although not necessarily equipped as the psychiatrists with medical training, should have something to contribute for the same reason. Both are experts. It may be charged that their professional contacts and concerns, being largely with abnormal mental conditions—which range to be sure from the definitely pathological to the mildest, if not purely imaginary, neuroses— affect their attitude toward normal human behaviour to the point where their analyses and theories imply motives more complicated than the ordinary person's experience seems to warrant. But not a few people will be found to hold with Dr. Harry Elmer Barnes, who recently declared that when it comes to the development of the science of mental hygiene the psychiatrists have played a larger part than the academic psychologists.

The group of psychiatrists from whom we have heard is too small to make any generalizations valid—except, perhaps, that as a class they are not greatly interested in the subject, the number who failed to reply being almost twice as large as the number who answered. The total replies were 21, but only 16 of these gave their opinion. On the other hand, only one of the five who wrote to decline did so on the ground of "insufficient data," whereas three-fourths of the academic psychologists plead ignorance. This may be indicative of a difference in attitude.

It might be said also that the 16 who expressed views revealed less hesitancy in making pronouncements than did the academic psychologists. Four of the opinions were undecided as to favour or disapproval of the practice, two for lack of information or first-hand knowledge. The other two were undecided, not because they felt a want of evidence but because they saw equal advantages and disadvantages, or believed that nudism might be good under certain conditions and bad under others. Of those with more decided opinions, Dr. George B. Wilbur, of South Dennis, Massachusetts, formerly of the Boston Psychopathic Hospital and the Psychopathic Hospital of the University of Iowa, was the only one who stated that his views were "preconceived ideas" since he had no practical experience with nudism. All the rest apparently felt they had sufficient grounds for their conclusions. A few in fact stated their grounds. Dr. A. A. Brill said that his opinion was derived "from what I have read and from my observations of two nudists." Another declared his view was based on his work "in the study of emotional interreactions of individuals in groups." Dr. Ira S. Wile, the pediatrist who is also a psychiatrist, explained: "I happen to have likewise been interested in the nudist movement abroad and have been in touch with some of the members in Germany, France, Sweden and Finland." Dr. L. Cody Marsh, of the Worcester State Hospital, had observed the "nudist sort of thing at first hand" in Russia.

The psychiatrists showed less hesitancy about being quoted,

only five out of the sixteen preferring not to have their names mentioned—and one of these, whose opinion was unfavourable, had no objections provided he could see the context before publication. (Lacking time for that, we are forced to cite him anonymously.) Most of the psychiatrists are not handicapped by academic affiliations, although one asked not to be quoted because of a "connection with an organization which might suffer for it." Two gave no reasons for desiring anonymity; the other said: "I do not care to be identified with the 'lunatic fringe' that will gather about proponents of the nudist cult." On the other hand Dr. Wile declared: "I have no objection at all to being quoted as I stand behind my views probably more vigorously than a manufacturer stands behind his wares."

The questionnaire sent the psychiatrists was a combination of that sent the physicians and of the one submitted to the psychologists, as it was felt their medical training might give them something to say on the purely physiological aspects of nakedness. The psychoanalysts without a medical degree— only two of whom expressed opinions—were not asked specifically about the effects of light and air or the health benefits of total exposure of the body. Four of the psychiatrists with medical degrees, however, disregarded these questions, and Dr. A. A. Brill stated they interested him "only in a general way and could be better answered by the general practitioner of medicine." Another New York psychiatrist answered the three in a single statement: "I may say that I believe it is very healthy to take sunbaths without any covering and to exercise unclothed in the open. Certainly this has a beneficial influence upon the physiology of the organism."

Of those who answered specifically regarding the benefits of exposure to the sun, three said "yes" without qualification— Dr. Beatrice M. Hinkle, Dr. L. Cody Marsh, and another New England psychiatrist. Dr. George B. Wilbur said "probably," and four answered in the affirmative with reservations. Dr.

G. V. Hamilton, of Santa Barbara, California, who is noted for his *Research in Marriage* and other works in social hygiene as well as for his studies in animal psychology, made the statement: "Yes. Rare cases get a dermatitis, but these need not qualify the value of the above generalization taken affirmatively." An anonymous New York psychiatrist replied: "Yes. There are, however, conditions or qualifications. Some individuals are so constituted that direct sunlight in more than moderate degree is harmful." Another of the anonymous—this one from New England—answered: "Yes, but it can be overdone." Dr. Ira S. Wile, who also qualified his affirmative statement, has already been cited in Chapter VIII, where he was considered as speaking as a pediatrist.

The health benefits of the circulation of air on the body were conceded by four without reservation—Dr. Hinkle, Dr. Hamilton, Dr. Marsh, and the anonymous New Yorker who qualified his statement regarding sunlight. The New England psychiatrist who made no reservations concerning sunlight answered this question: "Not necessarily." Another replied: "Yes, though I know of no very cogent evidence that it is." Dr. George B. Wilbur declared: "I think it would be well to dispel the superstition that it isn't beneficial. That would be the greatest benefit." Dr. Wile, it will be recalled, answered in the affirmative "with proper reservations for temperature, humidity, and the recognition that free circulation may be secured without nudism."

To the question, "Do you believe there are health benefits to be derived from total exposure of the body?" four also answered with an unqualified affirmative—Drs. Hinkle, Hamilton, and Marsh again, with one of the anonymous New Englanders. The other nameless New Englander said: "This need not be a matter of opinion. The factual evidence should be emphasized. My opinion is in the affirmative." One of the New Yorkers made the same reservation as for the first question—"Some individuals are so constituted that direct sunlight in more than a moderate degree is harmful"—and added, in connection with the practice of nudity in general: "I have no strong convictions, as I have no important data, on this point. As a rule, it seems to me we wear too many clothes, or too much clothing, at least for health and pleasure in some sports and recreations." Dr. Wile, it will be recalled, said there were "no greater health benefits to be derived from exposure of the genitals," and expressed the belief: "If one considers the physical side alone there is no great necessity for complete nudism" —thus agreeing with a number of the other physicians cited in Chapter VIII. One of the psychoanalysts, a woman, though not asked specifically concerning the physiological effects, replied to the question "Do you believe the practice of nudity to be beneficial to civilized man for reasons of health, æsthetic enjoyment, saner moral outlook, or on other grounds?" with the statement: "Health. Sunlight (natural or from lamps) has good effect, which should be increased with addition of outdoor air and exercise."

The psychiatrists gave less attention than the academic psychologists to the æsthetic aspect, although asked the same questions. Only four in fact mentioned it. Dr. Wile believed that: "So far as æsthetic enjoyment is concerned that is an individual reaction even under conditions of nudism." The other three felt the average of physical beauty was too low to afford much æsthetic pleasure. An anonymous New Englander said: "As a matter of æsthetics, nudity is frequently deplorable." Dr. A. A. Brill stated: "It would be æsthetically enjoyable if the average man and woman would be well built and would resemble those artistic productions that we are wont to admire for their artistic enjoyment, but a crowd of people such as one usually sees would rarely afford æsthetic enjoyment if we saw them naked. On the contrary, when I am in the subway or in other public places, I am very grateful that people are compelled to wear clothes." (It might be objected that the New York subway average is below that for America as a whole; certainly New York life is not conducive to a decent physique.) The views of Dr. C. P. Oberndorf, of New York City, on the æsthetics of nakedness will be quoted later, as they are not separable from his other remarks.

Three psychiatrists offered what some have liked to call "practical objections"—climatic handicaps, and insect pests. Two more, both of them on the whole favourable to nudism, mentioned the undesirability of compulsion in the matter. A New Englander asserted: "Evolution rather than revolution is the preferred technic." And Dr. L. Cody Marsh declared: "I only ask that should the movement altogether succeed that it does not compel me to go in bathing nude should I choose to wear a suit. Who can tell? The nudists may make us quite as uncomfortable as did the Puritans. Humanity must ever be on guard against its friends." (For the sake of nudism itself, as well as for liberty, we trust that the nudists will not adopt repressive measures and force Dr. Marsh out of his bathing suit, willy-nilly.)

Class distinctions in dress, touched on by one of the physicians (See Dr. L. Mason Lyons, Chapter VIII), were discussed at considerable length by Dr. S. D. Schmalhausen, the psychoanalyst and author of *Humanizing Education* and *Why We Misbehave,* as well as editor of an infinite series of stimulating symposia. Dr. Schmalhausen, preoccupied with the present economic mess of civilization and the crimes of Capitalism, cannot view any problem detached from the larger one of social and economic injustice. Thus he gave us a class-conscious proletariat-eye's view of nudism—and incidentally, as he explained, that of "a man who is always clothed even in his sleep." He chided nudism for the same limitations as did Dr. William J. Robinson (see Chapter VIII) and reproached nudists for fiddling while Rome burns, and for suggesting cake for a humanity that needs bread. "With the world's agony as a background for our thinking," he prefaced his remarks, "it would be frivolous to assert that the neo-modern cult of nudity is a matter of the first importance. Even a person possessed of a great sympathy for this hygienic and somewhat æsthetical movement in the direction of sexual simplicity and human amiability can hardly get himself worked up to a pitch of genuine enthusiasm for what after all must be construed as a playful footnote in the bitter reality of life." His extended remarks on the social implications of dress and undress follow:

"What I am primarily interested in is the functional correlation through the centuries between class status and the significance of clothes. Under the dominance of the aristocratic point of view, what could be more natural than the pomp and ceremony of eccentrically elaborate clothing the better to serve the subtle and insidious purposes of kings and courts and royalties and highnesses, the better to hoodwink the populace into a magically inculcated subservience in the presence of bejewelled and exquisitely begarmented superiors. I doubt very much whether the history of human exploitation, the narrative of force and fraud in human affairs, could be written with any sense of adequacy except in terms of the ceremonial charlatanry of clothes. The regal way of dressing not only catered lusciously to an illimitable vanity but had as its diplomatic and religious function the overawing of the multitude. The magic of exquisite and ceremonially astonishing clothes involved the principle of hypnosis; for hypnosis, in an ultimate psychological sense, means a relation between credulity on the one hand and prestige on the other, the rapport between superior and inferior being cemented by a truly infantile emotional dependence. Clothes have played an important role in the perpetuation of the superior-inferior relationship in society.

"The triumph of the bourgeoisie meant the considerable reduction of pomp and ceremony (the practical logic of *Tend to Business* not permitting such wide margins of indulgence and inflation), the substitution of relatively uniform clothing for marvelously variegated costumes. For all that, the wives of the bourgeois barbarians have done their stupid best to ape aristocratic fashions, to look like dolls and queens (rather than pigs and monkeys), to continue spreading the aroma of a false prestige among the lower orders of society by their pompous and expensive ways of dressing. It is interesting to contrast the bourgeois go-getter and his wife in relation to differences in elaborateness and ceremonial convolution of clothes. Business men tend to dress simply, monotonously, unexhibitionistically. They put upon their futile wives the burden of looking like exotic camels exuding perfume, radiating bejewelled magnificence, filling the envious air with their visible conspicuous costliness.

"Not until social evolution (more accurately, social revolution) brings a risen proletariate on to the stage of history do we meet with objective conditions that ruthlessly brush aside the hocus-pocus of upper class show off, the breast-fed vanity and mindless theatrical mummery of dominant class exhibitionists. The principle of genuine economic equality, attainable only in a communized social order, inherently and inevitably begets an honesty, a simplicity, a straightforwardness that of their own spontaneous urgency inaugurate a sexual behaviour, candid and natural, a relationship of the sexes to life that takes for granted the wholesomeness of nudity.

"At present nudity is still a cult and a queer ritual. Though it appeals in Germany to members of the working-classes, its essential status is still defined and stuffily circumscribed by middle-class persons whose social philosophy is anything but proletarian and egalitarian. . . . Once Communism triumphs in the world, nudity will come into its own *automatically!*"

That the majority of nudists in this country are middle-class in their social outlook is true and probably unfortunate, but it does not imply that nudism itself is essentially bourgeois. It simply reflects the fact that the American public is dominantly middle-class in viewpoint—even when in economic truth it belongs to the proletariate. If Dr. Schmalhausen wants the

[222]

nudists to be Communists, he cannot achieve his end by taking away their nudism. Rather, they will have to be converted to Communism by the same processes as the rest of the unregenerate American public.

As a rule the psychiatrists confined themselves rather strictly to the relation of nudity to mental hygiene in sexual matters, on which they agreed no better than did the academic psychologists. Of the four who felt they lacked data for a decision, or that the good and evil nearly balanced, one—an anonymous New York psychiatrist—answered the query as to possible advantages thus: "I have very little knowledge to go by. That clothing favours unfortunate tendencies to phantasy is probably true. That nudity—or near-nudity—has a chastening effect I feel pretty sure to be true in numerous instances." On the subject of objections, he said: "This is a broad question not lightly nor sweepingly to be answered, and I am not entirely clear about it. There are persons for whom there may be no objections. In other cases I can see clearly that there would be objections." (The present authors would disagree on one point only—that the psychological effects of nudity and near-nudity are identical.)

The other member of this group is a woman and a specialist in child guidance, who asked not to be identified. "I hope I am open-minded," she wrote, but as to nudism she had doubts. "It seems to me," she said, "that the whole matter of attitudes toward sex has very complex aspects, as we find from psychoanalytic studies and child psychology. Will not the attitudes toward sex already formed within the individual determine in any case whether nudist theory and practice will be accepted or rejected? If the answer is yes, we must presuppose that nudist groups will be composed of people who are relatively free from prudery and repressions—not those who need better sex attitudes. Unless, of course, some exhibitionists find nudism attractive."

We have commented on exhibitionism in the preceding

chapter. As for her other point, while it is true that until
nudism is well established and accepted few adults with set
attitudes toward sex will be attracted unless they are emancipated from conventional prudery and prurience, still, once
the movement does become widespread, many may be drawn
into it whose sex attitudes are susceptible of improvement.
Curiosity, not unmixed with prurience, has already attracted
some—and, incidentally, without disastrous results. A desire
for physical betterment, too, may prove stronger than very
real repressions. The influence of friends and relatives has
brought into even the American nudist groups both the extremely modest and those sceptics whose preconceived notions
on sexual matters were decidedly at variance with nudist
theory. Not a few have appeared among the nudists with little
more conviction than a willingness "to try anything once."
As the movement grows, there will be more who come in by
accident or out of curiosity.

Dr. Beatrice M. Hinkle, who was the first woman in the
United States to hold a public health position, and who later
at the Cornell Medical College opened the first psychotherapeutic clinic in America (incidentally she now specializes
in psychoanalysis), felt that without a prolonged study of
nudist groups, any opinion "is merely theoretic and expresses
the personal bias of the holder." Of the advantages of nakedness practised by both sexes in common, she said: "Have had
no experience in observing what benefits, if any, may accrue
under these circumstances." She considered it "might be advantageous under certain circumstances, but disadvantageous
under others." Her remarks in regard to objections were: "No
particular objections if undertaken seriously and purposefully."

Dr. Ira S. Wile, in replying to the question of the moral or
educational phases of nudism, stated: "The advantage lies in
opportunity for observation, naturalness in relationship, and
opportunity for the development of normal ideas and prin-

ciples. This does not essentially involve, however, general nudity. It may be supplied by nudity within the family. I have no objections to nudity on any basis if that is what people desire. Legal objections refer primarily to exhibitionism and efforts at debauching youth. Public disapproval is perhaps an outgrowth of fear, of taboos, and the necessities of environmental pressure, including climate." In a supplementary statement, he developed more fully the reasons for his conclusions:

"There is a vast difference between nudism in one group that is motivated, let us say, by the spirit of those who are members of a Youth Movement, and those who approach it bathed in lecherous sophistication. I have seen children who have been brought up in homes where nudism was practised, whose later development has not been any more successful from the standpoint of sex understanding or control than of those who have been raised in homes with puritanic concepts. I happen to have likewise been interested in the Nudist Movement abroad and have been in touch with some of the members in Germany, France, Sweden, and Finland. I believe again, from their statements, that generalizations are rather hazardous. To take that which is good in a movement and to expand it so as to cover the movement as a whole is unwarranted and unbalanced, and fails to meet rational demand.

"I am a strong believer naturally in honesty, frankness, and the abolition of irrational concepts concerning the normal relations of the sexes. I am completely in harmony with principles that would break down irrational taboos and restore normal mental attitudes as the basis for moral judgment. There is necessity, however, for recognizing distinctions between exposure of the larger surface of the body and complete exposure of the body. . . . If one considers the physical side alone there is no great necessity for complete nudism.

"If one thinks in terms of mental health, then one might say that ordinary nudism practised in the home would serve in large measure to impart necessary instruction pertaining to the anatomy, physiology and psychology, and cultural backgrounds of the sexes. The mere development of nudism for the purpose of common general exposure does not seem to me to be wholly supported by evidence in favour of its being improvement for ordinary behaviour. One must consider in part the anthropological background of the subject. Man's history appears to show definite values as the background of communal practice; and whether one has clothing to the extent of a G-string, a conch sheil, a grass plait, or a loin cloth, or a full skirt and trousers, there is evidence throughout man's cultural existence of some lack of nudity even though sexual customs permit of the widest freedoms. Under such circumstances one cannot say that nudism in itself is essential for mental clarity, or for establishing what is called a finer sense of morals."

Perhaps we had better leave the anthropological background for Dr. Briffault and the other anthropologists. We might make the suggestion, however, that where nudity in the home has not resulted in better sex understanding or control in the children's later life, the fault may lie largely in the improper sex attitudes they encountered outside of the home. The extension of nudist practices would diminish the danger of a sound home training being counteracted by less healthy attitudes in society at large.

Five psychiatrists condemned nudism with few or no reservations. The most concise and uncompromising blast of disapproval was from Dr. W. Béran Wolfe, author of *How to be Happy though Human,* and lecturer on mental hygiene. He declined to answer the questionnaire, but he stated his opinion of nudism in terms that left no ground for doubt: "In my opinion, nudism is psychologically a form of adult infantilism. Its principles may be theoretically sound, but in practice it is a neurotic manifestation of the prevailing hysterical hunger for panaceas, which besets the human race, no more deserving scientific approval than any other neurotic cult." (We cannot resist telling Dr. Wolfe that if all Americans were as un-neurotic as most of the nudists we know, we have grave fears the mental hygienists would be out of a job.) Almost as damning was the strictly Freudian interpretation of Dr. Isador H. Coriat, of Boston, whose opinion follows:

"I feel that the entire subject of nudism can only be adequately understood when it is linked up with the question of the psychology of clothes and also with social, biological, and instinctive factors both in primitive and civilized society. Of course the fundamental reasons for the use of clothing are decoration, modesty, and protection. Modesty requires a social repression of the fundamental exhibitionism of civilized man, because in children up to a certain age and in primitive communities there is no tendency to repress such exhibitionism. In primitive man clothing is used more for purely decorative purposes rather than to repress any exhibitionistic tendencies; therefore, for instance, if a naked savage wears a necklace he feels that he is sufficiently clothed and consequently there is no shame at the exhibition of the naked body. In the savage, too, clothes are sometimes used as protections against magic and spirits.

"I consider that nudism is a form of unsublimated exhibitionism and behind it there lies a strongly developed skin and muscle erotism which motivates exposure of the body. Of course in civilized society there is a tendency to repress this exhibitionism by wearing clothes. This tendency is essentially a replacement of the pleasure-principle by the reality-principle, because exhibitionism may be defined as a compulsive tendency for the conscious or unconscious purpose of attracting sexual interest. In the various articles of clothing, there may also be many deeply motivated phallic symbolisms. I feel that the desire for nudity is really a tendency to obtain as much gratification from skin and muscle erotism as possible, and hence tne satisfactions obtained by clothing are obtained at the cost of these skin and muscle pleasures. To go about nude is not only an unsublimated exhibitionism, but it is also a reaction-formation against the swaddling clothes of infancy and probably has its deeper motive in being independent of maternal protection. In the culture of nakedness in Germany this lost human mother is found again as a substitute in a more ample and satisfying form in Mother Nature, and therefore, nakedness in order to get 'back to Nature' is a substitution of one mother for another."

We are not qualified to pronounce on the working of the unconscious. The eminent psychologist, John Carl Flügel, author of *The Psychology of Clothes,* is probably the most competent authority to speak on the matter from the Freudian viewpoint. All the motives mentioned by Dr. Coriat as involved in nudity—skin and muscle erotism, the reaction against the swaddling clothes of infancy, the substitution of Mother Nature for the lost human mother—are stated by Flügel, who likewise discusses various unconscious motivations for dress that are equally appalling. Dr. Coriat has mentioned one of these—the phallic symbolization of various articles of clothing. Yet despite—or, perhaps it is by virtue of—his Freudian interpretations, Dr. Flügel comes to the conclusion that the fundamental motives for clothing are no longer valid (man no longer believing in magic, for instance, and being able to control his environment in respect to temperature and protection from the elements) so that humanity, having no good reason left for dressing, may, and probably will, go naked with impunity.

Dr. C. P. Oberndorf, of New York, stressed not only unconscious exhibitionism but æsthetics and the sexual stimulation of nakedness. His complete statement was this: "While it is desirable that the many prohibitions, distortions, and great mystery concerning sex which is now taught children be removed, the establishment of cults advocating nudism does not appear to be a particularly sound way to accomplish this end. Nor does nudism among adults seem to me a desirable means of

overcoming false modesty or advancing ethics to a higher plane.

"Nudism in temperate zones is impractical the year round because clothes furnish protection against changes in climatic conditions as well as ornamentation. During the few months in the year when it might be possible for people to go nude I can see little benefit from such a practice for the reason that no nude cult carries its practice to the ultimate possibilities. Apparently nudists are willing to expose the bodies to the gratification of sight but to none of the other senses—tactile, olfactory, and gustatory gratification is strictly enjoined. To my knowledge no nude cult includes promiscuity among its tenets. Thus association between members of a nude group does not offer greater freedom to the individual but really imposes upon him the necessity for greater restraint because he must check himself in the face of greater stimulation.

"From the æsthetic angle the cult of nudism seems to have little in its favour for most human bodies fall very short of the accepted standards of beauty. My impression is that constantly practised nudity in temperate climates would not lead to greater beauty of body but to a coarsening and roughness of the skin, increased hairiness of both sexes. Those individuals with whom I have come in contact who were strong advocates of nudity have nearly all been persons with strong exhibitionistic proclivities. These in turn were an over-compensation for an even greater unconscious modesty, just as excessive modesty is often an over-compensation for repressed exhibitionism.

"The best way to overcome the present day deleterious taboos concerning sexuality is through education beginning in earliest childhood. The parents should not withhold facts of anatomical difference from their children and should treat the household occurrences involving sex as undistinguished from other daily instances. But I see as little to be gained from the intentional parading of parents' nude bodies in front of their children as the withholding or condemnation of the sight of them."

Nudism Comes to America

Whether or not nakedness is so sexually stimulating as to call for rigid self-discipline has been frequently discussed, and further comment is superfluous. It is noteworthy, however, that despite the prevalence among the general public that the sight of the naked body is necessarily an erotic stimulus, Dr. Oberndorf is the only one of our psychiatrists who expressed it. As for the character of the advocates of nudity, we refer those who consider our own estimates too flattering to the statement of Dr. L. Cody Marsh, quoted later with the others of the favourable group. Dr. Oberndorf's fears of a coarse, hairy hide also seem unwarranted. As a matter of fact, the practice of nakedness in reasonable temperatures—and we are not talking of going bare in the arctic regions—enhances the beauty of the skin. Exposure to light and air, and the better elimination obtained when the action of the pores is unhampered by clothing, make for a healthier skin, firmer in texture, smoother, and freer from blemishes; it is more resistant—tougher, if you will—but not coarser. Nor is there physiological evidence that man would become hairier without his clothes. Ultraviolet light does stimulate the growth of what hair he already has, but that it would grow hair-cells where none exist is doubtful. If mere exposure will grow hair, why have not women after centuries of naked faces sprouted beards? Even if in the slow course of evolution man, as a result of nakedness, should develop into a furry animal, our æsthetic standards would doubtless evolve correspondingly, so that a thick coat of fur would be deemed a sign of beauty and a hairless man or woman as offensive to the eye as a hairless cat. But these questions, after all, are in the province of the physiologists and biologists.

Dr. A. A. Brill, of New York City, objected to nudism chiefly as too extreme a measure for the accomplishment of a desirable end. He wrote: "From what I have read and from my observations of two nudists, I feel that the cult is an extreme reaction to our modern sexual prudery. It has therefore a modicum of logic, but in its manifestations, it is extremely exaggerated. I do not believe that the practice of nudity is particularly beneficial to civilization for reasons of 'æsthetic enjoyment, saner moral outlook, or other grounds.'

"As for the saner moral outlook: I have advocated for a great many years that the sexual element should not be concealed from children, that parents should not try to hide their bodies from them, that the morbid sexual curiosity which one so often encounters in civilized children would not exist if the child would be accustomed to the sight of the genitals. In fact, I know a number of grown-ups who have a sane moral outlook because they have been brought up in the manner advocated. But I also know that those who were brought up differently are unable to throw off their sensitiveness about the genitalia and other parts of the body, no matter how liberal and educated they try to appear. In other words, to become a nudist does not solve the problem.

"Moreover, as civilization is at present constituted, it is impossible for people to discard clothes altogether except during certain seasons and in special places. Mankind has taken to clothes mainly through force of necessity. Consequently, one could see nudity only on rare occasions, which I feel would not remove the sex sensitiveness experienced by every civilized being. In other words, there is no possibility of nudism becoming an everyday affair.

"In brief, I see no special advantage morally, educationally, or otherwise for the practice of nudism. On the contrary, I see some objections to it as long as civilized mankind remains sexually sensitive—a fact which will continue for a long, long time—even if the law and public opinion should sanction nudity as demanded by the cults. Nudity is certainly more or less upsetting to the average person and as our main efforts at the present time are directed to helping the individual control his sex life, nudity would be more or less harmful to the individual. In other words, I feel that the only way to remove sex prudishness and sexual repressions is by the education of the child and not by such extreme measures as would tend to destroy the sublimations built up by organized society for thousands of years."

Nudism is less extreme than Dr. Brill apparently believes, since it does not involve forcing the participation of the "sexually sensitive" but seeks mere tolerance, rather than conversions, for the practice of nakedness on the part of those sufficiently educated to stand it. While Dr. Brill is right in asserting that clothes cannot be discarded altogether in our present civilization, the nudist contends they can be discarded often enough to condition himself to a sane mental attitude toward sex.

A New York psychiatrist connected with one of the medical schools considered nudism a danger, not for the actual harm it would do but because, failing to reach the roots of our sexual malady, it might distract attention from the real remedies. His view was this: "As far as concerns sunbaths, exercises, and games in common among persons of both sexes and different ages, as a sort of mental health movement, I cannot see any advantage in such a course. Indeed I believe that the advocates of this practice are deceiving themselves when they believe that such an altered mode of living will lead to a more rational understanding between the sexes or will promote a saner and more normal mental life. We know of civilized countries where there is no prejudice against both sexes bathing unclothed together, but I have heard nothing to warrant the view that life and ethics in those parts of the world are saner than elsewhere.

"Of course there is no denying that there is ample ground for criticism of the prevalent prudishness and ignorance in the world in regard to biological facts, especially of those pertaining to the sex life. But going about naked is one of those easy solutions that merely affords a superficial means of evading a deeper-lying maladjustment in the life of man. And so it is my view, based upon the work I have done in the study of emotional inter-reactions of individuals in groups, that the movement of the nudists, far from achieving its purpose of returning to a fundamentally saner life, seems to me to represent, like so many social movements current today, just another misdirected short-cut that fails to attain its goal. The real reasons for the distortions of feeling that characterize the inter-reactions among individuals socially, as expressed in part also in the sex life, lie much deeper and have to do with emotional habits and reactions which cannot be resolved by reverting to a program of living that consists in mere external divestiture. In fact, I believe that such external changes are apt to cloud the issue and to lead attention away from the long neglected need for more fundamental readjustments, both individual and social."

The tendency of the psychiatrists, even more than the psychologists, was to write long dissertations on the subject. One of the seven favourably inclined psychiatrists, however, could scarcely have been more laconic. Incidentally, he was one of the two in this group—both in New England—who did not wish to be named. Asked if he believed nudity for outdoor recreation and sports to be beneficial for reasons of æsthetic enjoyment, saner moral outlook, or on other grounds, D), he answered: "Not necessarily." Asked if he saw any moral or educational advantages in the practice of nudity by both sexes in common, E), he said: "For some people, yes." And to the query regarding objections, he stated: "No." The other anonymous psychiatrist was a bit more specific. His replies to questions D) and E) were: "Am dubious about it, as a practical measure. Theoretically I think it might have advantages. As a matter of æsthetics, nudity is frequently deplorable. Desensitization of prurient Americans would be an excellent measure. Probably could better be accomplished during this generation in the home rather than in public. As a move in the right direction the emphasis of 'nudism' is commendable."

His only objection was the need he had found for an impervious garb in Colorado.

Dr. Gilbert Van Tassel Hamilton, of Santa Barbara, California, replied thus to D) and E): "For all these reasons, and because it tends to develop in children a more direct and wholesome attitude toward sex. I believe that, if nudity were general among people of all ages, there would be fewer neurotics. Children who have daily familiarity with the sight of naked human bodies of all ages and both sexes are less apt to fall into difficulties with the 'Œdipus' situation." Dr. Hamilton had no objections.

Dr. George B. Wilbur, of South Dennis, Massachusetts, objected only to mosquitoes and gnats. To the question concerning advantages, he said: "It might have some effect in loosening up our hide-bound conventional ideas that pass for morality. But the institution of such a practice I should regard as a symptom that such a change had already come about. I am quite in favour of the movement in general. I see no good arguments against it. And it might possibly bring about some of the advantages that are claimed for it. Chiefly it will show up these also as superstitions. Largely I think it is a matter of convenience and taste. Most of the arguments for it, like those for women suffrage and other such panaceas are largely bunk so far as I can see. I am not including in this the argument that it would probably help to overthrow that large group of ideas centring around the belief that the naked human body is somehow peculiarly magical and wicked. But here again, as I said before, I should regard the establishment of such a movement on a large scale as evidence that such a change in public opinion had already come about. How? I am not prepared to say, but I guess I cannot deny a certain effect to propaganda after all." (This attitude, like that of Professor Max F. Meyer, see Chapter IX, is refreshing in a world prone to assume that the only choice is between joining the nudists and suppressing them and all their works.)

What the Psychiatrists Think

Dr. S. D. Schmalhausen, despite his strictures on the stuffy, bourgeois nature of the nudists, made a statement "on the more psychological and psychoanalytic aspects of nudity," wherein he argued so cogently and lyrically for nakedness that we persist in considering him favourable to nudism over his protests that the subject is not vital enough to be worthy of favour. Dr. Schmalhausen wrote:

"Perhaps some of us have been over-impressed by the psychoanalytic discovery that sex under repressive and puritanic auspices has suffered a hundred futile miseries, shames, disgusts, and degradations. Be it remembered that Freud has never argued for either the possibility or desirability of the elimination of the principle of repression in human behaviour. The choice is not between repression and license; the sensible choice is between repression that precipitates neurotic and psychotic states of mind and body *and* the repression which belongs in the internal discipline of a civilized person who must sacrifice a certain amount of natural impulse for the sake of social harmony and goodness.

"The question that immediately concerns us is the possible relationship between nudity and emotional wholesomeness. Which promises more genuine decency and moral excellence, in childhood, concealment with its accompanying consciousness of shame and guilt, *or* candid playful exhibitionism with its accompanying sense of naturalness and shamelessness? Nothing in retrospect seems so hilariously astonishing and amusing as the attempt on the part of the pompous guardians of the race to prevent boys and girls from knowing that nature at birth presented them with the free gift of sex organs. No student of culture yet knows whether the complicated attempt to conceal the simple sex organs had as its unconscious motivation to decrease or to increase sex-consciousness. As a matter of fact, it wildly increased it; as a matter of pretence it supposedly decreased it. The imagination cannot help pondering what the fig-leaf conceals.

[235]

Nudism Comes to America

"Prurience, pornography, puritanism, are the unholy trinity that have lorded it obscenely over the private mind of man (and of woman) because a certain number of over-sexed theologians and a few under-sexed saints foolishly agreed that the way to solve the sexual problem is to give birth to children in sin, to be ashamed of that fact for the remainder of one's life, and to instill in young minds a proper sense of degradation and misery. This insane solution of the sexual question has come close to wrecking human nature.

"Could anything be more natural and innocent—in a brand-new born babe!—than nudity? Would even the Pope expect a child to be delivered in a full dress suit? Nudity is natural; innocent: human. Why, then, have the elders of the tribe for so many moralistic and melodramatic centuries considered it the very weightiest problem in the living universe to supervise with ceremonial trepidation and hushed ritual the process of dressing and undressing? Why has the unclothed body, even of children, been under the ban, surrounded with suspicion and anxiety-haunted curiosity, so that long generations of grown-up men and women have actually been ashamed to look once more at the sex of their own children, the father fighting shy of femaleness, the mother of maleness, the children of both!

"Who can longer doubt that squeamishness, awkwardness, excessive sexual embarrassment, infantile curiosity lingering in the adult years, vulgarity truly vulgarizing, the cult of the toilet (especially in the adolescent years), silly misunderstanding between the sexes in love and marriage, taboo psychology, moral hardness and humourlessness, are each and every one of them traceable to the nasty inculcation in childhood of attitudes of concealment and evasion, attitudes which were possible and plausible because of the superstitious and most irrational cult of clothes (as the moral protectors and guardians of the immoral sex organs).

"I do not go so far as to assert that the wholesomeness and

[236]

liberating acceptance of nakedness in childhood, in adolescence, in maturity (whenever the circumstances and social desire permit), will *automatically* guarantee pure scientific objectivity in sexual thinking or completely devulgarize behaviour erotically. There is a wholesome as well as an unwholesome obscenity. Life without wholesome obscenity would be emotionally sterile, sexually colourless, humanly humourless. The cult of nakedness, as modern writers like to call it, should promote the more joyous and playful aspects of obscenity. At any rate, no student of the newer sciences of sexology, psychiatry, culture, can have the slightest doubt that the general unembarrassed acceptance of the sweet and lovable human body in its naturalness will solve some of the acutest of the neurotic dilemmas that confront those who have been moralistically and theologically trained in the puritanic philosophy of life.

"I myself am deeply of the opinion that both puritanism with its inevitable consequences of pornography and pruriency (let's not forget that the vicious institution of prostitution flourished most lustily in the ages of official prudery), *and* impuritanism, the far from lovely counterpart of repression in an age of brazen expression, will both vanish when a humanized society founded upon the scientific temper of mind, psychoanalytic candour, honesty in teaching, the rights of children to a free and æsthetically exhilarating expression of the body as well as of the mind, comes into existence.

"If men and women throughout the repressive and morally shamefaced centuries had devoted the energy they idiotically gave to repressing and concealing and tormenting the erotic impulses *to* the sane problem of ridding their social systems of injustices and cruelty, of exploitation and inequality, long ago the earth would have smelt sweeter, life would have flourished more happily, tolerance and humaneness would have dwelt among the peoples of the earth. When people's minds are constantly preoccupied with sexual immorality, they appear to have no energy or sense left for those deeper problems of life which in truth are responsible for most of what is wrong in the sexual situation. The social question is primary; the sexual question is subsidiary. . . ."

The idea with which Dr. Schmalhausen concludes had not occurred to us as an argument for nudism, the latter in truth seeming rather remotely related to our economic morbidity. But perhaps nudism, by taking our minds off sex, *will* contribute to our economic healing—provided the ingenious human mind, even freed from sexual preoccupations, does not find something else to keep it off the fundamental problems of society!

Dr. L. Cody Marsh, of the Worcester State Hospital, neatly divided humanity into Nudists (whom he exonerates from being necessarily neurotic), Nakedists (the Fishermen or Peeping Toms), and Clothists (the Comstocks and Sumners), and felt that only the last group would suffer from nudism. Dr. Marsh's statement was this:

"I am often asked, as a psychiatrist, to give a psychiatric point of view concerning the nudist movement. In this connection I have found three types of people. The first are the *Nudists* who are concerned with fostering the movement. Some of these are, to be sure, neurotic persons who have various conflicts of a sexual nature and they are working out these conflicts by their interest in this new philosophy of nudity. They are persons who have suffered from the excesses of the Puritan point of view. These form a scant minority of those interested in the movement. Most of those interested are well-balanced people who find in the nudist movement something which is valuable to the race as well as to themselves. Without a doubt the movement has value.

"The second group are the *Nakedists*. Possibly even these are not to be condemned. They are probably neurotic as a group and they are interested in nudity because it gives stimulation to their sexual interests. These too have developed symptoms as a result of puritanitis. However, from my experience and observation these last will find little in the way of satisfaction from the nudist movement. During the war while I was in Siberia with the A.E.F., I had an opportunity of observing the nudist sort of thing at first hand. When the Americans first arrived they were tremendously interested in the nude women bathers although the Russian men paid no attention to them. This was doubtless a Nakedist interest, but it shortly came to disillusionment, and then the American men took no more interest in nudity than did the Russian men.

"The third group are the *Clothists*. It is this group which suffers because of the nudist movement and seeks to 'expose' and suppress it. These are the most toxic with all that was pathological in puritanism. They have fears both for themselves and for others that the nudists will bring moral disaster to the race. Such a state of mind shows a marked moral insecurity, for one thing. It also shows that we have artificially charged the sexual organs with a morbid potential which they do not possess *per se*. In my opinion the Nudists are proving, to the amazement of many, that the frank nude are not sexually exciting. Both Nakedists and Clothists who came in contact with the nude in Russia learned this. One is tempted to think that the Puritans gratuitously contrived an unclean legend from their own spiritual uncleanness to fasten on the organs of sex. Biologically these organs are as clean as any other part of us."

The sufferings of the Clothists need not give us pause, since they find compensation for the pain occasioned by the thought of nakedness in the sadistic pleasure of trying to stamp it out. The greatest service the nudists could do them, perhaps, is to give them something to persecute.

Finally, we have the statement of Dr. Frankwood E. Williams, for fifteen years Medical Director of the Mental Hygiene Association and editor of *Mental Hygiene*. Dr. Williams went deeply into the possible effects of nudist practices on sex life. The crux of the matter, as he saw it, is not whether nudity will lead to license but whether it will impair or contribute to a normal, healthy, sex interest. If it impairs sex interest, of course, nudism would be a calamity; if it does not, the approval of nudism depends on how the nudists propose to treat that instinct. Should the nudists seek to repress it, they might do as much damage as those who try to discipline it by concealing veils. Dr. Williams's statement was as follows:

"That it should be possible for mentally healthy individuals, that is, individuals capable of reacting to situations on an adult rather than an infantile level, to go about nude without embarrassment, should they find occasion for doing so, would seem to need no argument. How could it be otherwise? What would there be to be embarrassed about? To obtain the physiological advantages of exposing the body to air and sun and the freedom of body movement in exercise and play may well be such an occasion. But where are such mentally healthy individuals to be found? From what we know of the rearing of the present-day adult there can't be many, and evidence that abounds on every hand in our social life indicates that there aren't many. Still there may be some—perhaps more than we think.

"However, just to strip off one's clothing does not prove that one is healthy minded. In an effort thus to lift one's self by one's bootstraps one may be reacting on a level just as infantile as the lady whose collar reaches her chin. These attitudes can be merely opposite expressions of the same thing; examples of such opposite expression are to be found readily in all fields of human behaviour. One cannot change one's psychological clothing as readily as one can change one's physical clothing. An attitude of being bold and brave may successfully cover but it does not change an individual's fundamental fear situation; an attitude of cocky superiority may cover but it does not change the fundamental feeling of inferiority; a marriage may cover but does not change a homosexual situation. This is not a particularly important point so

[240]

far as nudism is concerned, but it needs stating if for no other reason than to keep thinking straight. It would be foolish to demand at this time that no social movement should be initiated except on a guaranteed 'adult' basis. Social movements never have been and will not be for many generations.

"But whether or not the prude and the nudist may be the same under their psychological skins, there can be no hesitation in choice between them. The healthful solution of the problem of sex will eventually be found in the direction in which the nudist is going so that, regardless of the unconscious motives that may be activating him (and one does not question his conscious motives), his activity can be approved over that of his antagonist. Whatever will diminish the glamour and fascinating mystery with which we have come to cloak sex—to the point where it is frequently an obsession—is likely to be a social gain.

"One is less concerned with this point, however, than with another. In an effort to allay the fears of those who are shocked by anything sexual, nudists have taken great pains to show that nudity is not sexually stimulating, and that a nudist camp or gymnasium is just as 'pure' as a village church. If this is true—and, of course, we are assuming that the village church is as 'pure' as it assumes—then, it seems to me, this may be the most damaging evidence against nudism as a group movement.

"That nudity, in itself, is not sexually stimulating can be accepted; that individuals engaged in vigorous games or exercises are not preoccupied with sex can also be accepted. But not all time is so engaged. In the resting periods, the leisure hours, in the locker rooms, in the showers, there must be contacts that should be stimulating to mentally and physically healthy adolescents and young adults. If it is to be asserted that this is the case, that it is recognized and is openly discussed in an effort to find a satisfactory solution for such problems as it presents, then, that is one thing. If it is to be asserted

[241]

that this is not the case, then the questions must be raised: Have we to do here with a special group, homosexually determined? or, in the case of the young, what repressions, serious for the further healthful development of the individual, are taking place as a result of the group attitude?

"It would be difficult to conceive of any definition of health that would not include 'capable of being sexually stimulated under certain conditions by an individual of the opposite sex'; and it is difficult to see how these conditions can fail to be present in nudist groups. Among healthy people nudism should increase sexual appetite as it, no doubt, increases appetite for food. Unless a robust sexual appetite is to be considered undesirable, I cannot see this as an argument against nudism. The argument against nudism would be in case individuals were not affected by such conditions, for then one would have to question its social desirability as a movement in the belief that both society and the individual are best served by a healthy heterosexual development of the adolescent. What is to be done with this appetite once it is aroused is another matter, and perhaps it will be at this point that the nudists will have to defend themselves."

Dr. Williams is right in believing that the nudists are capable of sexual stimulation, and also in intimating that the effects on the sexual life are most important in the case of the young and adolescent whose attitudes are still plastic, and whose entire sexual future may be determined by influences at this stage. One has only to observe the young people in nudist groups to realize that there are no grounds for fearing their sexual life will be warped. Sexual attraction operates with them just as it does with any other youngsters, save that it is uncomplicated by a purely physical curiosity. We could cite numerous instances, such as the incipient "affair" between a charming girl of eighteen in an American nudist group and a young man a few years older who came out for a week-end. Although there were other young people of both sexes pres-

ent, they gravitated to each other immediately, went off together to swim or walk, and even when they found themselves
in a group they always remained apart, carrying on their own
private low-voiced conversation. In short, they behaved like
any young couple in a crowd who find themselves drawn to
each other. Whether a real love affair developed, we do not
know, having had only the one week-end in which to observe
it, but the start indicated no lack of sex interest on either
side.

Still more convincing of the effect of nudism on the adolescent were three young American girls, ranging from thirteen
to sixteen years of age, who had been brought up "nudistically" from infancy. Most of the men in the group during the
summer were married men of thirty or more—no doubt antique
and staid in the eyes of the youngsters. At any rate, the latter
displayed no interest in the men except as companions for
games and sports, and in general appeared bored by the company of all the adults save when swimming or a ball game
was in progress. But one week-end an attractive young col-
legian appeared. Instantly the three girls flocked about him
and followed him everywhere like a triple shadow. Whether
or not he joined them in games was a matter of indifference;
they would sit and talk with him by the hour. It was not
merely his youth, as a relief from the maturity of the group,
that attracted them; other girls who had appeared from time
to time exerted no such fascination.

We feel safe in asserting that nudists make no attempt to
control or check natural sex interest. They have reasons to
believe that with healthy minds that takes care of itself. They
know the natural sex instinct will continue to operate unim-
paired and unperverted but believe this, rather than being a
menace requiring control, is both desirable and essential. With
the artificial stimulations of prudery and pornography removed, there is much less danger of excessive and undiscrim-
inating eroticism, which is harmful whether repressed or

indulged. The absence of false excitations gives a chance for the sexual impulse to be selective. Dr. Williams says: "Among healthy people nudism should increase sexual appetite." Nudism does not, however, aggravate it to the point of making it blindly promiscuous; rather, by promoting both mental and physical health, nudism renders the sexual appetite normal, sound, and anything but neurotic.

Taking the psychiatrists as a whole—excepting Dr. Williams and a few others—the most striking feature of their replies, as contrasted with those of the academic psychologists, is a tendency not to withhold judgment for lack of first-hand experience but to view nudism in the light of their knowledge and theories of human behaviour in general. This may mean simply that they are less cautious and more confident of their infallibility, or it may be, as Dr. Barnes believes, that they actually know more about such matters.

᠁᠁᠁᠁᠁᠁᠁᠁᠁᠁᠁᠁᠁᠁᠁᠁᠁᠁᠁᠁᠁᠁᠁᠁᠁᠁᠁᠁

X I

WHAT THE ARTIST AND PHILOSOPHER THINK

THE DOCTORS, THE PSYCHOLOGISTS, THE PSYCHIATRISTS ARE, or should be, the experts on health and morals. But many others are especially qualified to speak on nudism, or various of its phases: the social scientists, the educators, the philosophers—all of those who study man and his nature in relation to his civilization and environment—and even the poets and the artists. Æsthetic objections being the final stand of the anti-nudists, the bulwark behind which retreat the prudish and the prejudiced when they have lost all the battles on other grounds, the poet and the artist, who should be qualified to pronounce on æsthetics if anybody is, might be allowed to have the last word.

The leaders in social thought most directly associated with the problems raised by nudist theory are probably the advocates of sane sex education, not all of whom are psychiatrists or physicians. The names of Mary Ware Dennett and Margaret Sanger inevitably occur in this connection. What they think of nudism we believed might matter. Mrs. Sanger declined to express an opinion on the ground that she had not given it "sufficient thought," though she added: "I have some knowledge of the benefits of nudity regarding children, but none to adults." Mrs. Dennett, writing on "Sex Enlightenment

[245]

for Civilized Youth" in the symposium, *Sex in Civilization,* as early as 1929 had seemed to hint at the coming of nudism, when she said: "They [the enlightened young people] will come to see the wide difference between the attitude of the girl who goes hipping along the street with her coat held tightly around the most purposefully jiggling part of her anatomy, and the open-air girl who plays with gaiety and bare-legged freedom in her swimming suit, or, presently, without it." In 1931, in her book, *The Sex Education of Children,* she discussed at length, in the chapter entitled "Privacy instead of Modesty," the subject of nakedness and modesty as related to sex education. She said at the start:

"The onset of popular education in bodily hygiene, the lessening—and ever lessening—of the number and bulk of garments, the prodigious interest in athletics, the delight in rhythmics, the furore for sunbaths, the nudity cult in Europe —all these have contributed toward the shelving of the old idea of modesty. Along with this development the newer ideals in sex education have appeared. . . . The frank recognition of the human body is being heralded in all directions.

"This change is altogether beneficial, except for the uncomfortable hangover of old concepts, which taints the new freedom in many instances, so that instead of the old-fashioned perverted sex-conscious modesty we have an equally bad perverted sex-conscious exhibitionism. Unless the real point of view can change along with the dropping of our clothes we are not much better off—except that our bodies get a needed airing." Modesty in its real—not the Victorian—sense, she pointed out, "can be completely nude and exhibitionism completely clothed, and yet neither be mistaken for the other by any normally developed person. It is only the obscene type of mind which tries to measure decency by the amount of clothing worn or by what is seen and what left unseen. The unobscene mind knows that such measures are meaningless, except as the making of them is a gauge of the point of view

[246]

of those who insist upon the measuring."

We sent Mrs. Dennett a questionnaire similar to the one used for the psychologists. She answered that she saw advantages, and no objections to nudity, and referred us to the chapter just cited from *The Sex Education of Children.* "You will see," she explained, "that my main emphasis is that one must *feel* right before nudity serves a good purpose. However, discussion tends to develop the right kind of feeling among many people, so here's to it, even if it is sure to carry along with it much of the undesirable atmosphere which envelops a good deal of the talk about sex these days."

In connection with the subject of sex education, it is interesting that when Alice Beal Parsons expressed misgivings as to the effectiveness of our modern strivings, in an article entitled "Should Parents Tell All?" in *Harper's Magazine,* October 1931, she did not question the advisability of a frank attitude toward the human body. Of her hypothetical mother's doubts concerning the daughter's enlightenment, she stated: "The mother hoped, too, that she would be unashamed, sufficiently accustomed to the sight of the human body without its fig-leaf that it would hold for her neither dismay nor shamefaced allurements, able to accept her own impulses as good and desirable, and to come to conclusions with life. Ideals and innocence of shame, however, cannot be imparted in last minute conversation." (Which is, of course, exactly the advantage that nudism has over formal instruction.)

On the questions arising from the subject of going naked, the social scientists can many of them speak with authority, but none with more authority than the anthropologists in general and Robert Briffault in particular. Dr. Briffault's replies as a medical man to the queries regarding the healthfulness of nudity were quoted among those of the physicians. For his views on the relationship of nakedness to sexual morality, he referred us to the chapter on "Modesty" in the third volume of his monumental work, *The Mothers.*

"It may be doubted," Dr. Briffault there declared, "whether the taboos of modesty have at any stage of culture had a restraining or regulative effect upon sexual relations. Ethnological and social history afford no indications that the development of clothing and modesty has at any time promoted sexual morality. . . . Pruriency and obscenity depend, like modesty, upon the breach of taboos and not upon natural sexual values. It is in the violation of the taboo that they find satisfaction. Where no taboo exists, lubricity is devoid of scope and has no existence." He specifically stated what the effect of general nudity would be if introduced into our civilization: "There can be no doubt that if complete nudity were once more to become general, it would, in spite of the traditional sentiments of the millenniums, cease after a brief while to produce either sentiments of offended pudicity or of stimulated lubricity. No feminine attire that has been devised is sexually less stimulating than complete unaffected nakedness, provided no contrast is suggested with the clothed figure."

On the questionnaire he stated, respecting advantages: "Every advantage ultimately, with the transient disadvantages attending any revolution." And as to objections, he said: "None, unless it be lowered sexual stimulation and excessive chastity." As a supplementary statement, he contributed the following: "I cannot, of course, see that those who regard the wearing of clothes as a moral obligation have a leg to stand on. Clothes are a matter of comfort and convenience. To dress for a swim or a game of tennis is as uncomfortable as to strip for a cocktail party. Both practices should be discouraged. Clothes are a source of irritation to the skin and to the sexual appetites. Occasional nudism would go a long way towards abolishing eczema and voyeurism. The question might, of course, be raised whether sex would continue to be delectable if it ceased to be nasty.

"The trouble with nudism is much the same as with disarmament. Is it much good unless everybody does it? Partial nudism

[248]

is a more effective sexual irritant than either complete clothing or complete nudity. So that the adoption of nudism by a secret, esoteric, and reprobated private society while people are clapped into jail for bathing without trunks is a different proposition from the abolition of superstitious fig-leaves. The women of ten years ago did more, it seems to me, towards that sacred cause than the nudists can do, and it is deplorable that the depression has, through the machinations of the couturiers, caused skirts to reach a new low level. Yet there can be no doubt that nudism is gradually creeping upon us. Children are brought up to it. Its future is assured. But it should, I think, be promoted publicly, not esoterically. The police is, after all, the sole bulwark against commonsense nudism. It should be fought for on the stage and on the beach, not in nudist reservations."

The fears of excessive chastity in a naked world have been so frequently discussed that no further reassurance can be added here except the categorical declaration that sex impulses are strong enough for sex to remain delectable even when it ceases to be nasty.

We also obtained samples of the views of a few social scientists and philosophers who, though less learned than Robert Briffault in the cultural history of nakedness, have evaluated many phases of our social order, and who have not hesitated to follow original and daring lines of thought. Professor John Dewey was one of those whose opinion we sought, but he replied that he was "not acquainted enough with the movement to have any valuable ideas to give," and some of the others declined on similar grounds.

Dr. Harry Elmer Barnes, formerly professor of historical sociology at Smith College and most famous perhaps for his *Genesis of the World War*, replied briefly but satisfactorily from the nudist point of view. "It [nudity] should promote a saner moral outlook," he asserted, "and for suitable persons health as well. I see no objections. I am more for sane clothing than for nudity, but am all for freedom for the nudists. If we advocate full nudity we may get as far as coatless men in summer at any rate." To the specific question of objections, he replied: "None, provided medical examination is given to those whose health may be imperilled by too sharp a transition."

V. F. Calverton, founder of the *Modern Quarterly*, who has written and lectured much on social subjects, likewise took a liberal if not ardently pro-nudist stand. He wrote as follows: "I believe that nudism would be excellent for outdoor recreation both from the point of view of health and æsthetics. I think that the practice of nudism by both sexes would certainly prove advantageous in the long run, especially since it would make people take that pride in their bodies which today they hesitate to do. No objection to nudism whatever except that it is not nearly so significant in my opinion as many nudists imagine. Quite obviously climatic factors would prevent nudism from being practised on a wide-spread scale in many places during many times of the year. I should not be interested in a nudist movement *per se*. What I am interested in is the development of a new social system, in which nudism might easily enough become an accepted practice. In other words, I do not think that nudism is a significant issue although I certainly have no objections to this practice by those who can find in it an element of spiritual profit."

Winifred Raushenbush, sociologist and writer on social subjects, had doubts, not as to the merits of nudism but as to the possibility of its being more than a passing fad in America. Her observations were: "I think that toleration of the right of the individual to go naked is gradually becoming part of the American mores and I believe that the effects of this growing toleration will be highly desirable. I should be willing to predict, however, that if nakedness is taken up as a serious-minded cult in this country, it will die of blight. If it arrives as a fashion, it may or may not survive. Near-nakedness was a phenomenon of the French Revolution, but it did not endure. Essentially nakedness runs counter to the grain of our acquisitive keeping-up-with-the-Joneses society. Not because they want to always, but because they must, Americans lavish much creative energy on building up a façade personality, consisting of a line, a gesture, a manner, clothes, a car, and what have you. To appear naked physically would be to appear without this cherished façade.

"There are indications that nakedness as a fashion may be imminent. Brassière, shorts, and a bolero were a high style sport fashion for women in 1930. The December 1931 *Harper's Bazaar* thinks we are stupid not to go 'a little Bolshevik'—without a stitch, my dear—in the summer! If nakedness arrives as a fashion, and if it survives, it will probably be practised by the younger and handsomer members of the upper middle-class—the medium style group—and by liberal and radical members of the lower middle-class. The urban poor will not be able, for the most part, to afford this seemingly inexpensive pleasure, and the high style group will quickly find other amusements."

On the other hand, a social scientist in a Western university, who preferred to be unnamed, felt misgivings regarding the desirability of the practice itself. Although he was not sure what its social implications would be, he feared that nudism might merely substitute new class distinctions for those of dress. He said concerning possible advantages: "I am not convinced that there are sound reasons for mixing the sexes, adult, entirely naked. The key to what resistance I feel is æsthetic, I think. Bodily symmetry would be as poor a basis for social classification as inherited wealth or prestige. There are obvious advantages in debunking our present codes, *provided* we can replace them with better." To the question of objections, he replied: "Yes, æsthetic and practical. Most people are physically unattractive, through no fault of their own. It is their right to exercise intellectual and æsthetic judgment in overcoming their handicaps. Because of climate, periods of physiological inopportunity, etc., nudity would not achieve the desired results." In a postscript he further explained his attitude: "I am really not very familiar with the movement. Of course the artificiality of line and colour in our present society comes to the aid of the rich and vulgar, able to hire an æsthetic talent they do not themselves possess. Any revolution, to do much good, must be thorough. I'm not sure about the general social implications of this one. For the young, before puberty, of course, nudity and thorough-going education are always advisable, to break up the tendency to prudery and filth. Still, there is a problem where adults are prudes and wear clothes."

Arthur Garfield Hays is not only famous as a lawyer but as a liberal and champion of minority causes; it is not inconsistent that he should be interested in the subject of nudism. Of the practice he has written as follows: "A few years ago I spent some weeks in the southern part of Russia, and there observed and engaged in what I called co-educational bathing. At first it was exciting and intriguing. I was much impressed by the fact that within a few weeks even the unexperienced could look at nude women with an eye to beauty and without any gross emotional upset. This is an illustration, if any were needed, that curiosity has considerable to do with pornography; that if the matter of sexual difference were the subject of casual observation, neither sex would be aroused by the view of the other. There is no reason why the hidden parts of the body should have a greater effect than the observation of the face. All one need do to arouse sexual curiosity is to hide any part of the body. If we want to avoid this, we should develop a race of people who find nothing startling in nudity. Thus I think the nudist movement is a good thing."

Professor Harry A. Overstreet, of the philosophy department of the College of the City of New York, whose studies in human behaviour are well known, was also consulted. Like the academic psychologists, he was hesitant about giving a verdict without more information but was unopposed to nudist experiments. He explained his stand thus: "I should hate to class myself among the prudes, but having had no personal contact with the nudist movement, I am unable to speak as a scientist. I hate to give opinions about a matter with which I have had no direct contact. My guess is that the increasing departure from the old habit of concealing the body is a thoroughly wholesome one. Whether this wholesomeness would continue in direct proportion to the exposure of the body, I do not know. It may be that there are limits beyond which we may not go without a distinctly sensory and spiritual loss. I should myself welcome experiments in nudism. Until we make experiments, our opinions are only guesses. I am sorry not to be able to make my statements any more specific than the foregoing. But I think that you will understand that my hesitation rises out of scientific caution. It is not that I am afraid of nudism, but I am very much afraid of venturing an opinion upon a matter that I really know nothing about."

The case of another professor of philosophy in an Eastern college, who prefers not to be identified, was quite different in that he had on one occasion actually participated in nudist activities in Germany. Particularly striking, in view of the scepticism of many of the theorists, are his remarks on the ease with which the taboo on nakedness is broken by normal people, and his description of the types of persons to be found among the nudists. He wrote of his own experience as follows:

"I suppose that everyone who has read about nudism without having had any practical experience with it in large groups of mixed company has wondered whether there might not be a vast and disconcerting difference between theoretical discussion and practical trial. Such apprehensions can hardly be overcome by argument—that is, by more theoretical discussion. The genuinely convincing case for nudism consists not of prattle about 'gymnosophistics' and such, but of the personal testimonies of not-too-gullible observers to the effect that it really works. The attitude of a great many can be summed up in the query of a friend of mine who had heard that I had been 'among the nudists': 'Do you mean to tell me that a lot of *really nice* people were there without any clothes?'

"The answer, in similar nutshell form, is 'Yes.' Really nice people seem quite capable, at least in certain parts of Europe, of enjoying life together without clothes when clothes would be nuisances, and of remaining really nice. The rest of what I have to say is merely by way of descriptive elaboration of that proposition.

"I have not observed the practice of nudism out-of-doors, but it was my privilege this summer to attend an indoor meeting of the Berlin branch of the *Reichsbund für Freikörperkultur* at the famous Wellenbad in Luna Park. This huge swimming pool with artificial waves is engaged each Saturday morning and Monday evening by the above nudist society, which has branches in nearly a dozen cities. At these times the whole building is reserved for the exclusive use of the members, who are selected with great care. Visitors are admitted only through the recommendation of a member, and very few Americans have visited this particular organization.

"One enters the men's dressing room as usual, the sexes being strictly separated, and after disrobing simply omits the hiring of the usual bathing costume. After a shower, one goes upstairs to the immense hall containing the pool, and surrounded by a large balcony with ample room for games and exercises. Fully a hundred persons of both sexes and all ages were engaged in vigorous gymnastics, led by a man on a large table in the centre of the rear balcony, who pounded a sort of drum in order to beat time for the various setting-up drills. There was nothing soft or easy about the exercises. They were done with a German thoroughness and seriousness, and yet seemed also to be enjoyed by everyone.

"When the community drill was over, the majority of the crowd came down and went in the water, especially during

[254]

the artificial-wave periods (the pool is quiet for fifteen minutes, and then there are fifteen minutes of quite boisterous waves). Those who were not swimming either sat about and chatted or played some of the games, ping-pong, quoits, and so on, available on the balcony. A number kept on with sundry gymnastic 'stunts' and exercises on the mats and apparatus.

"Anyone looking for signs of an orgy or a Folies Bergère tableau would certainly have been abysmally disappointed. Utter decorum prevailed. Only the convention of being clothed had changed; everything else seemed perfectly normal. The atmosphere was that of a gymnasium filled with congenial people interested in physical development and eager to have a swim without the necessity of dragging a bathing suit along through the water after them. Nakedness was absolutely taken for granted. There was not a trace in anyone's demeanour (and a foreigner would be the first to be conscious of it) that it was in any way a matter for curiosity.

"My experience was, then, almost painfully similar to those of others who have visited nudist gatherings. That is to say, it was surprising how easily one could get into the swing of things, and how soon one adopted the new attitude. Given a group of reasonably clean-minded people, the taboo can be broken without any disastrous consequences and with a great many benefits. It makes most sports and games more enjoyable, and creates a healthier attitude toward the human body all around. One does not have to make a principle, a theory, or a crusade out of it just because one sees that it adds to the joy of life on appropriate occasions.

"Two more notations: I was more or less on the look-out for the 'crank' type of nudist during my Berlin visit, and I am happy to say that I saw very few who seemed to be gritting their teeth and defying the world and going clothesless on principle. Most of the nudists I met seemed admirably balanced folk, most of them highly intelligent, and nearly all of them sharing the new German enthusiasm for physical development. Young married couples, I should say, formed the majority of the group. They were by no means all of one type, either grave or gay; both were represented. Neither are nudist groups made up exclusively of those whose bodies are well-formed and pleasing, or the opposite. While most them were, as one would expect, above the average in physical develop-ment, I saw no signs of acute exhibitionism among their number. Certainly, on the other hand, they were not, as they have sometimes been represented, a lot of stodgy and obese individuals.

"Nudism works, and works well. It can be practised with-out fanaticism, and is actually the accepted thing in circles made up of people who are not freaks, who we like to think are normal 'just like ourselves.' Of course it can be made into a preposterous mumbo-jumbo cult, and otherwise abused. But the burden of proof will eventually rest on those who want everybody, all the time, to wear clothes."

The present writers should like to add that this anonymous philosopher's impatience with those who would make naked-ness a "preposterous mumbo-jumbo cult" strikes a particu-larly sympathetic note!

Most amazing is the warm welcome that has been given nudism by a professor of philosophy in a college in the heart of the fundamentalist Southwest, a man who manages to recon-cile Methodism with political and social liberalism. To identify him would undoubtedly bring disfavour upon him, but of the possibility of nudism in the Southwest he has written thus optimistically: "Our great Southwest has been singled out as a part of the country that may in advance be expected to show itself hostile to pursuit of sun, beauty, purity, health and hap-piness. I want to venture a prediction; however it may be in other parts of our country, in our own Southwest before many years a vigorous movement for enjoying the sun and air un-fettered will appear." This is indeed a consummation devoutly to be wished, if scarcely hoped. A mental and physical airing

[256]

would be all to the good.

The benefit of the opinions of a few other academic men in scattered fields has been given us. The biologist of course has expert testimony to offer since he cannot be uninformed or indifferent to either the physical development of man or his relation to his environment. We present here the views of "A Biological Philosopher in a State University"—incidentally not one of our more radical institutions. It is noteworthy that this man is one of the few who has mentioned the psychic exhilaration of nakedness.

"Fresh air and sunshine are necessary to most forms of life, and human beings are no exception to the rule. The beneficent effects vary directly with the degree of intelligent exposure. Life guards soon acquire a healthy appearance that extends much deeper than their coat of tan. Primitive races generally are healthier than civilized ones, despite their lack of hygienic laws. Considering civilized man's favourable response to air and sunshine, it seems reasonable to assume that these elements may play an important part in the health of the naked savage. This point becomes more poignant when one considers that in most cases where primitive people have been forced to wear clothes, their health has been impaired.

"Civilized man is living in the most artificial environment of any non-parasitic animal. With steam-heated houses, closed cars, fur coats, and other such luxuries, the human body is put at no strain to keep the temperature regulated. As a consequence, man becomes physiologically like a slow-flowing stream meandering through placid meadows. The body needs an invigorating stimulation which will give tone to all of the various systems. Exercise in the fresh air and sunshine does this. Lack of garments affords greater freedom of movement and more exposure to the needed elements, besides producing a rejuvenating psychic effect on the individual. Man has spent most of his existence as an undraped creature, and it is in this condition that he is nearer to his natural environment.

Nudism Comes to America

Contrary to popular opinion, our immediate clothesless ancestors were not conspicuously hairy, and most of the naked tribes of men today are not as hirsute as the white clothes-wearing American. It will be seen then, that neither clothes nor hair are necessary as a protection against moderate climates.

"There are few who would object to nudism on the grounds of health, but many would throw up their hands in holy horror because of the moral effect of such a practice. This is where a better acquaintance is needed with the history of clothes and the morals of naked savages. Hand in hand with clothes for protection have evolved clothes for fascination. Certain parts of the anatomy have been concealed (not always the same parts) by different people in different ages. In time this part of the body becomes taboo and mystery enshrouds it. Human-like (one might even say animal-like) the uninitiated become curious and wish to pry into Pandora's box to see what the secret is. With this comes sin—for it is TABOO. To tread on forbidden ground has ever been sinful.

"There can be no reasonable objections on æsthetic grounds. Associating with various domestic animals as we do, to make such objections would be absurd. Who ever refused to take a drive behind old Dobbin for that reason? To the broad-minded person whose perspective extends beyond the horizon of his own little anthill, complete exposure of the human body during outdoor recreations offers much to be commended and nothing to be condemned. Sanely practised, nudism should produce healthier bodies and cleaner minds."

The connection between physics and nudism is less direct than the relationship between nudism and biology, although it should not be forgotten that Luckiesh, to whom we are indebted for much of the literature on the necessity of light to the human organism, is a physicist. So, this is "the point of view of a professor of physics in a Canadian university":

"There is very little for a physicist, as such, to say on the subject of nudism. He may perhaps be allowed to emphasize the presence of biochemically active radiations at the short wave end of the solar spectrum, and to point out that the still shorter rays, harmful to the eyes, are completely absorbed, mainly by the ozone in the upper atmosphere. The proportion of these desirable ultraviolet rays varies with latitude, with altitude, with the moisture content and the amount of smoke and dust pollution in the atmosphere. Clear skies, and the sun in general higher than thirty degrees above the horizon, are necessary for much benefit to the health from the solar rays alone.

"But these, of course, do not confer the only benefits to be derived from exposure of the whole skin. Moving air is more comfortable than stagnant, and it is obvious that this will be increasingly the case the more of the skin there is in direct contact with the air. It should take women less time than men to get over the initial fear of chilliness, since men have so much more clothing to remove! These effects and the absence of clothing constraints give an added joy to rhythmic movement and physical exertion. Anything that can give this in these days of multiplying sedentary and indoor occupations should receive every encouragement.

"If permitted to add my opinions as a person (and I am afraid I have not kept strictly to my own branch of science in the above paragraphs), I should like to start by saying that they, in turn, are tinged with the experimental. Our civilization teaches us many new and fine things, but it neither teaches nor encourages relaxation. Any aid in the development of the ability to relax more completely is therefore valuable, and it is my experience that nakedness, either indoors or out, is a great help. In quiet and security the mind and body relax together when one is taking a sunbath. Only by nudity can the full enjoyment of summer outdoor life be attained. So far it has been my nearest approach to 'Nirvana.'

"From the psychological point of view, experience teaches the observant that attention is always directed towards the unusual and the half-hidden. A bathing suit among nudists is as much an object of remark as is its lack among ordinary bathers. Wholesomeness of mind on sex questions naturally follows the theory and practice of nudism—and I speak here from eight years' experience as a theoretical and (whenever possible) practical nudist.

"The movement towards having one's most permanent costume recognized as equal among a number of costumes suitable for different occasions will have all the inertia of the conservative mind to contend with, and more. New ideas, or even the resurrection of old ones, are always a great shock to the unthinking and unenquiring majority. Prejudices are difficult to overcome, but perhaps not more difficult than the inability to recognize, or the unwillingness to admit, the soundness of reasoned arguments. We on this continent have not Germany's advantage of an enlightened government. We are in the power of the most prejudiced classes. We shall have business and advertising to fight, to say nothing of the Church, which will certainly follow the past in being blind to new enlightenment and real opportunities for service. With sufficient numbers, or financial support, we can only attempt to enjoy the air and sun in reasonably remote localities, or entrenched behind the laws of 'PRIVATE PROPERTY KEEP OFF!' "

While not a scientist, the Librarian of Princeton University, James Thayer Gerould, is amply qualified to speak as a student of both life and letters. This brief statement from him may be considered as representing the view of the tolerant and enlightened who see in nudism a possible weapon against pruriency:

"The philosophy and practice of nudism, as described in your book, seem to me to be sound both on hygienic and on moral grounds. Of the first, I speak from experience; of the second, from analogy. We have progressed a long way, during the last twenty years, from the ascetic conception of the human body; but my generation still finds it difficult completely to break with a tradition which, for hundreds of years, has sought to degrade and defile one of the most beautiful of human instincts. There is an ever increasing revolt against it. We are cleansing our minds and gaining in decency. Pruriency is the child of concealment. An exposure of the body which a few years ago would have been scandalous is today unremarked, with moral and physical results of great value. I am quite ready to accept the testimony of those who, like yourself, have practised it, that complete nudity very soon becomes as commonplace as the lesser exposure on the beach, the athletic field, and in the ball-room."

Having left the domain of science altogether, we ventured further into that of literature and sounded out a few writers noted for their social consciousness, those who, without being academic sociologists, have devoted themselves to observing, recording, and judging the larger social implications of our civilization. The opinions of such men of letters, who have frequently stepped into the arena to battle for social justice, would be more pertinent than those of the dwellers in ivory towers in the more rarefied atmosphere of pure literature. The name of Upton Sinclair is doubtless the one that would occur first. His replies to the questionnaire were the most laconic possible—"Yes," to all questions of benefits or advantages, and "None" to that of objections. But they left no doubt as to his stand, and he added: "I have been a sun-cure enthusiast all my life, but I have not had much time to practise it." Probably the name of Theodore Dreiser is the one that would occur next, but, fearing he would be unable to take his mind off Communism long enough to consider our questions, we did not approach him.

We did approach Floyd Dell. In an extended statement he developed numerous objections similar to those of the psychiatrists—his Freudianism no doubt being responsible—but some of them were entirely new, at least in their definiteness. His complete statement was this:

"My views are sympathetic but critical. I despise the conventional adult fear and hatred of nudity. I believe that childhood and adult (but not adolescent) nudity does have some of the values attached to it by the nude cultists. At the same time, these values seem to me to be fundamentally narcissistic, and to make a cult of nudity seems to me to be a somewhat neurotic thing to do. As between the widespread neurotic hatred and fear of nudity, and the neurotic cultivation of nudity, my sympathies are with the cultists—who are, in comparison, harmless. Perhaps it requires exaggeration to redress the balance.

"Most of the advantages lie in the getting rid of the contrary attitudes of fear and hatred of nudity. That is a positive gain. Beyond that, the advantages seem to me to be wildly though sincerely exaggerated. And some of its alleged advantages are, in adolescence, grave disadvantages. Its advantages, when real, are largely psychotherapeutic, in giving narcissism some socially (group) approved indulgence. These narcissistic values account for the deeply religious satisfactions which accompany the practice.

"In adolescence, boys need at least a loincloth, if not trousers, to conceal their special physical response to the attractions of the other sex. To deny them that is to inflict upon them a severer emotional discipline than even our present conventions demand. The worst of it is that they can, under group influence, repress their sexual feeling to the point of conscious unawareness of the sexual attractions of girls. This does not help them to grow up; it keeps them sexually infantile. The nude cultists who harp upon its moral advantages refer to this result. I disapprove of these results. The morality of the nudists is in this respect more puritanical than that of conventional people. In adolescence the practice of social nudity interferes with normal psychosexual development by requiring too much sexual repression in boys. It is like the Victorian ideal of 'treating all girls as if they were your mother or sisters.' As for girls, it seems to me that other psychological reasons connected with the physical developments of puberty attach ambivalent emotional values to the genital zone, and that genital clothing fulfils an adolescent psychosexual need for girls as well as boys. Genital shyness seems to be an adolescent fact, and one that should not be socially overridden. We do not, or should not, wish to prolong artificially the sexual indifference of childhood. But why not page Mr. Freud, and ask him what he thinks?"

It will be observed that Floyd Dell fears, even more than did Dr. Frankwood E. Williams, the sexual consequences to adolescents. The discussion of this matter in the preceding chapter may serve as a partial answer. We might add, however, that in our observations of many adolescent girls brought up as nudists, both in America and Germany, we have seen no sign of acute "genital shyness." It is quite true that a girl at this stage of development and unaccustomed to the nakedness of people of all ages probably would suffer from such shyness if abruptly introduced into a mixed nudist group for the first time. But it is the concealment of clothing, the unfamiliarity of the physical development in others, that makes for much, if not most, of the physical self-consciousness of puberty. Even family nudity may fail to abolish this self-consciousness if there are no other adolescent girls in the family; it is the limitations of the modern family—which may not contain even adults of both sexes—that often account for the failure of family nakedness to achieve the results of general nudism. In the case of adolescent boys, though we have had fewer opportunities for first-hand observation, we incline to similar conclusions. Much of the extreme sex-consciousness during puberty is wanting in boys who have been accustomed to mixed nudity all their lives. This does not in the least prevent a normal sex interest developing at this time, but when developed it does not take the exaggerated forms necessitating severe emotional discipline.

To Waldo Frank, the matter was much simpler. He wrote: "I'm not so sure about the æsthetic enjoyment, since the bodies of most modern people over *aet.* 25 are not much to look at; but I am sure there would be moral benefits—and benefits of health, too. As a lesson in moral honesty, nudism appeals to me most strongly. As a help in facing reality—to seeing onself and others unmasked, I should think the practice of nudity would be most efficacious. I can see no objections whatever."

Poultney Bigelow, that grand old historian, traveller, and pagan, was one of the first to greet nudism warmly. "Modesty," he has said, "begins when the last rag has left the body." As to the practice, he declared: "I have been 'nudisticating' for three quarters of a century and mean to keep it up in the Elysian Fields."

T. Swann Harding, who in his *Fads, Frauds and Physicians* and *The Degradation of Science* has charged at physicians and other scientists with such zest, was less certain. Expressing, as he said, mere "opinions and these are writ upon water," he stated: "I have made no systematic study of the matter and therefore cannot hold a belief. Possibly it would be beneficial; possibly not. I have no intellectual nor emotional objections. I have been nude in bathing with a considerable group of both sexes. My wife altogether lacks any emotional reluctance about appearing nude among intelligent people. I can claim no benefits, moral nor otherwise. Having never had any inhibitions on the subject it was just one of those things—just another thing I did. I do feel that a great deal of bunk is claimed for the benefits of nudity, just as those who try to divorce sex from physiology preach a lot of heavenly nonsense about its sublime spiritual character.

"I rather think it would be a social help if people generally were intelligent enough to practise nudity as indicated. But I also think this would take people of sufficient intellectual maturity to understand and appreciate the wonder and the grandeur of a book like Lawrence's *Lady Chatterly's Lover.*

What the Artist and Philosopher Think

How many are there who can do that? Who could even learn to do it? The chances are the cult would become evangelical and other-worldly, or that it would degenerate into something indulged in to get a 'kick.' I'm sorry to say that I have never given a damn for public opinion; that explains my social ineligibility. I can think of no possible objection—not even the legal—for people with discretion, I find, do as they please regardless. Twenty years ago under puritanism I found groups that did precisely as they pleased regardless of conventions and legalities. I believe in repressive laws because I believe the intelligent, the really intelligent, are sufficiently shrewd to do as they wish regardless. I think you will find this philosophy of the Greek Sophists not a bad thing."

We trust that Mr. Harding is wrong in one thing—that is, the chances of nudism becoming "evangelical and other-worldly." We have no fears at all that it might "degenerate into something indulged in for a 'kick' "—the kick that the lascivious expect being so disappointingly absent.

When it came to the joys of nakedness and, as it were, the pagan point of view, we felt that the poets were peculiarly fitted to speak. We found the delights of nudity given especially vital expression in the poem "Down With Clothes!" in the volume *Pregnant Woman in a Lean Age*, by Ralph Cheyney, co-editor with Lucia Trent of *Poetry World*.

Down With Clothes!

The world is too full of clothes.
A little, spanked girl is punished
By being made to stand in a closet
    crammed with clothes.
She wants to run out of doors without
    any clothes on at all.
She wants to feel the good, moist earth
    soft to her pattering feet.
She wants the green, lush grass to
    tickle her toes.

[265]

Nudism Comes to America

She wants the rain to stroke her back
    and her legs
With its long, cool, exciting fingers.
But she must stand in the closet and
    grow up
Suffocated by clothes.

The world is entirely too full of clothes.
The horizon is a clothes-line strung
    across the sky.
Great clouds of clothes between man and
    the sun.
Cities are clothes between man and the
    earth—
History yesterday's clothes, progress
    tomorrow's.
The world a clothes-closet.

Come, let us take off our clothes!
Let us begin, you and I!
You drop your dress,
One cloud the less!
Your petticoat descends.
We forget what fate portends.
Life makes amends.
Your clothing ripples down in haste.
Twin pillars light the desert waste.
So little yet revealed—
And yet the mind is healed!

.   .   .   .

"Truth is a nudist," Mr. Cheyney has said, and he began his statement of opinion regarding nudism with the fable: " 'Dear Mr. Whistler, don't you think that picture's indecent?' a lady is said to have asked of the master of that invaluable art of making enemies and masterpieces, to which he answered: 'No, madam, but your question is.' " Mr. Cheyney's views, eminently sane and felicitously expressed, were as follows:

"It is not those who advocate nudism who are indecent but those who oppose it. When my mother went bathing, she followed the opposite of the nursery rhyme, 'Hang your clothes on a hickory limb, but don't go near the water.' She wore stockings, gloves, skirts, and by sheer necessity bathed, not swam. Now that women wear one-piece swimming suits and very little of them, beach morale is no lower than it was in my mother's squeamish day. If self-reliance be a virtue for women as well as men, morals are higher today as well as skirts.

"Would I be favourable to the establishment of nudist camps in the United States similar to those now being conducted abroad? Emphatically, YES—and, were I not opposed to prohibition, I would like to see occasional participation in them a social if not a legal compulsion. Even if it were only for the sake of making people pay a little more attention to their own physiques—for to see the skinny and the pot-bellied, the pasty and the others made in 'His image,' but self-contorted to look like the devil, would be no æsthetic delight! At least, we should be good animals as the first step to becoming somewhat more.

"In my boyhood days there was a stump which when clothed in dusk became a bear that I feared. Not until we grow up enough to view each other and ourselves in the nude, revealed in the white light of truth, will we learn what we should fear and what we should foster.

"The frosted glass and furtive atmosphere were the worst thing about the saloon. Drinking *en famille* on European sidewalks with the pastor stopping at one's table for a sip seldom leads to drunkenness though it does foster what seems to be even more offensive to the Blue-noses: the joy of life. Defying Bluebeards and blue laws, let us sometimes take the skeleton out of the closet and the body out-of-doors and out of clothes."

A distinguished American poet of the older generation who asked that his name be not used—"My views are too unformed," he said, "for me to want to publish them"—has given us an intimate document of his own feelings toward nudism. If "unformed," it is revealing, frank, and thoughtful. What he wrote was this:

"I am unable to generalize about nudism. I know that I enjoy it in certain company—and that with certain other groups I could not bring myself to take my clothes off. I think it absurd for people to pretend that there is not a certain mild excitement involved. For me, it is about the same degree as seeing a very pretty girl in a scant bathing suit, or a 'daring' evening gown. Perhaps slightly less.

"I imagine that if boys and girls at summer camps were brought up to swim together naked, they would become perfectly accustomed to it when they grew up. But the poor little girl with flat breasts, and the very skinny boy, might suffer terribly from this enforced disclosure of their defects. I personally have never felt that playing around naked with a girl had the least tendency to lead me to make 'improper advances' to her. Perhaps it has the opposite effect—in that it satisfies a certain curiosity which would otherwise remain as a provocative itch.

"When you say 'pagan' you have about expressed the feeling I have for nudism. I myself enormously enjoy being on a picnic, or at a country house, with a few friends, and having everybody use swimming as an excuse for taking their clothes off. I should hesitate to disguise my perfectly frank pleasure with any such solemn terms as are used by some of the advocates of nudism. I very simply and straightforwardly enjoy seeing pretty girls running around naked; and though my enjoyment is not exactly a lustful one, it certainly is not a purely intellectual one. I just think that they are so damn cute!—and I also like the lack of prudery that enables them to do it so freely. There are two great objections to nudism. One is that persons who feel at all shy are in a very painful position when their companions suggest such a party. The other is that only young bodies are fit to look at."

What the Artist and Philosopher Think

While we did not consult William Ellery Leonard as to what he thought of nudism, his defence last summer in the Madison, Wisconsin, papers of men bathing in Lake Mendota clad only in trunks indicated that he believes decency is not to be gauged by the number of inches of clothing. The author of *Two Lives* termed the ruling against trunks "prurient meddlesomeness."

There was another interesting phase of this bathing suit war at the University of Wisconsin. The University had no rules for lake costumes, but the Dean of Men called on the city police to enforce the city ordinance (prescribing that bathers "shall be clad from the neck to the knees") on the complaint of girl students who were distressed by the sight of the shirtless men. When the Dean and the officials applying the ordinance found themselves in the midst of an uproar, and the words "morality" and "prurience" began to fly, their tactics were those of nine out of ten opponents of nudism. The request for complete suits, it was explained, was "for æsthetic reasons alone," and the Dean was quoted as stating: "I did not say it was immoral, or bad morals. I regard it purely as a question of taste."

It is time for an expert opinion on the æsthetics of nakedness. Standards of beauty, even of concrete visual forms, are of course subjective and greatly dependent on the habits and emotional bias of the possessor. But since it is the artist, who not only thinks and works in terms of visual beauty but studies the naked human form more carefully than anyone except the physiologist (who does not pretend to study it from the standpoint of beauty), the artist might possibly be better qualified than a Dean to say whether nakedness is æsthetically objectionable. So the last word in the conflict of American "expert" opinion, we have given to Roi Partridge, the American etcher.

"It has not seemed easy to explain why the artist approves of the unclothed body," Mr. Partridge declared in making his statement, "any more than it would be easy to explain why I should eat breakfast tomorrow morning. It is perfectly obvious to me that I should eat breakfast tomorrow morning, and perfectly obvious to me that to remove clothes is desirable æsthetically. If anyone questioned either, I daresay my first impulse would be to grow red in the face and sputter—which is much easier than being logical about it." His statement—which we hope will give the æsthetes food for thought—was this:

"To the artist the usual taboo and objections regarding the unclothed human body, if not incomprehensible, are at least ridiculous. Accustomed to using the nude as material for the exercise of his talents, he discovers early in his career, and he has the best opportunities to observe continually, that the conventional attitude toward exposing all of the body is not well taken. He finds that the body unclothed is not as seductive as the body clothed. He notes among his fellow workers, as among the models themselves, a matter-of-factness with respect to their occupation. He hears the oft spoken opinion that, under civilized conditions, the nude figure is not good looking, yet when he desires to create something exceptionally beautiful, he turns inevitably to the unclothed human body.

"Is not the nudist an individual, having disassociated in his mind all relationship of nakedness with evil, who desires to remove his clothes whenever it is a pleasure to do so or an advantage to health? To this attitude the artist will bring another —that of desiring to see clothes removed in whole or in part whenever this contributes to beauty. The artist also, in his inevitable liberalism with respect to the nude and his small respect for the proscriptions of religion or custom, will see no end of illogical absurdities in our present racial habits. The care with which a civilized woman covers the lower part of her breasts, while freely and even proudly exposing the upper part, seems to him quite as unnecessary and just about as logical as the care with which an orthodox Mohammedan woman covers her face. The civilized woman covers her breasts because they are secondary sex evidences, and sex to our twisted minds is a thing to be ashamed of. But so is the face evidence of sex; so are the eyes and lips that we so wantonly exhibit. The prohibitions of the censor, who permits moving pictures of the semi-nude savage woman but forbids the so-called civilized woman to be shown that way, will be derided by the artist, while he will rejoice over the youth of our age who are insisting upon less and less clothing at the beach, at the dance, and even on the street.

"A peculiarity of the artist's attitude has been his insistence upon nudity from early times to the present day; not only during periods of history when social customs have been favourable to it, as in ancient Greece, but also through the stuffy Victorian era, the era of voluminous bathing suits and still more voluminous moral proscriptions, when to expose the body was to become a social outcast. His insistence, through that inhibited age, upon the inherent and basic beauty of the unclothed body was one of the few contemporary evidences of an almost throttled sanity. In this way he has contributed to the breaking down of puritanic conceptions associating evil with nudity, and thus has been one of the most effective forces in the present day movement toward making nudity respectable."

XII

WHAT THE LAW SAYS

Iⁿ SPITE OF THE AMERICAN REPUTATION FOR LAWBREAK-
ing, most nudists in this country are anxious to know how the
law looks on their practice. Americans do not object to paying
fines now and then for violations that have good social standing—such as speeding or parking by a fire plug—but the respectability of nakedness is not yet sufficient to make an arrest for it seem trivial. The nudist who is concerned about his
reputation has a horror of being brought to court at all for
anything as unsavoury as "indecent exposure." He is fairly
sure that public nakedness is illegal, that somewhere in the
mass of legislation governing us is a provision designed to keep
him from going around without his clothes. What he is less
apt to know is whether such laws are so couched as to leave a
loop-hole for bona fide nudist practices, and whether they are
to be found in local ordinances, the state codes, or the Federal
Constitution. (Since the passage of the Eighteenth Amend-
ment, many people would not be surprised to find almost anything in the Constitution.) But in all likelihood he realizes
there is at least a possibility of forty-eight widely differing
laws in the forty-eight states, and he may hope that some of
the state codes are liberal toward nudity, though if he stops to
consider that for hundreds of years nakedness has been shame-

ful, he will scarcely expect to find nudity in mixed company approved by any statute.

Ever since the Pilgrims landed in Plymouth, the state legislatures, backed up by public opinion and the courts, have made laws against nakedness and exposure, on the theory that nudity is always for an improper purpose or has an improper and harmful effect on an observer of the opposite sex. Hence it is not at all easy to discover how the law applies to mixed nakedness when the purpose is proper. As obviously the legislators could not have had nudism in mind when they framed the laws, interpretation resolves itself into guessing what they would have intended had they conceived of such a thing. The field is unexplored, and there are no authoritative cases directly in point. The vast majority of the cases having to do with nudity deal with conduct relating to sexual intercourse or perversion. Therefore, we must ask the pardon of the nudists for unpleasant company in surveying briefly the development of the Common Law in England and the statutes in the American states. For often the court itself has hesitated to set down the facts but rather has treated them in vague generalities. It is not a pleasant field of law for the judge to administer or the jurist to analyze. Its episodes provoke violent mental nausea, and all concerned desire nothing more than to get the case out of the way quickly and quietly. When such procedure is the rule, we cannot expect a very consistent development of the legal principles involved.

The Common Law background is important not only because it is the basis of interpretation of all American statutes, but because a number of states have no specific statutes on indecent exposure and apply the Common Law. The *American and English Encyclopædia of Law* states: "At Common Law, an indecent exposure of the person is an intentional (that is, not accidental) exhibition, to more than one person, of the naked human body, or of the parts thereof which are commonly considered private." Generally the motive of the

[273]

exposure and the consent of witnesses are held immaterial, but it would be more accurate to say that the more public the exhibition the less necessary is an evil motive and the less significant the consent of witnesses. This is consistent with the treatment of the offence, where possible, as a common nuisance requiring no intent, and as an offence against the state rather than against the particular persons present. An exposure has been held not indecent either in itself or in its motive and yet, because it was public, punished as a common nuisance. A place not permanently public may be deemed so for the occasion if intruders are tolerated.

The Common Law on indecent exposure owes its origin to a case in the reign of Charles II, when the King's Bench first rose in righteous wrath to declare itself—though a temporal court—custodian of the people's morals, which had heretofore been left to the ecclesiastical courts. In 1657, Sir Charles Sedley stood forth naked on a balcony in Covent Garden and emptied bottles of urine on the heads of the crowds passing beneath. A more delicate statement might not make clear the true nature of the provocation that gave rise to the whole Anglo-American law of obscenity in conduct, speech, writing, art, and exposure of the person. Obviously here was a highly improper purpose and a public place.

In 1733 an English court refused to convict a woman for running in the street naked down to the waist, holding that nothing appeared immodest or unlawful, but it is doubtful that this case would have much weight today. Frequently cited are two later English bathing beach cases where the purpose—unlike Sir Charles Sedley's—was proper but the place was not. In 1809 a man was convicted for undressing to swim on a beach in the view of houses, and the court declared: "Whatever his intention might be, the necessary tendency of his conduct was to outrage decency and corrupt the public morals." Three quarters of a century later, in 1871, another man was convicted for the same offence under similar circumstances. Per-

haps the most cited American case on indecent exposure
involved a man in New Jersey in 1884 who persisted in urinat-
ing in his yard in view of his neighbours. The court, in affirm-
ing the conviction, approved the following charge to the jury:
"In order to convict the defendant you ought to be satisfied
. . . that the exposure was intentional, at such time and place
and such manner as to offend against public decency. . . ."
Here is an admittedly proper purpose, but the time and place
were not proper.

These are the foundations for the interpretation of the Common Law; their importance is evident when we find that nine
of our states appear to have no statutes bearing directly on the
subject, and that nineteen more merely repeat Common Law
formulæ, setting up the old offences in the broadest terms.[1]
Probably a good many others were not meant to do more than
declare the Common Law. Even where the statutes seem to
show a significant departure, indictments which cannot be
sustained under the statute are occasionally permitted by the
courts to stand good at Common Law, although customary
principles of interpretation would lead one to suppose that
the Common Law had been abrogated on the point by the
statute.

Those states which may be considered as without statute
are: Alabama, Delaware, District of Columbia, Illinois, Kentucky, Louisiana, Massachusetts, Tennessee, and Virginia. The
Delaware provision is typical: "Assaults, batteries, nuisances,
and all other offences indictable at Common Law and not
especially provided for by Statute shall be deemed misdemeanours." The only specific provision in these states is in
Kentucky, where it is unlawful to appear on the streets or
highway in a bathing suit. Where, as in Alabama, the section
on obscenity fully covers language, pictures, literature, but ig-
nores exposure, and the section on lewdness is limited to

[1] A complete list of statutes arranged alphabetically by state will be found in
the Appendix.

adultery and fornication, one could argue that the omission of nudity was intentional; but the argument would probably not succeed. These states have nuisance statutes which might cover organized nudist establishments. The Alabama law states: "Any person who shall erect, or continue, after notice to abate, a nuisance which tends or threatens to injure the health of the citizens in general, or to corrupt the public morals, shall be guilty of a misdemeanour." The form of indictment provided in Massachusetts has the broadest of possibilities: "That A. B. in a public place in said Boston, wherein were great numbers of people, did indecently expose to the view of said people his body and person naked and uncovered." Virginia has a "lewdness and lasciviousness" statute much like those next to be considered, but because of its title it has been construed as applying to cohabitation only. An indictment for exposure purporting to be under the statute was held good at Common Law.

The nineteen states that practically declare the Common Law are: Colorado, Connecticut, Georgia, Iowa, Kansas, Maine, Michigan, Minnesota, Missouri, Nevada, New Jersey, North Carolina, North Dakota, Pennsylvania, Rhode Island, Vermont, Washington, West Virginia, and Wisconsin. Eight of these—Colorado, Georgia, Kansas, Missouri, New Jersey, Pennsylvania, Vermont, and West Virginia—repeat almost verbatim the following formula: "Any person who shall be guilty of open lewdness, or any notorious act of public indecency, grossly scandalous and tending to debauch the morals and manners of the people. . . ." Such were the terms in which exposure was spoken of at Common Law, but the number of epithets varies somewhat. Vermont couples the fewest words with the heaviest sentence in the Union—five years or three hundred dollars. If any of the statutes are a little too vehement to apply directly to nudism, the courts may follow the lead of Virginia and go back to the Common Law alone.

What the Law Says

West Virginia adds a clear picture of that summary procedure which in any state will probably bother nudists more than indictments and supreme court decisions: "If any person shall, in the presence of a constable and in his county . . . improperly or indecently expose his person . . . such constable may without warrant or other process, or further proof, arrest such offending person and take him before some justice of the county, who, upon hearing the testimony of such constable and other witnesses, if any are then and there produced, if, in his opinion the offence charged be proved, shall require the offender to give bond or recognizance, with surety, to keep the peace and be of good behaviour for a term not exceeding one year."

Iowa, Maine, Michigan, Nevada, and Washington use the same formula as the eight states previously cited, except that they append a definite reference to "any open and indecent or obscene exposure of his or her person or of the person of another." North Dakota speaks in similar generalities, but does not insist on the lewdness or lasciviousness. (The constitutionality of the North Dakota statute was questioned in 1916 for vagueness.) Rhode Island throws the nudist in with tramps, vagrants, and prostitutes: "every person who shall speak or behave in an obscene or indecent manner in any public place, or within the view of others." Texas puts him into different company: "Whoever shall go into or near any public place or into or near any private house and shall use loud and vociferous, or obscene, vulgar, or indecent language, or swear or curse, or yell or shriek, or expose his person, or rudely display any pistol or other deadly weapon, in a manner calculated to disturb the inhabitants of such place or house. . . ." (This breach of the peace idea is reminiscent of Sir Charles and the debate over the bottles.) Texas also treats exposure in connection with obscene literature and the like. Minnesota has only a nuisance statute quite similar to that of Alabama, but there it is clear that only the indecent act is required and not an establishment for indecent purposes.

The Connecticut, North Carolina, and Wisconsin statutes belong in the class declaring the Common Law, but their breadth is worthy of notice. Wisconsin, for example, says only: "Any person who shall publicly expose his or her person, in an obscene or indecent manner. . . ." Perhaps Iowa and Texas should be placed in a class apart, since their use of the word "designedly" suggests an intent not required at Common Law. They are on the fence between the Common Law and the class of statutes next to be considered.

New York is probably the founder of the largest school of American legislation, but with the passage of time and the influence of Anthony Comstock the New York statute has become the least typical of its school. The statute which California copied from New York in 1872 has become the model for eleven other states. California says: "Every person who wilfully or lewdly either: (1) Exposes his person or the private parts thereof in any public place where there are present other persons to be offended or annoyed thereby; or (2) Procures, counsels, or assists any person so to expose himself or to take part in any model artist exhibition, or to make any other indecent exposure of himself to public view or to the view of any number of persons such as is offensive to decency or is adapted to excite to vicious or lewd thoughts or acts; is guilty of a misdemeanour."

This same statute has been enacted verbatim in Idaho, Montana, Oklahoma, South Dakota, and Utah. The western circuit is continued by Arizona and Oregon, which omit the subsection on procurement; and by Wyoming which omits the "lewdly." The Comstock trend of legislation breaks into the Middle West in Ohio, where the statute is identical with that in Wyoming; and in Indiana, which omits both "wilfully" and "lewdly." Mississippi and New York retain the adverbs and a procurement clause but omit the "other persons to be annoyed thereby." These statutes, with their more definite provisions as to intent and place or company will lend far more confidence to the nudist than does the Common Law.

Six statutes have earned separate classification by their attempts to define a public place: Maryland, Nebraska, New Hampshire, New Mexico, South Carolina, and Texas. Three of these might seem definitely to exclude nudist practices from the scope of the statute. Maryland limits to trains, steamboats, docks, and stations; perhaps it should have been classified as a no-statute state, which will turn to the Common Law. Nudists should not assume that they would be legally safe in staging a naked protest demonstration in front of the Baltimore dwelling of H. L. Mencken, though presumably he does not inhabit a railroad station or a steamboat dock. The New Hampshire law reads "in view of a dwelling house or a public road." This is rather like the German laws, which are held not to apply to nudist grounds that are properly screened from view. New Mexico limits to villages, towns, or cities. The remaining three begin specifically but end in general terms.

Canada's old statute said: "in the presence of one or more persons . . . in any place to which the public have or are permitted to have access. . . ." But by legislation passed in 1931, as a result of the fanatical outbreaks of the Doukhobors, the Canadian Parliament made it an offence punishable by three years imprisonment for a person while nude to be found without lawful excuse upon any private property not his own, whether alone or in company with other persons, or to appear upon his own property so as to be exposed to public view; and nudity was defined as being so scantily clad as to offend against public decency or order. No evil intent is required, but a public place or public view is insisted upon. It does not appear that the place is made public merely by the assembling of the nude Doukhobors therein; otherwise the words "public place" and "public view" would be without meaning in the statute. If this is true under so rigorous a measure against excessive practices, nudists under laws in effect in the United States may well gain a feeling of new security from this latest outbreak.

The statutes reach their highest degree of certainty in Arkansas and Florida, especially in the latter, where the statute reads: "Exposure of sexual organs. It shall be unlawful for any person to expose or exhibit his or her sexual organs in any public place or on the private premises of another, or so near thereto as to be seen from such private premises, in a vulgar or indecent manner, or to expose or exhibit his or her person in such a place, or to go or be naked in such a place: Provided, however, this section shall not be construed to prohibit the exposure of such organs or the person in any place provided or set apart for that purpose." One might almost believe that this statute was drawn up with nudism in mind, and that the specific intent was to exempt nudist parks or enclosures. However, it would be an exaggeration to say that there is any active trend in the legislation on this subject. It is simply that, as changes do come from time to time, they have been from Common Law generalities to something slightly more definite; and the more definite the statutes have become the more ease of mind they afford the nudists—not because the newer statutes were intended to sanction nudism, but because the old Common Law was not designed to forbid it, and the closer legislators get to saying what they mean the clearer this becomes.

But let not the nudist put his trust in any statute—the law has other resources. Police power, temporarily at least, may sanction such summary procedure as that authorized in West Virginia; or local ordinances may supply the specific provisions wanting in the state code; or again, the offence may be treated as a common nuisance regardless of intent, or the courts may fall back on the Common Law. But the great fundamental uncertainty that menaces the nudist is what constitutes indecency. The indefinite and changing nature of the moral standard has nowhere been more apparent than in the courts nor more vigorously recognized than by judge and jurist.

This uncertainty as to what offends morality produced its most positive judicial effect when the Indiana Supreme Court decided during the Civil War that: "We are of the opinion that for want of a proper definition, no act is made criminal by the terms 'public indecency' employed in the statute." But Indiana was off technically on the wrong foot.. The statute abrogating Common Law crimes in general provided that all offences must be defined *by the legislature.* The Civil War Court had misinterpreted this to mean that all offences must be *defined* by the legislature. So seventeen years later, with the opinion in Ardery v. State, 1877, Indiana launched the longest series of decisions on the subject to be found in any state. This opinion has been quoted so often throughout the United States that it deserves space here: "Immediately after the fall of Adam, there seems to have sprung up in his mind an idea that there was such a thing as decency and such a thing as indecency; that there was a distinction between them; and, since that time, the ideas of decency and indecency have been instinctive in, and, indeed, parts of, humanity. And it historically appears that the first most palpable piece of indecency in a human being was the exposure of his or her, as now commonly called, privates; and the first exercise of mechanical ingenuity was in the manufacture of fig-leaf aprons by Adam and Eve, by which to conceal from the public gaze of each other their, now, but not then, called, privates. This example of covering their privates has been imitated by all mankind since that time, except, perhaps, by some of the lowest grades of savages." (It may be noted that the Indiana statute has since been put in a slightly more definite form.)

Soon the Federal Courts, in a case having to do with the mailing of a doctor's work on sexual perversion, likewise based their position on Adam and Eve, deciding in United States v. Harmon, 1891: "There is in the popular conception and heart such a thing as modesty. It was born in the Garden of

Eden." An often quoted non-biblical decision regarding indecent exposure was handed down in Vermont in 1846: "No particular definition is given by the statute of what constitutes this crime. The indelicacy of the subject forbids it, and does not require of the court to state what particular conduct will constitute the offence. The common sense of the community, as well as the sense of decency, propriety, and morality, which most people entertain, is sufficient to apply the statute to each particular case, and point out what particular conduct is rendered criminal by it." In short the objection of uncertainty has long been considered in discussions both heated and cool. Although this objection will become more glaring than ever when the law is applied to nudism, nudists will probably save their breath by admitting that as a ground for defence uncertainty has fallen beneath a substantial weight of authority.

What "Supply and Demand" is to the economic parrot, "Act and Intent" is to the student of criminal law. What is the act, and what is the intent necessary to make nakedness an offence against the state? With regard to the *act,* if there is such a thing as a degree of nakedness which is indecent in itself— and the tenor of the statutes implies there is—the nudists have crossed the line. Of course the cases do not deal with the amount of exposure permissible, for in them it has usually been limited to the sex organs; perhaps the old judges themselves would have thought total nakedness less indecent. But on the whole the words "indecency" and "obscenity," in their substantive, adjective, or adverbial forms, are used apparently not as modifying and limiting the act coming within the statute but as vituperative epithets with which the act is branded. "Lewdness" and "lasciviousness" have quite a different effect. Lewdness without a lewd intent is almost a contradiction in terms.

As to the question of *place,* clearly the "public place" so often referred to does not have to be a place publicly owned or even publicly frequented in the ordinary sense, such as a theatre, a church, or a beach. It is probably enough for the public to have access to the place, even if technically they are there as trespassers, though a place could scarcely be called public if trespassers were not customarily tolerated. The question most discussed—whether there must be more than one, or the possibility of more than one observer—is immaterial to the nudist. But does it make any difference that all the observers of nudist activities are not only consenting but participating? Certainly consent cannot generally be said to nullify this offence. For instance, there is the stand taken in United States v. Bennett, 1879: "While there may be individuals and societies of men and women of peculiar notions or idiosyncrasies, whose moral sense would be neither depraved nor offended by the publication in question, yet the exceptional sensibility or want of sensibility of such cannot be allowed as a standard by which obscenity is to be tested. Rather is the test, 'What is the judgment of the aggregate sense of the community reached by it?' "

There is much reason for the view that consent does not excuse, as otherwise the disgusting exhibitions in peep-shows and bawdy houses—for which the witnesses not only give their consent but pay—would be beyond the reach of the law. The public may feel that the individual needs protection from himself; yet if all the witnesses are also participants, the desire to protect them from the subversive influence of the exhibition largely disappears. The courts have repeatedly made it evident that they have little use for complaints by peepers, even where gross lewdness is involved, and that the offence must really be public. To be sure, Missouri in 1915 and Virginia in 1929 went contrary to this trend and upheld convictions in instances where all those present were participants, but the details of these cases were unusually revolting to the moral sense of the community. Those states whose statutes read "any place where there are present other persons to be offended or annoyed thereby" seem to take as positive a stand on this issue as could be asked. They are Arizona, California, Florida, Idaho, Indiana, Montana, Ohio, Oklahoma, Oregon, South Dakota, Utah, and Wyoming. Of these, the Florida statute is the clearest of all.

That the same stand may be taken under the Common Law, or in states where the statutes make no such express provision, is indicated by judicial dicta in Massachusetts, Wisconsin, and elsewhere. The clearest decision on the subject without statutory help came from Canada in 1916: "It is of the essence of the offence that it should be committed 'in the presence of one or more persons'; and this is not satisfied by holding that the man who participates in the offence is 'a person' contemplated by the statute. It is enough that one person should be shown to be present, but it must be a person other than those engaged in the offence."

Nothing has been said directly as to the nudity of the sexes in common, which is probably the most critical question. The truth is that little can be said. There are no authoritative cases of mutual exposure between the sexes except in connection with intercourse, and no definite reference to sex in the statutes or opinions except where intercourse is clearly in mind. Mixed company may increase the indecency or obscenity in the opinion of the public—it may even increase the inference of evil intent—but it adds nothing to the publicness of the exposure. Discretion suggests that for the present at least nudists keep their activity not only out of sight but out of mind, in order not merely to keep themselves out of court in the first place, but to get themselves out if they get in. In general, since they will not stir up quite the degree of aversion that drove Virginia and Missouri off the modern trend, nudists may fairly hope for reasonable immunity through the legal requirements that the offence be public.

Intent and *motive*, however, are very different matters and offer less security to the nudist. Bishop's *New Criminal Law* states: "Obviously this offence is not committed where the

[284]

mind is pure." But unfortunately this decisive statement by so respectable an authority cannot be supposed to mean exactly what it says—and if it could, it would have to be considerably discounted. Bishop's subsequent statements reveal that he, like many others, was unable to imagine that the mind could be pure unless the exposure was accidental. Just what state of mind is required is not clear, and the doubt is increased by careless use of the terms of criminal law. Criminal intent, whether general or specific, means little more than that the act was not purely accidental. It seems evident that both general and specific intent are required—which fortunately saves the difficulty of trying to draw the distinction here. The nudist's nakedness of course is not accidental; he cannot escape the charge of criminal intent on that ground. Does the law go further and require an evil motive? The English bathing beach cases and numerous instances of literary censorship indicate that a pure mind does not necessarily nullify the offence. An early New York decision that "mere nudity in painting and sculpture is not obscenity . . . the proper test of obscenity is whether the motive in a painting or statue, so to speak, as indicated by it, is pure or impure" seems to be in the minority, or at least it has not been generally applied in analogous fields.

But in the statutes, the word "lewdly" is frequently found. It is consistently defined in the cases, as well as in the dictionary, as pertaining to "those wanton acts, between persons of different sexes, flowing from the exercise of lustful passions, which are grossly indecent or unchaste," or "that form of immorality which has relation to sexual impurity," or "unlawful indulgence in lust, eager for sexual indulgence." Here certainly a special intent or motive is stipulated, and one that would absolutely exclude the nudists. But there is reason to fear that if this point were pressed too far, the courts, wanting a statute on general indecency, would turn to the Common Law, although as a matter of fact they have consistently required that "lewdly" be alleged, and they have quashed, rather than referred to the Common Law, indictments which have failed to do so. The states specifying "lewdly" are: Arizona, California, Idaho, Mississippi, Montana, New York, Oklahoma, Oregon, South Dakota, and Utah. Connecticut and Maine use the word "wantonly," which would probably be given a similar interpretation. New Jersey, Vermont, and West Virginia statutes speak of "lewdness" only, which seems to imply a lewd intent.

"Wilfully," "maliciously," "designedly," are also familiar in the statutes. In legislation of other fields these words are no more than key words, indicating that the act must not be accidental. Arizona, California, Idaho, Maryland, Mississippi, Montana, Nebraska, New York, Ohio, Oregon, South Carolina, South Dakota, Utah, and Wyoming employ "wilfully"; South Carolina uses "maliciously"; and Iowa, Michigan, and Texas use "designedly." Some statutes specify a more definite *intent*. Arkansas says: "Every person who shall appear in public places naked, or partly so, with the intent of making a public exhibition of his nudity"—which has been expanded by interpretation to "the intention to outrage public decency by an exposure of his nudity." On the other hand, eighteen states are entirely silent as to special intent.

In all the cases we have been able to find in which the motive was not evil—only three, and those not dealing with mixed nudity—the defendants were discharged somewhat impatiently. If both sexes had been involved, however, the outcome might have been different. As far as we know, the American League for Physical Culture is the only regularly constituted nudist group that has learned from experience something of how the law may be applied to nudism. Twice they were arrested and charged under section 1140 of the Penal Code of the State of New York (once in a rural county and once in New York City). In the first instance, they were recharged and fined five dollars apiece for disorderly conduct; in the second, their case was dismissed, the magistrate holding that lewdness must be proved, and that mere nakedness, even in mixed company, does not necessarily constitute lewdness. In other words, the question is whether nudity in mixed company must be lewd in itself—a decision that depends on the magistrate's viewpoint, until there is a decision by a court of last resort.

In their second trial, the American League nudists were also given an intimation that place and company may be a factor. The prosecuting attorney moved that they be recharged under section 43, which reads: "A person who wilfully and wrongfully commits any act . . . which openly outrages public decency, for which no other punishment is expressly prescribed by this chapter, is guilty of a misdemeanour." But the City magistrate held that since the nudists' gymnasium was inaccessible to the public (the police had to obtain their evidence by looking through a hole in the skylight), their activities could not "openly outrage public decency." This should serve as a warning to nudists to make sure that outsiders cannot gain access to their premises.

Perhaps in time the present statutes will, as Morris Ernst has said, "be whittled away in so far as they ban nudist activities" once the public has come to recognize that the latter are not indecent and obscene. But if nudists are premature or go to extremes that will arouse an unaccustomed public, the courts will find it easy enough in most cases to convict them. Then to get rid of those precedents, legislation would be necessary, demanding a political influence—nudist lobbies—which the movement might be a long time acquiring, especially after a bad start. If, however, the nudists develop their program discreetly until public opinion is convinced of their good motive and good sense, they will have nothing to fear from the state, and there will be no statutes to be repealed and no authoritative cases to be overruled, in order to give their proper activities the full sanction of the law.

‎ᴜᴜᴜ

CONCLUSION

Nudism has come to America, and its presence has not passed unnoticed. The newcomer has been denounced by a few, ridiculed by many, and welcomed warmly by others. Its future remains uncertain. Perhaps it is not yet fully naturalized, and there may still be danger that it will be deported as an undesirable alien; or perhaps—what would be no less disastrous and is a more likely fate—it will be taken up wholesale as a fad, sweep the country in the dazzling and ephemeral train of fashion, and as swiftly sink into oblivion, joining the forgotten shades of mah jong, cross-word puzzles, and Coué in the limbo of American crazes. But its brief career among us has not been in this direction. Progress has been slower and healthier, and those Americans who are the nudists are not faddists. The time may still come when we shall go naked to be fashionable, but as yet nudism is far from stylish, being in fact scarcely respectable. At present, an interest in nudism requires a personal independence of public opinion and social pressure rather than a thoughtless yielding to mass psychology. The start is sound, and with this beginning the practice of nudity may well be here to stay and to prosper, and—like many another immigrant—to become so completely a part of our national life that not even the superpatriots would dream of calling it un-American.

It is still beset by hazards—the possibility of counter-campaigns by our moral watch dogs, and the danger of legal coercion under loosely couched statutes whose framers never dreamed of such a thing as decent nakedness. Likewise, there are hazards from within the movement, and these are even more perilous. Nudism may be jeopardized by the rashness of its exponents: if it parades itself too brazenly, or attempts to bully and use compulsion, it will wreck itself. Caution and circumspection are necessary. But a frank and open attitude is equally essential. The nudist ought neither to feel guilty nor to behave as if he did, for he can only cast suspicion upon his practices by whispers and conspirator-like surreptition. While not intruding his beliefs on the unreceptive, he should, if he is challenged or has the misfortune to be "caught," display the courage of his convictions. Nothing is so disarming as a matter-of-fact and straightforward attitude. A calm and unashamed nudist is apt to make others see that there is nothing either dreadful or shameful about him after all.

Until the movement has an assured status, both social and legal, nudist groups must also exercise discrimination in admitting members. Nudists should bar the psychologically unprepared, whose conduct may annoy fellow members; the indiscreet, who may inadvertantly arouse the animosity of neighbours; and the petty and vindictive, who make trouble in any group and who in this case have too ready a weapon of revenge in betrayal to officers of the law. There is no danger that nudism will degenerate into licence, but it is possible for its name to be used as a cloak for orgies. That, the nudists cannot control, save by so conducting themselves as to win the respect of public opinion and enable the latter to distinguish between nudism and lubricity under a pseudo-nudist whitewash. Above all, nudism must not allow its direction to fall into the hands of fanatics who would make a simple, healthful, and jolly practice part of an involved and solemn doctrine, "a mumbo-jumbo cult" whose extravagant claims would repel any reasonable person and excite the laughter of anyone with a sense of humour.

The American movement, if it continues as it has started, is in a fair way to avoid most of these hazards. The nudists at present are sane, well-balanced people, capable both of using judgment in the admission of members to their groups and of earning the respect of the public. They have shown no tendency to make nudism a cult. American nudism might be called humanistic, were it not that this word has taken on a peculiar and restricted meaning as a result of the late literary controversy over the so-called humanists; at least it has the same pagan freshness and naturalness and joy that made the spirit of Renaissance humanism. This is not to imply that American nakedness for recreation and outdoor sports is unthinking, or a purely instinctive exuberance of animal spirits. The nudist in this country has consciously thought out the bases for his practice. He is fully aware of its hygienic, psychological, and social implications, and he can justify his conduct by sound theory; but he does not let the theory either swell into a monster so remote from reality as to lead him into quixotic and dangerous excesses, or set in a harsh dogma so puritanical and unworldly as to confine him in a straight jacket.

Frequently German *Nacktkultur* is allied with naturism and is but one phase of a movement for a "natural life" that involves vegetarianism (in its extreme form a raw fruit and vegetable diet), strict abstinence from tobacco, alcohol, and drugs (including those of the physician), and a dependence on "natural healing." The American is less likely to feel that he must dispense with his cookstove along with his clothes, or that a naked man must forego meat, smoking, and all the other comforts and indulgences of civilization. Furthermore, German nudism often tends—as indicated by the name *Freikörperkultur*, or "Free Physical Culture"—to be gymnastic and literally physical culture rather than recreation and relaxation. Regimented gymnastics, performed as a matter of principle, have less attraction for Americans. In this respect, our nudism seems closer akin to the more light-hearted and unsystematized French movement. The Germans undoubtedly enjoy their exercises and consider them recreation, but such is not our, or the French, idea of fun. In Latin, as in Anglo-Saxon eyes, this dutiful devotion to gymnastics invests *Nackt-kultur* with a solemnity verging on the ludicrous. French *Nudisme* is more obviously characterized by a *joie de vivre* less alien to the spirit of the American movement.

Both German and French movements are organized on a national scale, the local clubs usually belonging to large federations. There is nothing of the sort in America, nor have any effective steps been taken to affiliate the existing groups into a national association—a thing difficult not only on account of the distribution of the clubs through a large and uncentralized country, but on account of the wide diversity in nature and organization of the local groups themselves. A federation would demand some semblance of uniformity in its member clubs. As they are now constituted, the only sort of national organization possible would be not a central governing board but a clearing house that might issue a publication and act as information bureau for local groups subscribing to its services. If the opponents of nudism in this country should organize for a systematic and powerfully backed drive, the only way to meet it would be with a united front. In such an eventuality, a strong national organization might be formed. But as yet there has been no mustering of hostile forces.

American nudism can hope to prosper unmolested and trust that opposition will decrease through the development of public tolerance as the real nature of nudist practices becomes better known. The greatest assurance of the growth and duration of the movement in America lies not in national organization but in the appeal of the practice itself, the delights and benefits of unhampered enjoyment of sun and air and water.

Nudism Comes to America

Nakedness in nature satisfies such a fundamental craving of the human organism that, once tasted, it becomes a habit. This is the chief guarantee that nudism will not be a passing fad.

THE END

APPENDIX

STATUTES

The States having no Common Law offences apart from the statutes are: Georgia, Indiana, Iowa, Kansas, Louisiana, Michigan, Nebraska, New York, Ohio, Oregon, Texas.

ALABAMA: "What nuisances are indictable: Any person who shall erect, or continue, after notice to abate, a nuisance which tends or threatens to injure the health of the citizens in general, or to corrupt the public morals, shall be guilty of a misdemeanour."

Section on obscenity has nothing except on language, pictures, literature. Lewdness is limited to adultery and fornication.

ARIZONA: "Every person who wilfully and lewdly exposes his person or the private parts thereof, in any public place, or in any place where there are present other persons to be offended or annoyed thereby. . . ."

ARKANSAS: "Every person who shall appear in public places naked, or partly so, with intent of making a public exhibition of his nudity, or who shall make any obscene exhibition of his person, shall be deemed guilty of a misdemeanour."

Interpreted as two distinct offences, 20 Ark. 156.

CALIFORNIA: "Every person who wilfully and lewdly either: (1) Exposes his person or the private parts thereof in any public place or in any place where there are present other persons to be offended or

Appendix

annoyed thereby; or (2) Procures, counsels, or assists any person so to expose himself or to take part in any model artist exhibition, or to make any other exhibition of himself to public view or to the view of any number of persons such as is offensive to decency or is adapted to excite to vicious or lewd thoughts or acts; is guilty of a misdemeanour."

CANADA: "Everyone is guilty of an offence and liable on summary conviction to three years' imprisonment who, while nude, (a) is found in any public place whether alone or in company with one or more persons who are parading or have assembled with intent to parade or have paraded in such public place while nude, or (b) is found in any public place whether alone or in company with one or more other persons, or (c) is found without lawful excuse upon any private property not his own, whether alone or in company with other persons, or (d) appears upon his own property so as to be exposed to public view, whether alone or in company with other persons. For the purpose of this subsection anyone shall be deemed to be nude who is so scantily clad as to offend against public decency or order."

COLORADO: "If any person shall be guilty of open lewdness, or other notorious act of public indecency, tending to debauch the public morals, or shall keep open any tippling or gaming house on the sabbath. . . ." $100, 6 months.

CONNECTICUT: "Any person who shall, wantonly and indecently, expose his person shall be fined not more than $100 or imprisoned not more than six months, or both."

DELAWARE: "Assaults, batteries, nuisances, and all other offences indictable at Common Law, and not especially provided for by statute, shall be deemed misdemeanours. . . ."

DISTRICT OF COLUMBIA: "Whoever shall erect, establish, maintain, use, own, occupy, or release any building, erection, or place used for the purpose of lewdness, assignation, or prostitution . . . is guilty of a nuisance . . . which may be enjoined or abated."

Appendix

FLORIDA: "Exposure of sexual organs: It shall be unlawful for any person to expose or exhibit his or her sexual organs in any public place or on the private premises of another, or so near thereto as to be seen from such private premises, in a vulgar or indecent manner, or to expose or exhibit his or her person in such place, or to go or be naked in such place: Provided, however, this section shall not be construed to prohibit the exposure of such organs or the person in any place provided or set apart for that purpose. . . ."

GEORGIA: Public indecency treated under lewdness statute identical with that of Colorado.

IDAHO: Identical with that of California.

ILLINOIS: Common Law.

INDIANA: "Whoever, being over 14 years of age, makes an indecent exposure of his person in a public place or in a place where there are other persons to be offended or annoyed thereby. . . ." Fine $5 to $100.

IOWA: "If any man or woman, married or unmarried, is guilty of open and gross lewdness and designedly make any open and indecent or obscene exposure of his or her person or of the person of another, every such person shall be punished. . . ."

KANSAS: ". . . and every person married or unmarried who shall be guilty of open, gross lewdness or lascivious behaviour, or of any open and notorious act of public indecency, grossly scandalous. . . ." 6 months, $500.

KENTUCKY: "That it shall be unlawful for any person or persons to appear on any highway or upon the streets of any town or village having no police protection, when such person or persons are clothed only in ordinary bathing garb."

LOUISIANA: No statute.

[295]

Appendix

MAINE: "Lascivious cohabitation; lewdness; indecent exposure; penalties . . . ; and whoever wantonly and indecently exposes his person shall be punished. . . ." 6 months, $25.

MARYLAND: "Any person . . . who shall wilfully act in a disorderly manner . . . by indecently exposing his person on or about any steamboat wharf, dock, or public waiting room, or in or about the station grounds of any railroad of the State, or in or on any steamboat, street car, electric car, railroad car, passenger train, or other public conveyance. . . ."

MASSACHUSETTS: Form of indictment for exposure of person (under no specified statute): "That A. B. in a public place in said Boston, wherein were great numbers of people, did indecently expose to the view of said people his body and person naked and uncovered. . . ."

MICHIGAN: Identical with that of Iowa.

MINNESOTA: "A public nuisance is a crime against the order and economy of the state, and consists in unlawfully doing an act or omitting to perform a duty, which act or omission . . . (2) Shall offend public decency. . . ."

MISSISSIPPI: "A person who wilfully and lewdly exposes his person or private parts thereof in any public place, or in any place where others are present, or procures another so to expose himself, is guilty of a misdemeanour. . . ." 20 days, $50.
 Note—"lewdly" necessary to charge.

MISSOURI: Identical with that of Kansas.

MONTANA: Identical with that of California.

NEBRASKA: "Whoever, being of the age of 14, shall wilfully make an indecent exposure of his or her person in any street, lane, alley, or other place, in any city, town, village, or county. . . ." 90 days, $100.

NEVADA: "Every person who shall be guilty of open or gross lewdness or make any open and indecent or obscene exposure of his person, or of the person of another, shall be guilty of a gross misdemeanour."

NEW HAMPSHIRE: "No person shall, within the view of a dwelling house, or of a public road, expose his person indecently. . . ."

NEW JERSEY: "Any person who shall be guilty of open lewdness, or any notorious act of public indecency, grossly scandalous and tending to debauch the morals and manners of the people . . . shall be guilty of a misdemeanour."

NEW MEXICO: "That any person who shall hereafter indecently expose his person in or upon the streets or other public places in any unincorporated village, town, or city in this state shall be guilty of a misdemeanour. . . ." 30 days, $25.

NEW YORK: "A person who wilfully and lewdly exposes his person, or the private parts thereof, in any public place, or in any place where others are present, or procures another so to expose himself, is guilty of a misdemeanour."

NORTH CAROLINA: ". . . or if any person shall make any public exposure of the person or other indecent exhibition, . . . or if any one shall permit such exhibitions or immoral performances to be conducted in any tent, booth, or other place owned or controlled by him, he shall be guilty of a misdemeanour."
  Test of immorality: "tendency to shock the moral sense of the average, normal head of a family."

NORTH DAKOTA: "Every person who wrongfully commits any act which grossly injures the person or property of another, or which openly outrages public decency and is injurious to public morals, although no punishment is expressly prescribed therefor in this chapter, is guilty of a misdemeanour."

OHIO: "Whoever, being over 14 years of age, wilfully makes an indecent exposure of his person in a public place or in a place where there are other persons to be offended or annoyed thereby . . . shall be fined not more than $200 or imprisoned not more than 6 months or both."

OKLAHOMA: Identical with that of California.

OREGON: Identical with that of California except that words there (subsection 2) applying to the procurement of others here apply to exhibition of self.

PENNSYLVANIA: "If any person shall commit open lewdness or any notorious act of public indecency tending to debauch the morals or manners of the people, such person shall be guilty of a misdemeanour." 1 year, $100.

RHODE ISLAND: ". . . tramps, vagrants, prostitutes . . . every person who shall speak or behave in an obscene or indecent manner in any public place, or within the view of others. . . ."

SOUTH CAROLINA: "Any person who shall be guilty of wilful and malicious indecent exposure of his person on any street or highway, or in any place of resort, shall be guilty of a felony."

SOUTH DAKOTA: Identical with that of California.

TENNESSEE: Common Law.

TEXAS: Criminal Code 1927, Art. 474 "Disturbing the peace. Whoever shall go into or near any public place or into or near any private house and shall use loud and vociferous, or obscene, vulgar, or indecent language, or swear or curse, or yell or shriek, or expose his person, or rudely display any pistol or other deadly weapon, in a manner calculated to disturb the inhabitants of such place or house, shall be fined not to exceed $100."
Art. 475 "A 'public place' as used in the two preceding articles is any public road, street, or alley of a town or city, or any store or workshop or any place at which people are assembled or to which people commonly resort for purposes of business, amusement or other lawful purposes."

Appendix

Art. 526 "If any person shall make, publish, or print any indecent and obscene print, picture, or written composition manifestly designed to corrupt the morals of youth, or shall designedly make any obscene and indecent exhibitions of his own or the person of another in public, he shall be fined not exceeding $100."

UTAH: Identical with that of California.

VERMONT: "A person guilty of open and gross lewdness and lascivious behaviour shall be imprisoned not more than 5 years or fined not more than $300."

VIRGINIA: "Lewd and lascivious cohabitation. If any persons, not married to each other, lewdly and lasciviously associate and cohabit together, or, whether married or not, be guilty of open and gross lewdness and lasciviousness. . . ."
Applies only to cohabitation (Cf. 152 Va. 965).

WASHINGTON: "Lewdness. Every person who shall lewdly and viciously cohabit with another not the husband or wife of such person, and every person who shall be guilty of open or gross lewdness, or make any open and indecent exposure of his person, or of the person of another, shall be guilty of a gross misdemeanour."

WEST VIRGINIA: Official Code 1931, Ch. 62, Art. 10, p. 1537, §6 "If any person shall, in the presence of a constable and in his county . . . improperly or indecently expose his person . . . such constable may, without warrant or other process, or further proof, arrest such offending person and take him before some justice of the county, who, upon hearing the testimony of such constable and other witnesses, if any are then and there produced, if, in his opinion the offence charged be proved, shall require the offender to give bond or recognizance, with surety, to keep the peace and be of good behaviour for a term not exceeding one year."
Ch. 61, Art. 8, p. 1492, § 4 "If any persons . . . be guilty of open and gross lewdness and lasciviousness. . . ."
Progressive punishment for successive offences.

Appendix

WISCONSIN: "Any person who shall publicly expose his or her person, in an obscene or indecent manner, shall be guilty of a misdemeanour. . . ."

WYOMING: Identical with that of Ohio.